THE REAL THINGS

THE INTIMATE JOURNEY OF A WORKING MUSICIAN FROM BILL GRAHAM TO BILLY GRAHAM TO INSTAGRAM

BRENT BOURGEOIS

FOREWORD

The first time I heard Brent Bourgeois perform, he was in a band called Uncle Rainbow, fresh out of Dallas, new to California, and playing the club circuit—working toward what they believed would be their debut record. A Doobie Brothers connection had carried them west. I remember having two reactions at once: love and fear.

Love, because they were extraordinary. Fear, because they were so far ahead of anything in the Sacramento music scene that the message was unmistakable: get your thing together or get left behind. I took it to heart. I had work to do. Brent had arrived fully formed. This flex hints at why *The Real Things* is so good.

There is a ridiculous accumulation of coincidence suggesting that, in some cosmic sense, collaboration and friendship were not optional for us. We've been friends since our early twenties—lived much of the music business together and shared family and life at almost every turn. We are both keyboardists, singer-songwriters, producers, autodidacts, writers, and polymaths by necessity. We both began playing professionally as teenagers. Brent was born in New Orleans; my people are from Louisiana. We championed each other, competed just enough to stay sharp, traded gear, musicians, songs, and chances at a paycheck and the golden ring. He reached commercial pop success before I did. I took the longer, more experimental road. He had an infuriating habit of getting it right the first time.

In one way, reading *The Real Things* felt uncannily like reading pieces of my own life—except I learned far more about Brent than I ever knew. I heard serious and comical stories I'd missed. I saw patterns only time reveals. In short, I was there for a lot of it and yet came away surprised, enriched, and entertained.

What I most want a reader to understand is this: Brent is an honest-broker storyteller—not merely for the amazing anecdotes, but for the craft of writing and pure transparency. These are stories that musicians and music book readers love, yes, but they also work as allegory and a whole-body dose of hard-earned wisdom and humility. This book is not a celebrity memoir. It is a working musician's story, written by a true artist who has actually done the work.

Brent was born to be a musician. A few lessons, perhaps, but mostly a true self-learner, and already a high-level professional as a teenager. There was nothing he could not play, sing, or shape into truly imaginative music. While Uncle Rainbow fell short of its original ambitions, Brent was not to be denied his place in pop history. *Undeniable talent* is not a phrase I use lightly—but that's him and his story. You contribute to the Top 40 Pop canon and Billboard charts, then some part of your work is done. The band Bourgeois Tagg and Brent's overall career have done both.

What this book offers is something rarer than ubiquitous names and success stories, though. It offers an honest picture of a sustained life in music—through records and tours, triumphs and reversals, heroes met, and systems and toxic religion survived. It shows how talent, perseverance, and adaptability once made lasting music careers possible. And, it's as real as it gets about the cost of the business to family and health—spiritual and physical.

I was impressed with Brent in the late 1970s. I am still impressed today. No fear, though, now. All love and respect.

The Real Things is not just a great book by a great musician. It is a roadmap to reality—how to build a sustainable artistic life—and how to recover from both your victories and your failures, with grace and humility.

Charlie Peacock—Grammy Award-winning music producer and author of *Roots & Rhythm: A Life in Music*

INTRO

"The funny thing is life goes by
So quickly, slowly, that
I can't see the changes in me"

It was 1987 and we were just passing through Nashville on the Bad Animals tour with Heart, staying in a nice hotel for a change rather than sleeping on the bus. I was sitting in the lobby by myself, reading a magazine, waiting for the bus, sporting the mid-80s Flock of Seagulls haircut in vogue then, especially as it was morning. An older Black man cleaning the floors circled around me a couple of times, looking back furtively. Finally, he stopped the machine and said, "You somebody famous?"

Surprised, I laughed, and said, "No."

Not buying it, he replied, "C'mon, man, I know you somebody famous!"

"I promise you I'm not," I told him.

"Just tell me who you are then," he said, "'cause I know you're somebody."

Finally taking the bait, I said, "Brent Bourgeois. My name is Brent Bourgeois."

"Brent what?"

"Brent Bourgeois," I answered again.

"Boo-zh-wah," he said slowly, looking around the room, disappointed, rubbing his bald head, trying to digest the name. "Never heard of you."

Fifty years. Fifty years as a survivor, even a thriver in the music business. Fifty years as a keyboardist, bandmember, background singer, lead singer, songwriter for myself, songwriter for others, solo artist, music director, producer, orchestral arranger, A&R executive, worship leader, sideman, main man, playing funk music, Christian music, Devil's music, jazz, rock, writing music for the biggest tech company in the world, and *never* working an honest day in my life. Married for forty-two years with four grown children supported by nothing but my singing, playing, and producing music. My wife, Mary Ann says, "Why would you *ever* retire? You will just end up doing it for free!" She has a point.

This book is about those fifty years plus a few more. One day you're the youngest person in your class, the youngest in your band, the youngest to play in a bar; then, in a flash you're in a hotel going to a 50th High School Reunion. Time means the most when you have the least of it left to lose. My son Adrian encouraged me to write down my memories while I still had time. While I still had memories. While I still could write. My mother was diagnosed with Alzheimer's Disease when she was sixty-five. I just turned sixty-seven. Like most people I know, I did not keep a diary or journal. I made a few attempts over the years, but I mainly just embarrassed myself and gave up after a good month or so. Even a simple calendar would have come in handy for an effort like this. But no.

Why would I write a book about my life? Who will read it? What have I done? I'm not famous. What's the hook?

This is a nuts-and-bolts, warts-and-all look at a lifetime in music. There are plenty of famous people in it. There are club gigs, theatre gigs, arena gigs, and stadium gigs, European tours, North American tours, bus tours and flights on Lear jets, basketball with a Prince, close encounters with a Princess and a Beatle, Todd and more Todd, altar calls with Billy Graham, management by rock royalty, and finally, working for tech royalty. The "cat-with-nine-lives" analogy is overused, but when I count them up, that's about how many I've had in music.

I fear I'm a dying breed. They're not gonna make 'em like me anymore. I'm one of the last of the cowboys, or maybe like the last surviving Civil War Veteran. "Grampa–you made a *living* playing music? Your *whole* life?" It's almost impossible to make a living making music today. This book is about being on the ground floor through all the changes in the music business, from getting paid my first salary in a working band at the age of fourteen, ascending to the industry's top in the 1980s and early 1990s, and then cratering to the outhouse a mere ten years later. It is about being a shapeshifter, a chameleon and a Mr. Magoo. It is about five distinct eras of my life: New Jersey in the 1960s, Dallas in the 1970s, California in the 1980s, Nashville in the 1990s, and California again in the 2000s and beyond.

It is about choices–some I'm glad I made, some I wish I had made, and a few I wish I hadn't. It is about temptation, and the pitfalls of being an addict and a local hero at the same time. It is about my talent being way ahead of my brain for a long while. It is about sometimes being the most talented guy in the room, but most of the time just being the luckiest, stumbling and bumbling forward, Magoo-like, into the next good thing.

This book is also about the struggle to become a worthy husband and father while being a constantly working and in-demand musician, songwriter, and producer. For that I am as lucky as I am good.

The best choice I ever made was to follow a young woman outside of a club to her car, much to her surprise, and possible dismay. We have been together for forty-six years and have four wonderfully well-adjusted grown children. I am maybe most proud of being a loving and conscientious father, present when it counted the most and getting my priorities, for the most part, right.

And finally, there is the struggle with religion and spiritu-ality, which will end something like this: "Hey y'all! I finally figured it out!!" And then I die. I have been tied up in knots, in and out, up and down and all over the place with religion almost my whole life. As I write this, the Sermon On the Mount speaks most powerfully to me; Christianity does not. My struggle with religion in general, and Christianity in particular, is detailed within these pages.

With that, I begin in New Orleans...

1

EARLY SNAPSHOTS:
NEW ORLEANS

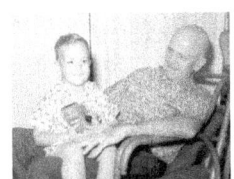

Snapshot: (1960) I have been told when I was two years old my parents or my older brothers would lift me up at the front window and I could name the brand of every car that drove by our house. I have no memory of it. It became a parlor trick to show off to their friends. No one taught me, I obviously couldn't read yet, and no one ever figured how I did it. And as I grew older, I never knew the brand names of any cars.

Snapshot: (July 1961) I'm in the car with my father and his father, PaPa, arriving at a hospital for the birth of my sister Becky. I couldn't go inside because "mommy was sick." My mother had to stay longer because of complications during the delivery. Becky was the last child she would have.

Snapshot: (1961-63) We had a beautiful 1910 Chickering baby grand piano in our house. Some of my earliest memories surround that piano. I remember my mother playing "Für Elise," Liszt's "Liebestraum," and other classical pieces. I also remember my older brothers and sister practicing their piano lessons.

Snapshot: (Summer 1963-64) We would occasionally go to a bigger swim club called Timberlane, although we had a neighborhood community pool. I remember three things about Timberlane: 1) They had a high dive, and the first time I dove off the high dive was the scariest moment of my young life. And I belly-flopped, which *really* hurt. 2) My two older brothers, Bruce and Brian, horse-playing around with me and holding me underwater until I felt like I was going to drown. 3) The first time I saw young Black children playing in the shallow end of the Timberlane pool. Our own neighborhood was lily-white, so our neighborhood pool was as well. I was confused about seeing these Black kids in the pool. Nothing was said, there was no overt prejudice in our home– but it made an impression on me because it was unusual to this five-year-old white kid in the 1963 South.

Snapshot: (Friday November 22, 1963) I was picked up early from nursery school that day because "something terrible happened," but my memory of the Kennedy assassination really begins on the following Sunday. We were all gathered around the TV when Jack Ruby shot Lee Harvey Oswald in the underground garage at the Dallas police station. We were glued to the TV for the funeral as well.

· · ·

Snapshot: (1964) One day at recess in kindergarten we were outside throwing things into a small pond. I picked up a rotting wooden stake with a rusty nail, and when I threw it, the nail got deeply wedged into my left thumb. I was rushed screaming and crying to the doctor where a large, scary nurse pulled the nail, with stake attached, out of my thumb. I still have the scar. A more frightening accident happened at a bowling alley. There, my two-year-old sister Becky got her hand stuck in the ball return. She wears those scars, too.

Snapshot: (1962-64) PaPa and MaMa (pronounced PUH-paw and MUH-maw), my father's parents, would come over every Sunday evening with warm glazed donuts. What a wonderful memory. PaPa, whose name was Earl Bourgeois (he pronounced it "Oil"), was a kind, easy-going man who saw the good in everything. My grandmother was a quiet woman who always seemed troubled by something. I found out when I was older she was then in the initial stages of Alzheimer's disease, or what they called at the time "hardening of the arteries." She ended up in a nursing care facility soon after we moved away from New Orleans.

Snapshot: (1961-64) There were great differences between my two sets of grandparents. I remember spending the day at MaMa and PaPa's house. I can vividly recall the scent of moth-balls, an indefinable musty but not unpleasant smell of lived-in fabrics and a house full of old, settled things. I loved their little organ they let me pound on. It had buttons that played chords. PaPa had metal World War I toy soldiers that were a real treat to set up and knock over. He had a little push mower, which even at that time seemed old-fashioned. PaPa had had a few heart attacks, and he had fallen off a ladder. He used to talk about "when the doctors sawed me open" and that never failed to make a deep visual impression on me. MaMa would make us fried baloney sandwiches on white bread with a little bit of mustard or split a couple of wieners and fry those presented in the same way. Like Proust's madeleine, I can taste that in my mouth now. I had my first cup of coffee there, Sanka, with lots of milk and sugar. Every time I said, "Hey!" MaMa would reply, "Hay is for horses!" They had a fig tree in the backyard that I loved to climb. One time I misplaced my foot and nearly fell out of the tree. I thought I almost died.

MaMa's name was Gertrude Gelzenlaueter, the most German name there ever was. A visit to these grandparents usually meant a companion visit to my Aunt Gloria's house. She lived right around the corner from MaMa and PaPa. Gloria was my father's older sister and she looked like a heavier version of him. I don't have a fond memory of Aunt Gloria. She always seemed a little bothered when we came over. She smoked three packs of cigarettes a day and her house was always smoky. I had two cousins living there as well, Kathleen and Bud. They were much closer to my older brothers in age, so I didn't know them very well and they didn't spend a whole lot of energy getting to know me or my sisters either.

Snapshot: (1961-64) Visiting my mother's parents was a different experience. They lived off St. Charles Avenue in an exclusive part of New Orleans. My grandfather, Clarence Dowling, who we called DaDa (pronounced DEH-deh), was an important judge. His brother Richie Dowling was the District Attorney of Louisiana. I always had the impression that, when at their house, children were to be neither seen nor heard. I constantly got in trouble. Of course, I was a little brat, teasing my poor younger sister Becky almost without ceasing. If I wasn't supposed to touch something, which, at their house, meant anything, I touched it. I saw my first baseball game on the television in their living room. DaDa was watching the Saturday Game of the Week, and I still remember that it was the St. Louis Cardinals vs. the Chicago Cubs, and I know it was at Wrigley Field because I remember the brick behind home plate and ivy in the outfield. We had to stay at NaNa (NAH-nah) and DaDa's house during hurricanes because they lived on higher ground. I never knew there *was* such a thing as higher ground in New Orleans, but the wealthier parts of town were built on slightly elevated terra firma. When we got home from one hurricane, a large tree in our backyard had fallen over and struck the side of our house.

We would occasionally have Sunday Brunch after church at their country club in Metairie, which was another chance for getting in trouble. My grandmother NaNa (whose maiden name was Helen Kurakar) would pinch my ear for teasing my sister. These two grandparents not-so-secretly wished that my mom and dad would have stopped having children after my two older brothers. My mother's older sister was Aunt Dottie. She looked and sounded like my mother except she had a sharper edge. My two cousins on that side of the family were Henri and Petey. Henri was older and almost unapproachable, but Petey was like another brother to us.

Snapshot: (1961-64) I have fond memories of Mardi Gras and the brilliantly colored and lit-up floats and parades with marching bands. The Black bands, with their fantastic steps and their high-flying baton-twirlers, were the best. There were also some floats like the Zulus with their Voodoo dancers that were scary to a five or six-year-old. We would dress up like

Indians and yell, "Hey mister! Throw me something!" We always ended up with piles of beads and doubloons. Both sides of my family were deeply involved in the societies called Krewes that made the floats and costumes for Mardi Gras. It was a big deal and there were balls and planning parties all year long. It was also something I took for granted as a kid. I thought everybody had Mardi Gras.

Snapshot: (1964) The only time I ever got spanked, I was five or six-years-old. I broke a 7Up bottle in a rain gutter by the side of the house. When asked whether I had done it, I lied. I wasn't spanked for breaking the bottle, but for lying about it. The coverup is always worse than the crime. Lesson learned.

Snapshot: (1962-64) My best friend between the ages of four and six was a boy who lived a few houses down named Scotty Tangney, a spunky, ginger-haired little fellow with a lot of freckles. He had a funny way of talking that we never forgot. For the rest of our lives, my siblings and I would recall Scotty knocking on our front door asking, "K'I pee pay Bent Boowa?" Me and Scotty Tangney decided one day to dig a hole to China in our backyard. We had a detached garage, and behind that was a bit of ground where we started to dig. We put a lot of effort into this project and dug for days. As far as I can remember, we dug a hole about the size of a small army helmet. Not long after that, my sister Coral ran away from home but came back crying after a few minutes because she wasn't allowed to cross the intersection at the end of our street by herself.

. . .

Snapshot: (1962-64) My mother cooked yummy red beans and rice and the best Cajun gumbo. Both meals took all day to cook. Living in New Orleans, we were spoiled by fine food, and learned to eat spicy foods young. My love of red beans and rice has never diminished. My mother would get us to eat vegetables by pouring melted cheese, garlic, and butter all over them. We ate fish sticks on Friday because we were Catholic. Occasionally my father would bring home a big bucket of crawfish and dump them out on newspaper at the kitchen table and we would pull the heads off and suck out the insides. Things like that are normal when you're a little kid. In Louisiana, that is.

Snapshot: We lived nearby The Levee and were always driving in one direction or the other next to The Levee. I heard about The Levee all the time. The Levee was a steep grassy hill that you couldn't see over from the car. I don't think I ever put two and two together that on the other side of The Levee was the mighty Mississippi River. It was just The Levee.

Snapshot: We had a set of The Encyclopedia Britannica including the wonderfully exotic World Atlas. I would lie on the floor and look at all the countries in the atlas for hours, tracing with my fingers faraway places like Czechoslovakia and Morocco, Pakistan and Albania, all with distinctly different colors. This was the beginning of my life-long love of geography. We also had a nice cabinet record player, and I would lie under the dining room table and stare at the fabric pattern on the cabinet doors while listening to Louis Armstrong, Pete Fountain, Al Hirt, or the soundtrack to *My Fair Lady*.

·   ·   ·

Snapshot: My brother Bruce had his own little record player in the room that he and Brian shared, and they would listen to Elvis, Rickey Nelson, Fabian, Dion, Chubby Checker, Fats Domino and Little Richard. In 1964, my whole family watched The Beatles on *The Ed Sullivan Show* a couple of times. We watched the *Ed Sullivan Show* on CBS every Sunday night. I remember seeing Edie Gormé and Topo Gigio, Brenda Lee and Paul Anka, Tony Bennett and Connie Francis, and the guy who spun plates. He'd get twenty plates spinning up on twenty different poles. That guy never knew that someday he would become a metaphor for having too much to do at one time. Disney's *Wonderful World of Color* was on Sunday nights too on NBC. If you wanted to watch one and then the other, you had to get up and change the channel on the TV set yourself.

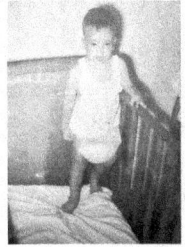

Dirty Diaper

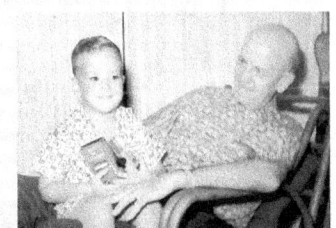

3 years-old with PaPa

At Timberlane Pool

4 year-old champion

About to dig a hole to China

Looks like I got what I wanted

With Scotty Tangney and my brother Bruce

New Orleans, 1960-1964

2

A KID IN NEW JERSEY

Despite my love of geography, I'm pretty sure I didn't know where New Jersey was. At six-and-a-half years-old, you're just going where your parents go. The first thing I remember about moving was being in the car on the long journey north, sometime after Christmas 1964, during the winter school break. We had two cars, my mom drove one, my dad the other. We traveled through Louisiana, Mississippi, Tennessee, Virginia, Washington, D.C., Maryland, and Delaware before we finally arrived in New Jersey. Along the way, I made a booklet out of construction paper of all the states we visited, gluing maps, emblems, trinkets and mementos on each page. Those were the days of no seat belts. We would lay on the floor in the back of the car, my little sister Becky cramming into the space between the top of the seats and the rear window. Becky could fit anywhere–she would take baths in our small bathroom sink.

When we got to Morristown, New Jersey, it was the middle of the winter and there was two feet of snow on the ground. I had never seen snow in person, only in books and in the movies. We were moving into a new neighborhood called Cromwell Hills, full of brick and clapboard Colonial-style homes. Because our house was still being built, we were temporarily settled into a rental home in the neighborhood. We made a snowman on the first day. The property had a large hill as a side yard, and we bought sleds and zoomed down that hill for days. What a culture shock!

At my new school, Normandy Park Elementary, I was supposed to be enrolled in the first grade. Born in the middle of June when the school year was over, I was always among the younger students. I was instead moved directly into the 2nd grade. Maybe it was the booklet of states that I presented to the principal, or a test I took, but suddenly, I was thrust into a new classroom in the middle of the school year with kids considerably older. The difference in age of a year and more in emotional maturity is much greater at that age than as one gets older and the gap melts away. This promotion had lasting effects on my childhood. Thankfully, I wasn't on the small side. In no time, I was labeled as "hyperactive," describing half the boys in that school. My dad called me a "bull in a China shop." I'd get deportment checkmarks on my report card– "can't sit still," "talks too much," "class clown," and testy hand-written remarks like, "He would do so much better if he just tried a little bit." My way of fitting in was to make people laugh. I was always cutting up for attention. In modern language, the definition of ADHD.

My first magical memories of living in New Jersey were trips we took to New York City. The whole family went to Radio City Music Hall to see *Mary Poppins* in the winter of 1965. What another culture shock! Upon arriving, my dad bought tickets for the *next* show, and we stood for two hours in a long line that wrapped far around the corner of 50th Street, shuffling our feet in the cold, slushy snow. The smells! I have always associated certain smells with New York City, none more than the Con Edison aroma of the subway coming through the metal sidewalk vents. Combined with those coming from corner vendors selling pretzels, hot dogs and roasted chestnuts, people smoking, with maybe a little urine mixed in, nothing has ever smelled the way Manhattan does. My dad would go across the street to the Horn & Hardart automat and bring back hot chocolates and coffee.

When it was finally our turn to go in, the view walking through the large brass-plated front doors was one of the most breathtaking sites in the world. It was all red velvet and gold, sparkling diamond chandeliers, massive and brilliant Art Deco at its finest. Even the velvet ropes keeping the crowd in line at my height were gorgeous. After we found our seats, assisted by ushers dressed in their finery, the organist played on the Wurlitzer pipe organ, the largest ever built for a theatre. The Rockettes then pranced out and dazzled the audience with their perfectly timed show-stopping kicks. And this was just the warmup to the movie! We took in a Radio City Music Hall show about once a year, seeing *The Sound of Music*, a special showing of *The Wizard of Oz*, and at least one Christmas Spectacular. Always, it was standing outside in line (or "on" line as they say in New York) for the length of the first show, getting hot chocolate at the automat, and then finally going in.

That summer, my father took me to my first two major league baseball games. One was on a cool night in May to see the once-mighty New York Yankees play the Washington Senators at the old Yankee Stadium. The Yankees were *the* dominant team in baseball since the early 1920s when they had a guy named Babe Ruth, but 1965 was the year it all fell apart. They had a team full of legendary but hobbled and aging players.

Mickey Mantle was limping on two bad knees, Whitey Ford had suddenly grown old and lost his fastball, Roger Maris couldn't stay healthy, and ol' Yogi Berra was now a coach. (These "old" guys were in their mid-30s!) None of this mattered to me–I was seeing all it all for the first time.

The only thing that rivaled Radio City in amazing first impressions was walking through the entrance of the legendary Yankee Stadium to our seats and seeing the emerald green grass, the baby blue balustrade topping the stands, the monuments in center field, and the smell of beer and cigar smoke that wafted through the air. One of the greatest moments of my life. My dad had gotten us seats in the lower deck just behind third base. Large steel pillars held up the upper decks obstructing some sight lines. We were on the outside of one of these pillars and had a great view. I brought my glove, as every kid does for the minute chance he might catch a foul ball. In the middle innings, Mickey Mantle came up to bat. Mickey was the greatest switch-hitter of all time, and in that at bat he was hitting from the left side of the plate, which meant that we were in a prime position to receive a foul ball off the bat of the mighty Mick. Sure enough, Mickey hit not a pop foul, but a screaming line drive right at us. Six-year-old me was too scared to even try and catch such a thing, but there was a guy right on the other side of the pillar who reached out in front of my dad and me and caught the ball bare-handed and held it up proudly like all fans do, to wild applause. What I will never forget is that his hands dripped blood down his arms, but he didn't seem to care at all. He had snared a foul ball off the bat of the great Mickey Mantle.

The other game my dad took me to that summer was at Shea Stadium, home of the woeful but lovable New York Mets. After the Brooklyn Dodgers and the New York Giants broke the hearts of many New Yorkers by leaving in 1958 for California,

New York was awarded a National League expansion team, the New York Metropolitans, in 1962. Their uniforms combined the orange and blue colors of the Giants and Dodgers. They had, for their first manager, the wacky and ancient, ever-quotable former skipper of the Yankees, Casey Stengel. The Mets promptly lost the most games in one season in major league history, but everyone loved them. I started following baseball just as the Yankees were in decline, so my first favorite team was the Amazin' Mets. In 1965 they were a little better than when they started, but they were still pretty awful. The game my dad took me to (I'm hearing the voice of the immortal broadcaster Vin Scully breaking in on this next part.) *"on a warm night in August against those villainous traitors, the Los Angeles Dodgers, who would go on that year to win yet another World Series. Pitching for the Dodgers on that summer evening in Flushing Meadows was the best pitcher on the planet, the almost unbeatable Sandy Koufax, in the midst of his greatest season ever. Against the mighty Koufax the Mets countered with a rookie named Tug McGraw, making the second start of his career. In some unfathomable twist that proves the chaos of the universe, the Mets and Tug McGraw beat the Dodgers and Sandy Koufax 5 to 2."* And I was there! Tug McGraw went on to become one of the best relief pitchers in baseball for almost twenty years and was the father of country music star Tim McGraw.

Our house on Chimney Ridge Drive in Cromwell Hills was called a split-level. From the garage, you walked into the family room, a level below the front door. It was up seven steps to the main level containing the kitchen, the living room and the dining room. The Chickering baby grand piano resided in the living room, and the record player (my dad's domain) sat in the dining room. Both the front door and the side door out of the kitchen took you down several steps to the yard. We used to catch the school bus right out that side door by our mailbox. Up seven more steps were three bedrooms, two bathrooms and a laundry closet. These consisted of my bedroom and the bedrooms of my two sisters, Coral and Becky. Coral had a bedroom with her own bathroom. Seven steps higher and you had arrived at the master bedroom and bathroom. My parents had another TV in their bedroom. And seven *more* steps took you to the attic, which my dad single-handedly converted into another bedroom for Bruce and Brian when they were around. As is a rite of passage for all little boys with older brothers, I found my first *Playboy* magazine hiding in there. I also listened to *Sgt. Pepper, The White Album,* and *Abbey Road* for the first time on a nice stereo in that room. My father Harry was a handy guy. Not only did he build that whole bedroom by himself, but he also built a brick front walk and our patio too. I didn't inherit that trait.

When we moved in, we got a dog to go with the house. His name was Boxer, but he was a mutt. He might have been part boxer, but he was more Rhodesian Ridgeback than anything, and those dogs are fast. The houses in our neighborhood had no fences, so we had to be careful with Boxer. One of my constant childhood memories was of someone (*never* me!) forgetting to close the back door all the way and Boxer tearing out of the house through the garage down the street and then into the car my steaming mad dad would go, muttering and gripping the steering wheel tightly, up the hill several blocks to one of about five houses. Everyone in the neighborhood knew Boxer's tendencies towards the lady dogs.

In our ample front yard, my dad would put Boxer on a long chain tied to a metal stake in the ground. Over and over and over and over again Boxer would go tearing after a car only to get yanked at the end of the chain and flipped on his back. He never learned. A couple of years later my sister Coral was riding in her boyfriend's VW Bug while my dad was out watering the front yard. Boxer was chasing cars when the Bug came ripping around the corner right in front our house and flipped on its back! Boxer thought it was a cute impression, but my dad did not.

The mid-1960s was a wonderful time to be a kid in a neighborhood like ours. The streets and fields crawled with kids riding bikes, jumping ropes, throwing balls, and playing hide-and-seek, hopscotch and kick-the-can. In the winter we built snow forts and had snowball fights. There were just enough woods around for an eight-year-old kid to feel insecure. Along with many Irish and Italian Catholic families with five or seven or even eight kids, there were quite a few Jewish families, including a good friend of mine, Alan Einstein. There was always a quiet, somber and mysterious feeling when I went into his house. His grandmother lived with them, but we weren't supposed to talk about what happened to the rest of her family.

Our corner lot was across from the football field, and next to that was a small baseball diamond surrounded by large trees. If you hit it into the trees on the fly it was a home run. Across the street from the baseball field was the Cromwell Hills swim club. The swimming pool was packed from Memorial Day to Labor Day and had a good swim team. All my siblings were fine swimmers, none better than Becky, who would go on to swim in Texas youth state swimming tournaments in the butterfly. Even though the pool was right there, we kids would still swim in the muddy drainage ditch near our house when it overflowed.

I had a mustang bike with a banana seat (and no helmet of

course!) On a weekend day or during the summer when the weather was nice we would emerge from our houses about 10:00 in the morning (sometimes after swim practice) and be gone until dinnertime. No adult supervision necessary. My mom had a dinner bell she rang from the front porch of our house that I could hear from a long way away.

My best friend, Eddie Costello, lived next door. He was a thin little guy with white-blond hair. His mother looked and sounded like Edith Bunker, although I wouldn't make that connection for another ten years. Eddie had a board game called Strat-O-Matic Baseball and it was playing it a *lot* in the summer of 1965 that really stoked my interest in America's pastime. All the boys began collecting baseball cards and I ended up with hundreds, and then thousands of them. Willie Mays, Mickey Mantle, Hank Aaron, Sandy Koufax, Warren Spahn, Yogi Berra—I had them all. I built card houses ten stories high.

On Sunday mornings, all the Catholics in our neighborhood attended the same local church. We never had any choice in the matter, just like eating fish sticks on Fridays. I remember being in the car one Sunday morning, driving down our street and knowing which houses were neither Catholic nor Jewish. These houses were quiet and dark, the garage doors closed, the large Sunday morning paper still out in the driveway. I asked my dad about this, and he said they were probably Protestants, and all I could think about these Protestants was that they couldn't possibly be as religious as we were because they didn't *have* to go to church. I didn't know what they were protesting about either.

When I was ten, I became an altar boy. That volunteer position followed me around for much of my young adult life, because people would occasionally say to me, "You're no altar boy!" and I would reply, "Well, yes, as a matter of fact I was." I tasted my first wine in the back room of the church. We went to Confession once a month, which was strange because I had to make up fibs to tell the priest so he could then tell me to say ten Hail Marys and ten Our Fathers, a circular logic I never understood.

We also went to Catechism, or Catholic Sunday School, on Wednesday nights. Our teacher one year was our neighbor, Mr. Sitter, a drinking buddy of my dad's. Mr. Sitter told us one Wednesday evening that it didn't matter if you grew up in the jungles of Africa, or the mountains of Tibet at *any* point in time after Jesus was teaching, you would go to Hell if you didn't profess your faith and allegiance to Jesus Christ whether you *had heard of Him or not*. That was the moment the skeptic in me was born. How could you go to Hell if you'd never even *heard* of Jesus? That was one of those times when an adult said, "Because I said so!" It wouldn't be the last.

I was good at sports on a neighborhood level, and we played them all as the seasons unfolded. But baseball, the sport I was best at, was always the most important. We played sandlot baseball endlessly on our little field as soon as the snow melted in spring, on the hottest days in summer and in the rain, on into the fall. The games always devolved into heated arguments, a problem when boys umpired them-selves. "He was out!!" "He was safe!!" He was OUT!!!" "He was SAFE!!!" I don't think we ever actually finished a game, but a good night's sleep seemed to iron out the last dispute and we never failed to play the next day. I also concocted a wiffle ball stadium in our back yard. It was perfect for me because I was a lefty, and the garage roof was in right field, and if the ball hit the roof, it was a home run. I led the league in home runs every summer. I would persuade my poor little sister Becky to pitch to me at dusk so I could run up my home run totals.

I started playing Little League when I was seven. I was always good but never great, and I wanted *so* badly to be great. I once pitched a no-hitter but lost 6-5 because I walked eleven guys. During one game I was standing next to the dugout getting ready to bat when there was a close play at the plate and the boy behind me slammed his bat right over the top of my head in frustration. I was knocked out cold and woke up in the hospital. I made the All-Star team in my last season, and we lost in the state finals to Wayne, New Jersey, the eventual winner of the 1970 Little League World Series in Williamsport, Pennsylvania. But I was an alternate and didn't play. That was my baseball career.

The best pitcher on that team, Matt, was a big, husky kid from our neighborhood who could throw hard. He and I were what is called today "frenemies." Depending on what day it was, he'd either be at my house playing, or he'd be sitting on me, punching me in the face. One day we were skipping stones in the flooded ditch near my house, and he threw a fastball with a sharp stone from three feet behind that hit me squarely on the back of the head. I had a concussion, was bleeding profusely and had to get eleven stitches.

My parents' first two tries at having children turned out, from their perspective, splendidly. Bruce and Brian were prototypical 1950s-early '60s kids who dressed up as cowboys and played football in the backyard with their crewcuts and Johnny Unitas Colts jerseys on. They both went to Catholic schools, both were straight A students, and both Valedictorians of their high school classes. Who knew parenting was so easy?

When my sister Coral became old enough to have a voice, it

was clear she was different. Straight academics didn't come easily to her, nor was she that interested. Inside was a restless budding artist my parents weren't equipped to handle. She was the first sibling to get in trouble in and out of school, paving the way for her younger siblings to follow. Coral was caught between two eras of parenting: the first–hands on, tight discipline, good grades, good behavior. The second–five o'clock cocktails, lax supervision, and *laissez faire* parenting. By the time my younger sister Becky and I came along, my parents had had it; we were largely on our own. But Coral was stuck in between, and it was often painful. When we moved to New Jersey, Coral got her own room, bathroom, TV, and phone, which she paid for with a waitressing job. It was the first time I heard that cry of many young teenage girls to their parents, "I HATE you!!" She was sent to a girls' Catholic high school but disliked it so much they transferred her back to Morristown High.

Coral was a social butterfly who didn't find her calling until she majored in Art in college. When we moved from New Jersey to Dallas, she wanted to turn around immediately and go to a New York Art School, but my dad made her pick a college in Texas, so she went to North Texas State University in Denton, thirty miles up the road. As soon as she graduated, she moved to New York City and has thrived as an artist in the Northeast her entire adult life.

I was a child prodigy, a savant at one thing–playing the piano. Not that I was some genius kid pianist, that wasn't it. I had perfect pitch from as young as it was possible to have it and could tell you what key a song was in on the radio, what key the blender hummed at each speed, and what note the ping pong ball made when it was hit. After my siblings had their piano lessons I climbed up on the piano and played what-ever they had practiced. I heard a Beatles song and picked it out in seconds. When I was given piano lessons, it drove my teacher and my parents crazy because I wouldn't practice the song in the book but waited for the teacher to play it and then played it right back at her. I couldn't turn it off. I heard a cricket chirping and could tell you the two or three tones its legs were making. There were giant bullfrogs the size of a softball that used to populate our front stoop in the summer, and I could pick out the notes of their bellowing. It really made me different from other kids.

In elementary school the band teacher would play a cluster of notes at the very bottom of the piano and I could name them all. He banged on a music stand, and I told him what note it was. The school brought an audiologist to our school when I was in fourth grade to check me out. She had a bulky, early version of a cassette player and asked me to put headphones on while she played the first note from the cassette.

The audiologist said, "That's a 'C'–you tell me what the next note is."

She played the next note from the machine, and I said, "F sharp."

"No," said she, "it was four steps higher–C, D, E, and F. It was an F."

I replied, "No-it was more like a flat F sharp. The 'C' wasn't really a 'C' either."

She smiled at me condescendingly. When I insisted, she asked if there was a piano nearby. The school nurse pointed her down the hall to the auditorium stage, and we marched over to the piano. Sure enough, the tape was running sharp, and the "C" was almost a "C sharp," so the "F" was almost an "F sharp."

It was a great equalizer for me, the thing that allowed me to be on the same level as all the older kids in school. All the classes in my elementary school from third grade and above put on a class play every year. In fifth grade I asked if I could write the fifth-grade play. I wrote a Charlie Brown musical, simply so I could be Schroder and play piano in it.

My parents were never shy about showing off this singular talent of mine. This was the beginning of their "cocktail years." My mom and dad and most of their friends were successful functioning alcoholics to a greater or lesser degree, and life around Cromwell Hills, especially when the weather was nice, was a floating cocktail party. I never saw my dad drunk until many years later close to retirement, and my mom would get warm and fuzzy, but she wouldn't be drunk either. But some of the neighbors were a different story.

At least once every month some couple in the neighborhood, including my parents, would have a party at their home on a weekend night. Most of them had pianos so I, along with my brother Brian on acoustic guitar, became the entertainment in someone's smoke-filled living room. I remember sitting with Becky on the steps leading to our bedrooms one Saturday night when it was my parents' turn to host. The smoke was so thick you could barely see the living room. And sure enough, when the booze got as thick as the smoke, Dad summoned me and my brother to pull out a set of songs for an inebriated audience. Picture a middle-aged man, oversized glasses, short hair slicked back, tie askew, paunch well developed, leaning over the piano with a cigarette in one hand and a highball in the other shouting, "Hey! You know Washington Square? Or how 'bout Alley Cat?" "Woo boy!" "Wow Harry! They're good!"

We lived in a real-life version of *Mad Men*. My dad got up early in the morning and took the Erie-Lackawanna Railroad into Penn Station in New York City and then walked to his office at General Electric on 42nd Street. He would do the reverse to get home, and usually arrived back at our house around 6:30 in the evening. My sister and I rushed to the garage door to greet him with, "Did you bring us anything?" He'd rummage around in his suit pockets and fish out a golf divot or tee, a Mr. Magoo pin, a paper clip, or a nickel and we'd accept it excitely, only to drop it on the floor two minutes later. When he left for work the next morning, he'd pick up whatever it was we dropped, put it in his pants pocket, and do it all over again that night.

My dad also indulged in a curious habit that had a lasting effect on my music career. On the walk back to Penn Station from his office, he often stopped at a midtown record store and picked up a couple of the popular 45s of the day, not caring what they were, so we ended up with the most eclectic mix of 45s I have ever seen or heard. The Top 40 back then was a mixed bag, and we had them all. But the one thing that held all those singles together were the hooks. No matter what style or genre, every one of them had a memorable hook. And I was a musical sponge.

Here's the problem when something comes too easy for you. It becomes difficult, especially when young, to develop the discipline to work as hard as the person who really wants to be good at it. This goes for sports as well as the arts. I wanted to be good at baseball, and I spent a lot of time trying, but I never was better than average. As I got older, that wasn't nearly good enough. Playing music was something I was always better than everyone else at, and it just came naturally, so I never worked hard at it. My parents struggled with this, always trying to get me to practice, but when I did sit at the piano, I just improvised, made stuff up and then was out the door to play with my friends. At one point when I was twelve, my exasperated parents bought me an accordion(!), which I have to this day, in the hopes that it would spark some interest in me to actually practice something. It didn't.

Around the same time, they hired a professor of jazz from the local university who came to our house to teach me, which was an unheard-of thing. He did it because I was a unique talent, but I was largely unteachable. He showed me all the jazz chords, and how they were written, and the theory behind it all and gave me assignments for the next week. I never practiced what he wanted me to practice, but if he played something I would play it after him. I have often wondered where I might have gotten to in my career if I had ever developed true discipline.

My brother Brian had *the* paper route in Cromwell Hills for the evening papers and it was a large one. In the mid-to-late '60s, the newspaper was a very important part of everyday life. There was no 24/7 news, no cell phones, and no internet. There was the morning paper, and there were minute-long news updates every hour throughout the day on some radio stations. Then there were the evening newspapers and the nightly half-hour news on the three networks on TV. That was it. As a result, the evening newspaper held a great deal of vital information that you couldn't get anywhere else. People impatiently waited for that paper to be delivered in a timely, predictable cadence. Brian walked the route and delivered *The Newark Evening News* and *The Morristown Daily Record*. He was the responsible type, and as long as he did the paper route our neighbors had few problems. When Brian went off to college at Brown University, ten-year-old me inherited the paper route. My parents thought it would be a good way to instill some responsibility in me and I could make a little money, especially in tips. Oh, the baseball cards I was gonna buy!

I was a failure as a paperboy, as the quality of newspaper delivery in the neighborhood immediately went down. In my defense, it was a difficult job for a ten-year-old. All the news-papers went into a canvas bag with a shoulder strap. It was *really* heavy at the beginning of the long, hilly route, which had to be on foot because I placed the newspapers inside the storm doors. In the winter, I had to trudge through two feet of snow and no matter what snow boots I wore or the number of socks in which I padded my feet, I would come home with frozen, numb toes and feet. In the summer, the paper route was the very last thing I wanted to do after playing outside with my friends until dusk, becoming the burden of my young life, mostly put off until it was almost dark. Oh, how many times did the family phone on the wall ring with a neighbor complaining that they didn't get the paper. These were people we all knew, some of them well. *"The paper is late!" "Where's the paper?!?" "What's wrong with that kid?!?"* To quote my dad, "It was a 4-star disaster!" I kept up this disaster for three miser-able years until we moved away, which was loudly applauded by our long-suffering neighbors.

My brother favored a malt shop near our neighborhood called *Friendly's*, where they had the best and largest chocolate milk shakes on the planet, including a huge one, called a Frib-ble, which was served in a mug almost the size of a blender. If you ate three Fribbles in one sitting, you'd get your name up on the board–quite an honor. Brian was a quiet guy who was infa-mous for his endless appetite–odd because he wasn't a large kid. He had his name permanently etched in the Fribble Hall of Fame. I also remember him being thrown out of more than one all-you-can-eat restaurant. He would finish everyone's food at dinner if there was anything left over on our plates and ate more bananas than anyone I ever knew.

1968 was a watershed year for everyone. The Vietnam War was on the nightly news, and race riots in the streets of major American cities, including Newark, not far from us. I wasn't yet ten when Martin Luther King was shot in Memphis Tennessee. I watched Bobby Kennedy climb up on the back of a truck and announce to a Black crowd in Indianapolis where he was campaigning that King been killed by a white man. "But I had a brother and he, too, was killed by a white man," said RFK. Ten days before my tenth birthday Robert Kennedy, too, was killed by an assassin's bullet while we watched on my parents' TV in their bedroom. He had just won the California Primary and it looked like he was on his way to win the 1968 election. The Democratic Convention in Chicago that August may have been the ugliest scene of all.

I floundered through sixth grade and started doing things that would get me in trouble. There were still a few houses being built at the end of our neighborhood, and a couple friends and I would go into the open shells after the construction workers had left for the day and just mess things up for fun. It was small-time stuff, but it was cruel and thoughtless. I got caught and my parents had to pay the damages, which I paid back with money from the paper route. Some other friends had BB rifles and one time we climbed up in trees and shot at a front-room window in a house across the street from our neighborhood, which was dangerous and stupid. Why I did I do these things? Peer pressure. Showing off. Because somebody else did them and I didn't want to seem weak. I was a goof-off in school and did the absolute minimum to get a few As and mostly Bs. The remarks on the report cards were always the same. "He could be such a good student if he would apply himself just a *little*." I was more interested in making people laugh, but they didn't have grades for that.

It was the summer after sixth grade I discovered *girls*. I belatedly noticed that boys in my grade were buying faux-silver ID bracelets with their names engraved on them and giving them to girls. I didn't know any girls to give an ID bracelet to–I didn't *have* an ID bracelet to give. So, I went down to a jewelry store in Morristown and bought with money from my paper route a twelve-dollar ID bracelet with *Brent* engraved in script. Now I had the problem of whom to give it to. Most of the girls in the neighborhood were taken but there was a freckle-faced girl named Patty up the hill that was still available. She was a real-life Peppermint Patty, kind of a tomboy–in fact she played Peppermint Patty in the fifth-grade play. But then again, all the girls in our neighborhood at that age seemed like tomboys. I gave her my ID bracelet, but I don't think we ever talked once, and she gave it back to me soon after that. Later that summer, I played the piano in a youth version of Up With People that met in the basement of the local YMCA. There was a pretty girl singing in the choir named Janie–I didn't know her either, but I asked her to wear my ID bracelet and she did–for a couple of days. The next time we met for practice she gave it back to me because her father wouldn't allow her to wear it.

On the evening of July 20,1969 my whole family sat in our family room watching CBS's Walter Cronkite guide America through the momentous and historic event of man landing on the moon, the giant achievement of our age. My whole family minus me. I was upstairs in my parents' bedroom watching the upstart Miracle Mets on their TV, on their way to a stunning World Series victory that Fall. Near the end of July, they were still making their way towards first place in their division, playing the second game of a crucial double-header in Montreal, having lost the opener, and had to win the nightcap. The moon landing thing was pretty cool and all, but the Mets needed me. What kind of fan would I be if I abandoned them? While my entire family yelled and urged me to come down quickly, conveniently there was a commercial break between innings, so I raced down and saw, "Once step for man...blah, blah, blah..." and as soon as I could raced back upstairs for the top of the sixth inning.

Also that summer, Brian bought a ticket and convinced my parents that it was safe for him to go to The Woodstock Music and Arts Fair. After all, it wasn't that far away from where we lived, and nobody had any idea beforehand that it was going to turn out to be this huge life-changing event. They expected *maybe* 50,000 people. I almost convinced my parents to let me go with Brian, but they demurred, and boy were they glad they did. We watched the whole thing unfold on television and my mom and dad were fearful for Brian's well-being as over 500,000 stoned but happy hippies showed up. There was no way to contact him, and it poured at least one of the nights and mornings. But what a show he saw. The movie and albums they made of the three-day concert, from Richie Havens to Jimi Hendrix, were touchstones for me as a musician, and are forever burned into my memory.

I entered Junior High as an eleven-year-old. We were now going to school with a new set of kids from the other side of town. The first morning, before we even went inside the new building, my friend Matt, who was the biggest, toughest kid from our elementary school, got into a fight with Andy, who was the biggest, toughest guy from their elementary school. I think it has been that way for thousands of years. It was Biblical.

My first new friend from the other school was Rusty Trevena. I had one skill that he didn't possess, at least not yet–I was an accomplished musician for my age, and he was just learning how to play the guitar. But he loved music almost as much as I did, and he was the first friend I could hang out with and talk about popular and rock music. I did my first recording with Rusty one weekend afternoon. I had discovered a nice reel-to-reel tape machine hiding in a closet in our house and we recorded Carole King's "It's Too Late" by putting guitar and piano on the left side, then the bass and vocals on the right side. My first multitrack recording!

If I was going to play the keyboards with anyone else, I needed to own my own music equipment. The first instrument anywhere near my price range was a red Doric Combo Organ. This was the sound in the popular song, "96 Tears," by Question Mark and the Mysterians. Needing something to play it through, I bought a black Leslie 825. A Leslie is a rotating speaker cabinet, usually wooden, that you see next to most B3 organs. Stepping on a foot pedal made the speaker speed up or slow down, getting that signature vibrato effect. To pay for this, my dad instituted a strict system that would follow me well into my teens, loaning me the money with monthly due dates for payment. I paid for both items with my paper route. I was ready to join a band! The only problem was there weren't any bands for an eleven-year-old to join. There was one guy in our neighborhood, Joe Breitenbach, who was an excellent guitar player, but he was a lot older than me and played in real bands making real money.

The first cool gig I saw in person was on a Friday night in the YMCA basement. They turned this otherwise plain room into a psychedelic scene with black lights, strobe lights and weird fluorescent painting, the band covering their amps in tie-dye and paisley cloth. I felt so grown-up being there I was hooked. But there wasn't a lot of action for a young keyboard player, no matter how talented he might be.

I did get one audition with high school friends of Coral's who had a multi-racial horn band called Mocha. I saw them perform and thought they were fantastic. They played Sly Stone songs! Her friends knew how talented I was, and they

needed a keyboard player, so they swallowed hard and audi-
tioned me. Although I think I played the songs okay, it was a
bridge too far–there was just too much of an age gap, so they
decided against inviting me to join the band. I was crushed.

In the classroom, it was unfortunately more of the same with
me. I was a cut-up, always trying to get people to laugh,
getting in mild trouble, talking too much, never staying still,
and doing the minimum to get Bs. In science class, I almost set
the classroom on fire messing around with the Bunsen burn-
ers. I liked being in gym, where I was always the quarterback in
football because I had a strong arm, and I was slow. In concert
band I played the baritone horn, an oft-forgotten member of
the brass ensemble; like a cello is to a viola, the baritone horn
is to a French horn. It had the range of a trombone, and the
fingering of a trumpet. The band teacher had to rummage
around to find pieces that featured the baritone horn. I wish I
had been half as good in math or science as I was at the baritone horn. I come from a math-oriented family, and I've heard
it said over the course of my life that music and math are two
sides of the same coin, and the only evidence that I have to
disprove this is my track record in math at school. Then again, I
never looked at music logically.

Girls continued to be a mystery to me; a puzzle I had no
answers for. This was an area in which my younger age came
negatively into play. The guys who were successful with girls
at that age were all the most physically advanced, whether the
tallest, the biggest or the ones whose voices were changing
and sprouting fuzz on their faces. I couldn't compete with any
of that. I wasn't small, but I hadn't begun to physically mature.
I was still a boy. At that age I would develop a crush on a girl,
and the feeling was never reciprocated. There was one girl who

was in the same Study Hall as me, sitting all the way across the auditorium. She was in the local newspaper because she won a youth horseback riding competition, and I thought she was the most beautiful girl in the world. I would sneak as many peeks at her as I could. She made it impossible to study. I would *never* have thought to talk to her, except *maybe* to utter a quick, "hi!" to her in passing in the hall. She never knew of this obsession, at least I don't think she knew, but who knows how obvious 12-year-old boys are when they think they are being surreptitious. There were others along the way, but the story was always the same.

I was on the fringe of the "cool" kids in junior high because I was decent at sports, and I was the best musician in the school. Otherwise, I don't think this cohort would have had anything to do with me. One of the cool kids, Robbie, who of course was tall, well-built, and physically maturing, played the drums. In ninth grade we finally formed a band with Robbie on drums, Rusty Trevena on guitar, and (believe it or not) Jim Morrison on bass, the more famous Jim Morrison already being dead at that point. This was my ticket into the "cool" kids' club. We played dances in the school canteen. I think a few girls might have even thought I was okay.

The culmination of my ninth-grade school year was the class play, *Cheaper by the Dozen*. I played the lead, the father, and during intermission I ran down to play piano in the band, hair slicked back, and mustache firmly glued on. I was voted "Most Likely To Succeed" by my classmates in the ninth-grade yearbook. My life in New Jersey was ending. My father got another promotion, which meant another transfer to a new location. This time we were headed to Dallas, Texas. But there was one more story.

. . .

The lawn-mowing duties had been passed down to me, at least when my dad didn't do it himself. With our large front and back yards, it was quite a job. It was a hot summer Saturday; I was about to turn fourteen. Our house had already been sold and was awaiting closing. I had just finished mowing and had brought the lawnmower back into the garage to fill it up with gasoline for the next time. As I was filling it up, some gas spilled on the garage floor. I decided to spill a little more. I moved the lawn mower out of the way, found some matches and lit the wet gasoline on the garage floor, thinking it would just be a little puddle of a flame. Instead, the whole garage caught on fire. I quickly ran inside and yelled for someone to call the fire department. Luckily, they came fast, and the damage was limited to the garage. I convinced my parents that a spark from the lawn mower had started the fire from some gas that had leaked to the ground. This almost-tragic incident sparked the lyric from "Changed," the first song on the *Bourgeois Tagg* album almost fifteen years later:

I was filled with creative desire
I set my mommy's house on fire
I was strange

———

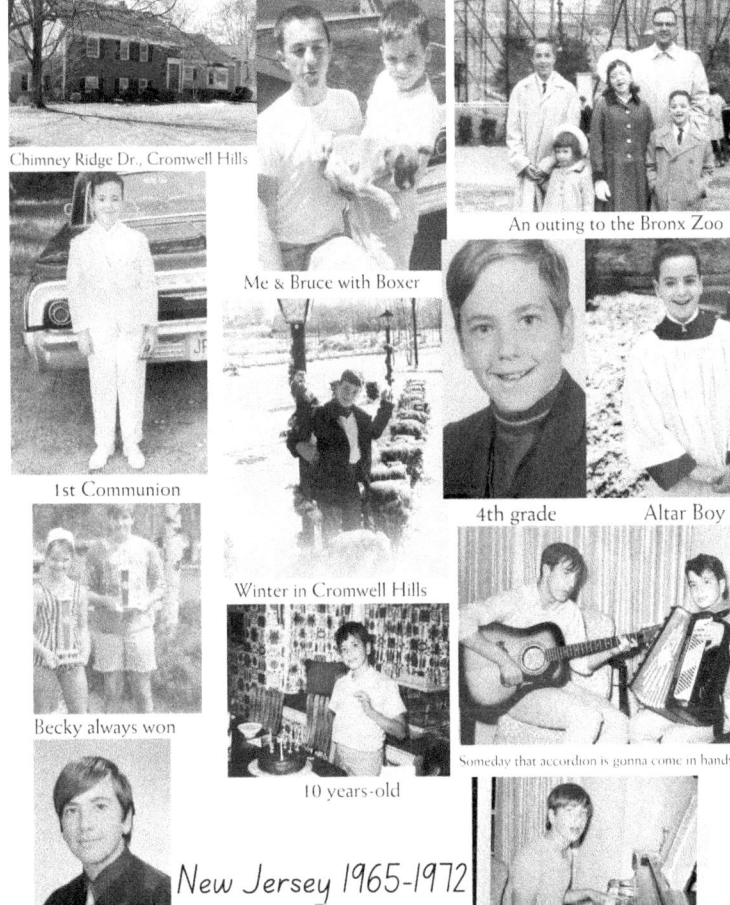

Chimney Ridge Dr., Cromwell Hills

Me & Bruce with Boxer

An outing to the Bronx Zoo

1st Communion

Winter in Cromwell Hills

4th grade

Altar Boy

Becky always won

10 years-old

Someday that accordion is gonna come in handy

New Jersey 1965-1972

9th grade

11 year-old pianist

3
DALLAS–THE BEGINNING OF A MUSIC CAREER

Harry Whit Bourgeois was born in New Orleans, Louisiana on New Year's Eve, 1925, and grew up in a working-class family during the Depression. His father, Earl, was an accountant. Like many other families during that time, they didn't have much, but they never lacked anything important, either. Harry, too, had a paper route. Growing up in the Depression, he was a frugal man right until the day he died even though he had plenty of money, going to one store to buy bananas, one store for paper supplies, buying cheap beer and box wine, and often driving out of his way to save a few cents per gallon on gas.

He played the clarinet in high school, and his high school band, featuring Al Hirt on trumpet, performed at the 1939 New York World's Fair. Harry met Helen Mae Dowling in a drafting class at Tulane University in New Orleans when both were sixteen. College in the early 1940s was sped up to get the boys out of school and into the service. He turned eighteen on the last day of 1943 and enlisted in the Merchant Marines, getting in on the tail end of World War II, making a couple of convoy trips to France and Italy before the war ended.

After he was discharged, Harry finished his degree in Engineering at LSU, and continued courting Helen. They were married in September 1947. Around the same time, he secured a job as a sales manager in the Lamp Division of General Electric in New Orleans. In May 1949, my brother Bruce was born and then in 1950, Harry was called back into the Service at the outset of the Korean war. He became a Marine Diving Instructor and the small family moved for a short stint to New Jersey. When his service commitment was up, they moved back to New Orleans in time for son number two, Brian, to be born in November 1951. As would happen to the family several more times, Harry got a promotion, which meant a transfer, and this time it was to Nashville, Tennessee where their first daughter, Coral was born in June 1954. Further promotion sent him and the family back to New Orleans where I was born on June 16, 1958. Three years later, in July 1961, my sister Becky was born, completing the family. And three-plus years after that, via another promotion/transfer for Harry, we moved to New Jersey.

Harry was a conscientious father and husband, seeing his primary role as a provider. He came of age during the time that men, particularly white men, were large and in charge. There was very little pushback to that idea, not in our house, at least not until my sisters got older. He was a Catholic who took his religion seriously. I was told that when other seamen got off the boats in France or Italy to do what young men do, Harry went straight to the closest Catholic church. I never heard him swear or make a disrespectful comment to or about a woman or look at another woman in any kind of a leering way, even on TV (although when he got well into his senior years he would comment, "That Maria Bartiromo is a *fine*-looking woman!") He loved Helen monogamously, deeply, and forever. He most showed that love when my mother was diagnosed with Alzheimer's Disease at the early age of sixty-five, and my dad took care of her in their home for the next thirteen years. It darned near killed him, too.

Despite being born and raised in the Deep South, my dad was not a racist. He had the personality of a patrician, which extended to all genders and races. An early memory of mine was my father talking to *his* father like he was the one in control. Harry was married to a woman who exceeded him in higher learning and had two independent-minded daughters whom he encouraged to find their own way. He insisted that four out of his five children go to college, and yet was open-minded enough to understand that I was different, and my arc was set as a musician; college would only slow down my path to success. When my mother was sick, there came into his house a succession of strong-willed Black women as daytime helpers. He treated them all with the same patrician-like atti-tude—a little condescending, like he knew more than anyone else about everything, but always had a twinkle in his eye, and was quick to laugh at himself.

My dad also had a quick temper, and his voice when infuri-ated was very intimidating. He never raised a hand in anger to us—he didn't have to. He got mad over seemingly little things, like not putting tools back in their proper place. But he soon cooled down and forgave.

He had a generous, sentimental side as well. My sister Becky got pregnant when she was not yet sixteen. For a conservative, religious man of his generation, this would have been devastating news. Becky told my mom first when Dad was out of town and then she flew off to New York to be with older sister Coral and await her father's wrath. Instead, he called her and said he wanted her to keep the baby, and they would support her in every way they could.

Harry was stubborn and methodical. He loved trading in the stock market in later years and would plot his trades on graphs like the mechanical engineer he was. He worked at General Electric for almost forty years, moving all around the country for them. I never thought to ask him whether he *liked* his job. It paid well, but he never talked about what he did for a living; he was much more interested in what his children did for a living. He was proud of his artistic ones–Coral's art lined the walls of his home, and my music was always in the mix on his stereo.

He was politically conservative. As he got older, Fox News was constantly playing on his TV, vying only with CNBC for his attention. I heard him say, "If you're not a liberal at 25 and a conservative at 55, there's something wrong with you." (There's clearly something wrong with me.) He always had a book in his hand, and he loved to take his bass boat out on a lake and do some fishing. He jogged and played tennis until his legs could take no more; I often heard him lament in his later years, "I'm falling apart! Everything hurts!"

He drank a lot of alcohol; more and more as he got older. A full bar dominated the family room of Harry's home in Dallas, and sitting on a stool behind it playing bartender was his happy place. He would have a beer or two for lunch, take an afternoon nap, then start drinking after 5:00. Harry encouraged everyone to drink along with him, often whether they wanted to or not, or if they had quit drinking long ago. He would fill my mother's glass with wine, which she drank to humor him, or maybe to keep up with him when he got sloppy and monologue-ish. Over about thirty years he went from being a hefty social drinker to a full-on alcoholic. As he took care of the love of his life, who disappeared day by day as he helplessly watched, alcohol became his great coping device, and I didn't blame him for one minute as long as he didn't get behind the wheel of a car. I am the most like my father of all my siblings in both looks and temperament. I consider this a mixed blessing.

Harry was forty-seven when he moved the family to Dallas. It would be the last home he owned. In 2014, eight years after Helen died, he moved to an assisted living facility in Houston near my brother Brian, as it became too difficult for him to cope with such a large house. From what my brother told us, he managed the assisted living facility as much as he could. He died there on St. Patrick's Day, 2015 at the age of eighty-nine.

———

HELEN

Helen Mae Dowling was born in New Orleans, Louisiana on June 14, 1926, the daughter of Clarence and Helen Vivian Dowling. She had one sister, Dottie, who was four years older. She grew up in better financial circumstances than my dad, as Clarence was a well-known lawyer and then judge in New Orleans.

A trailblazer, she was sixteen when she entered the Engineering Program at Tulane University and was teaching their college students three years later. There are many "firsts" and "onlys" in my mom's academic career. Suffice to say she broke through the male-dominated mathematics field at a time when most young women weren't allowed in the room.

Helen and Harry's love match was not particularly encouraged or endorsed by her parents, most likely because they would have preferred a partner with a more upscale resumé. Love won, and they were married on September 6, 1947. In keeping with the temper of the times, Helen's mathematics career was put on hold while she birthed five children over

twelve years, following Harry around the country as he got
called back into the Service and then promoted within his
company. She was a loving and faithful wife, a true Catholic
believer, and she never lost her love for math and teaching.

She was my biggest fan, to a fault. I couldn't sit down for five
minutes at the piano before she came in and said, "What is
that? It's beautiful!" I remember being so frustrated at her lack
of discernment that one day I started pounding out some
atonal nonsense and sure enough she came in and did the
same thing. I could always be honest with her. She would
rather hear the truth, even if it was something of which she
disapproved. She was a warm, intelligent woman and was a
great listener. She had to be, married to my dad. She deferred
to him in a way that most women wouldn't dare do in our
time. But she stuck up for her children whenever she thought
reinforcement was needed against our father. She moved
around the country constantly at the whim of her husband's
company. They didn't ask her. Her parents were never happy
that she left New Orleans, and I don't think she was happy to
leave New Jersey.

Mom thought mathematically, geometrically. She would
cut her eggs into precise quarters. She would notice when no
one else did that "all the left-handed kids are on one side of the
table" or "you are all sitting in your exact birth order" or "it's
boy-girl-boy-girl." Helen was a favorite of the young men who
came to band practice at our house. They knew how to secure
favors with flattery. "Ahh, Mrs. B., I love what you're wearing!"
cried one with a full laundry basket in his hands. "Sure smells
good Mrs. B! What are you cooking?" cried another hungry
one. She was not shy about noticing a handsome man. She,
too, enjoyed all kinds of music, and seemed just as at home

with Frank Sinatra as the Beatles. She found it easier to raise sons than it was to raise a different generation of daughters, as she was a woman raised before the advent of Women's Lib.

Helen had few social interests outside of the house other than swimming laps at the Y. She didn't garden, didn't play tennis like the rest of the family, didn't jog or go for walks, and didn't visit friends very often once we moved to Dallas. She went to church every Sunday, and I do remember her playing bridge. Her life revolved around her family and teaching college mathematics at the local junior college. She taught and thought about math for almost fifty years. I didn't inherit that trait.

Around 1993, I began hearing stories from my siblings that mom would walk into the kitchen holding a fork with no idea why, or where it belonged. Tests revealed Alzheimer's Disease. It was a long, slow goodbye, made much longer by the love and care exhibited by my dad. Instead of being placed in a nursing facility, she stayed until her dying day in her loving home, surrounded by the pictures, the music, the art, and the things she knew and the man she loved. Late in the progression of the disease, when she spent most of her time in a wheelchair with her head down sleeping, we wheeled her to the piano and I played for her. She perked up and smiled. I put her fingers on the piano that she had played most of her life. As she plunked the notes, a twinkle of recognition came over her face. She remembered. She died in 2006.

———

I had mixed feelings about moving to Dallas. Whenever you are moving *to* a new place you are moving *away* from your familiar climate, accents, habits, patterns and accepted ways of life. I was moving away from friends, sports teams and girls I was starting to like. It was also a rare opportunity to recast, readjust and reinvent myself as a person more to my own liking. I had the chance to start over.

I knew nothing about Dallas, other than it was the place that Kennedy was shot, and it was home to the Dallas Cowboys. Not exactly a great resumé. My dad was being transferred there to run the Southwest Region of the Lamp Division of General Electric, or GE. I used to ask him how come, with all the technological innovations happening, like sending a man to the moon, they couldn't invent a light bulb that didn't burn out so quickly? He replied, "Oh they can! But why would they? It would put us all out of business! Hahaha!"

We arrived in the summer, another culture shock. Texas in the summer is hot and dry, with occasional torrential rainstorms. It was often said, "If you don't like the weather in Texas, wait five minutes." My parents bought a spacious brick ranch-style house in (then) Northwest Dallas. The first thing we all noticed not far up the road was a succession of fast-food restaurants. I never remember going to a McDonalds, or a Burger King, a Taco Bell, a Kentucky Fried Chicken, or a Jack-in-the-Box in New Jersey near where we lived. But here they all were, in a row. In 1972, we viewed it as a major plus.

The other thing I noticed when we first moved to Dallas was the number of futuristic steel-and-glass new buildings sprouting up all over the city. Obviously, coming from New York, there was no skyline like it. In fact, on a clear day we could see the progress of the building of the WTC Twin Towers from our Cromwell Hills neighborhood. But Dallas's mid-level structures were everywhere next to the freeways, and every time we drove somewhere there seemed to be several new ones. These were the glory days of the Texas oil boom that spawned the hit TV series *Dallas*. One more thing: My lifelong love affair with Mexican food probably started the first week we lived in Dallas.

Following standard family procedure, I was sent to Jesuit High School for tenth grade. I had, until then, escaped being sent to Catholic school, but now it was my turn. From many angles, it was my most forgettable school year. The curriculum was difficult, and it was all boys. I made the swim team but was the worst swimmer on the team. Joining the marching band was another decision I immediately regretted. I made no lasting friends that year, and was generally miserable. Only in retrospect did I realize what an advantageous thing it was to spend a year at a prep school. It enabled me to graduate a year early from high school, but I couldn't see that far ahead. I did play my first electric piano, a Fender Rhodes, in the band room at Jesuit. I was immediately convinced that I had to have one, arranging for a new loan with my dad. The Fender Rhodes electric piano became my constant companion for many years to come.

Sometime in the spring of 1973 I saw an ad in a local music rag looking for a keyboard player to join a working horn band named Pariah Past. They played songs by Chicago, Blood, Sweat & Tears, Tower of Power, and other pop and rock music that featured horn sections. They had a booking agent and played a regular schedule of gigs. I hadn't yet turned fifteen, but I convinced my mom to let me audition. She had to drive me there, Fender Rhodes in her trunk. I passed the audition! They swallowed hard and hired me.

If there was a starting point to my music career, this was it.

These were young men in their early twenties for the most part; the lead singer was twenty-four. The youngest guy in the band was Mark the drummer, almost nineteen. The horn players were all guys from North Texas State University, a

renowned jazz school. The guitar player was already losing his
hair. It was life changing. From that moment, I never looked
back. At age fourteen, I was a working musician.

I didn't talk my parents into doing it, but this working
band of twenty-somethings from Day One started practicing in
our house on Duchess Trail. If there was one person who could
have, it would have been the handsome, smooth-talking, kind-
hearted, bearded, long-haired, great listener, ladies' man with
a million-dollar smile who happened to be the bass player in
this group, Bruce Yamini. I saw Bruce charm the pants off
many a young lady at gigs, and convincing my mom to do this
would have been child's play for Mr. Yamini. Bruce was the
bringer of the laundry basket, and a smile and a wink was all
he needed for clean laundry by the end of practice.

The "why" was simple for my parents–the devil they knew
was better than the devil they didn't. The band had to practice
a lot to work me in, and I'm sure Mom and Dad had visions of
wild pot parties and booze-fests at some remote practice facility. So, Pariah Past set up this large operation in the study right
off the kitchen. The room had originally been intended for my
brother Brian, but he was still in his senior year at Brown up in
Rhode Island and was headed after that to the University of
Texas to get his PhD. This eight-piece horn band was really
loud. There could be no conversation if you were in the
kitchen. The window in the practice room wasn't fifteen feet
from the window in our next-door neighbor's house. I'm sure
the neighbors, a nice older couple named Mr. and Mrs. Traffi-
cano, weren't expecting this when they moved into their quiet
suburban home. They were either saints, or they were deaf.
This room became the practice room for every band I was in
until the day I moved to California.

I believe the band's lead singer, John Barnes, a more typi-
cally handsome and arrogant diva type, was embarrassed to

have a fourteen-year-old boy in the group. I really don't blame him. He wasn't above sitting at my dad's bar, though, and sharing a drink with him. The horn players set up right behind me, both in practice and at the gigs. Alan, who played trombone right over my left shoulder, had a leaky spit valve, so over the course of a rehearsal or performance my keys and shoulder would get well-sprayed with his spit. It sounds funnier in the telling. Randy Drummond pointed his trumpet right at my head. I am lucky to have any hearing left at all.

Being in this band changed everything and made the second half of the school year (the spring of 1973) a new experience. I began to grow out my hair and bought some cool new shirts at J Riggings in the mall. Every Friday and Saturday night we played at college dances, homecomings, senior proms, and frat parties all over Texas and Oklahoma. I was good enough to play with them, but I was still just fourteen. We were loading the gear out of a venue one night when someone started passing around a joint. Wanting to fit in, I took my turn. Within minutes, I was absolutely paralyzed and had to sit on the curb with my head in my hands while everyone else finished the load-out. It was embarrassing.

Somebody had to pick me up and take me home from all those far-flung college dances and parties, and that task usually fell to Bruce Yamini. Bruce would drive up to our house in his yacht-like Buick with a big smile on his face and his leather bag (I had never seen a man carry a purse-like bag but on him it looked great) and off we went. The car had a great stereo system, and he would light up a joint and proceed to blow my mind with the most amazing music: Weather Report, Miles Davis, Herbie Hancock, Chick Corea, John Coltrane, McCoy Tyner, and Mahavishnu Orchestra. I got ten years of incredible jazz education riding around in that Buick for six months. By the time the band broke up, I was a 15-year-old jazz aficionado and had the perfect instrument in the Fender Rhodes. I talked my parents into buying me an upright piano to put in my bedroom and started buying nothing but jazz records, soaking it all up and taking it all in, practicing for hours with those records. By the fall of that year, I had taken a huge step with my playing, and I owed most of it to Bruce Yamini.

That summer of 1973 I discovered Skyline, a public magnet high school. There were twelve "magnets," or trade professions that you could major in while going to high school. One of those was music. I was in! It would turn out to be the best school year of my life.

The first morning of school, waiting for the bus, I met Sharon. I had grown up a lot over the past nine months, and this was the first time I felt comfortable enough in my own skin to have a conversation with a cool girl. She was all blue jeans and turquoise, a natural blond with a Texan accent and hippie-like flair–Austin in the flesh. I now had something to talk about: I was in this working band, playing gigs every weekend, and we were both headed off to this unknown adventure at a music-type high school.

Also on that bus was a guy named David Glick–gay, Jewish, with a great personality and a wonderful sense of humor. The three of us became fast friends and hung out as much as we could when we weren't in school. Sharon was my first love. We were boyfriend and girlfriend for the whole school year. Seventeen-year-old Sharon was way ahead of fifteen-year-old me in many ways of the world. She was always a bit mysterious, disappearing for days at a time, and it was only later that I found out she was visiting older guys out of town. Suffice to say I learned a lot from her. Once the school year was over, she didn't really break up with me, but was never home and didn't answer my calls. We would call that "ghosted" nowadays. I sat on Coral's living room floor in Denton, wiping a tear from my eye, and she said, "You'll get over it. There are many fishes in the sea." It was a prescient thought for a young, sort-of good-looking, local musician about to start playing regularly in the Dallas club scene.

The school year was like college. I had only two academic classes, English and History, to go along with a bunch of music courses. Because of my year at Jesuit, I didn't have to take Math, a real blessing. I played the piano in the school jazz band, with my new-found jazz chops. The other pianist in the class was a guy in the grade below me named Michael Weiss. In terms of recent jazz piano history, let's just say I was Drew Bledsoe and he turned out to be Tom Brady.

Another member of that jazz band was guitar player Danny Neal, a guy I reunited with a few months later. The head of the program, Mr. White, was a warm and patient fellow who understood that I was out performing in clubs most nights and was only semi-coherent at the beginning of each school day. He cut me a great deal of slack, even coming out to shows later in the year. It felt like Sharon and I glided over the top of Skyline High School as honorary captains of the music program.

There were a couple of bumps along the way. Students who could drive were allowed to leave the campus at lunchtime, and David, Sharon and I would do that when David had his car. One day, we were on a local freeway, possibly smoking something illegal, when the red lights of the Dallas Highway Patrol lit up the car. I nobly volunteered to take the "lid" of pot that wasn't mine and crammed it down in my pants. I was searched and taken downtown to Dallas police headquarters. The only person that could come and get me out was my dad. As generous as he was with his alcohol, he didn't understand marijuana or any other illegal recreational drugs and viewed them all with contempt. I will never forget the silent ride home in his car, his hands white-knuckling the steering wheel, smoke issuing from his ears. His silence was worse than anything. When we finally got in the house he exploded. "How could you DO such a thing?!?" I was young, dumb and entitled.

The other incident came out of the blue at the end of a normal day towards the end of the school year. For the first time in my young life, I felt like I was one of the cool kids and generally floated about a foot off the ground. I remember thinking more than once how great life was. Suddenly, walking towards our bus, I stumbled through a whirlwind of Black students who were chanting and yelling obscenities. They didn't care at that moment who I was or how cool I thought they would think I was if they only knew me–they just started pummeling me, sending me around the circle for everyone to take a shot at. I ended up on the ground and they began kicking me. I was very fortunate to end up with only a black eye and some bruised ribs. It was so random; at least it was for me. For them, obviously there were seething resentments, unresolved issues, and long-standing systemic problems. I was unfortunate enough to find myself an inconvenient punching bag representing my race. I was on the ground thinking; *Don't you know I'm one of the cool guys?!? I love Marvin Gaye and Stevie Wonder! I have a Clavinet for chrissakes! I listen to Richard Pryor!* None of that mattered. There was rage, and I was in the wrong place at the wrong time.

I realized very late in the year that my junior year in high school would be my last. This is where the one year at a college prep school came in handy. It suddenly dawned on a guidance counsellor, then me, that I was one class shy of graduating high school in the summer of 1974, just before my sixteenth birthday. So, I signed up for the requisite Civics class at the beginning of the summer, and six weeks later I was done! There was no graduation ceremony, no gown, nothing. I didn't go in for the school events. By the time I was eligible to attend our school's prom I had probably played at a hundred of them. I was just there until I wasn't.

———

Coral & Becky 1st
Day in Dallas

13 years-old
Marching Band Geek

With Rusty
Trevena

15 years-old

13 years-old
1st Date

14 years-old
with Mom

Brian & Brent

Brent, Sharon, & David Glick

Early Dallas
Days

16 years-old
to the Prom

With Bob Lincoln

Steve Mitchell & Eric Tagg

Ken Murphy

With Debbie Lovelace

Dallas Friends 1974-1976

4
UNCLE RAINBOW

I have a lousy memory for dates, not a great defect to have when attempting to write a book like this. I'm no Proust. I know people who can say, "Remember in November 1981, you were playing at Smokey Mountain, and you were wearing that funny-looking jacket?" Or "Remember in the fall of 1976 when you put on that stupid buffalo hat at Bowley & Wilson's Alley?" The answer is no and no. My wife will say, "I remember what I was wearing to the eighth-grade dance." I should have handcuffed a journal to my right arm. I remember my wedding anniversary, and I can remember my wife's, my kids' and my siblings' birthdays. But that's about it. This is the point in the narrative where everything gets a little hazy.

When we first moved to Dallas in the summer of 1972, a good young bass player lived nearby named Richard Bannister, and we jammed early on with guitarist Mike (Junior) Clark, who is still, fifty years later, a fixture in the Dallas blues scene. When I formed my first band, The Baked Bears, around the beginning of 1974, Richard got the call to play bass. I snagged

Mark Boatman, the drummer from Pariah Past, and Lewis Hutchinson, an odd fellow but a very good guitarist. I found out about a singer in another band who might be interested and went to watch him at a gig. Richard Oates, a tall, handsome guy with a strong Texas twang who looked a bit like Mick Jagger, was really good. I liked him right away. He was in an average cover band, and he was primed to be poached. Bands were like that. If you had something better to offer—more money, better gigs, a better setlist of songs, or even a better P.A. system—you could easily steal away someone from another band. We talked after his gig, and he came by the rehearsal room a couple of days later to check things out. It was the beginning of a long and close relationship.

When I met Richard, he was newly married to Cindy Ziglar. If the name Ziglar rings a bell, it's because her father was the well-known Christian motivational speaker Zig Ziglar. Zig was famous for such lines as, "You need a checkup from the neck up!" "If you aim at nothing you will hit it every time" and "You cannot climb the ladder of success dressed in the costume of failure." Richard Oates, his new son-in-law, was rough around the edges, had a mouth full of false teeth and arrived every day in blue jeans with holes in both knees, long before they became a prized fashion statement for young women. He smoked, drank beer, cussed even more than the rest of us, and pretty much embodied the exact opposite future wanna-be Zig Ziglar son-in-law. Cindy saw something in Richard that went beyond sartorial splendor. Zig and his charming wife Jean in time came to love and accept Richard for who he was—a man who chose a different way to make a living and one who was deeply in love with their daughter. Ironically, many years later, Richard put on a suit and tie and became a vice-president in the Zig Ziglar organization.

One of the first times Richard came over to my house, he had just bought a souped-up 1969 GTO and took me for a ride around the area. When we got back to the top of our street, and were about five hundred yards from my house, I said, "C'mon Richard! Let's see what this puppy's got!"

"Nah," he replied, "Probably not a good idea."

"Aww c'mon! What's it gonna hurt? Just to my house!"

"Alright" he reluctantly agreed, and he floored it, the tires spinning and smoking. We sped down the street and he slammed on the brakes, screeching, and laying rubber just as we got to my house, where my dad was out watering the lawn. That's how Richard met Harry.

I started spending most nights out at various Dallas music clubs, able to get into such places at the age of fifteen or sixteen because things were much looser in the mid-70s. Being a young musician with a rock-shag haircut and the beginnings of a swagger might have been the equivalent of being a pretty girl in those days. The "older" waitresses certainly treated me like that.

Mother Blues, Gertie's, Fannie Ann's, and Sneaky Pete's all had live music at least five nights a week. I saw local blues guitar legend Freddie King at Mother Blues; his daughter Cookie played upside-down left-handed guitar. Freddie, holding court in his dressing room, coke bottle dangling from his neck and surrounded by a few of us young acolytes, once opined that "jazz is all the wrong notes played too fast!"

Further down Lemmon Avenue at Gertie's, while standing one foot in front of a tower of PA speakers, I watched guitarist Jimmy Vaughn, the older and at that time better-known brother of Stevie Ray, play a smoking set of Texas blues and rock. To this day it's the loudest live music I ever heard, the thumping of the kick drum literally punching me in the chest. I couldn't get enough of it.

I saw bands that would soon be our peers: Texas Rose with Bob Lincoln, Lynx with Jimmy Wallace, Daniel with Alfred Brown, and the funkiest club band ever, Buster Brown, a mixed racial group of young men mainly from a small town in upper Texas. Their keyboard player, Kelly McNulty is still the best white funk singer I've ever heard. At the same time, they had a Black lead singer named Otis, or the Big O. Otis and the band did a version of the Stylistics' "Betcha By Golly Wow" that melted me. Their bass player was named Widetrack. And they had two guys who would figure in my future: George Lawrence on drums, and Little John Sanders on saxophone and vocals. Buster Brown was always one of those "what-if" bands. What if their drive to succeed had matched their incredible talent? They always seemed to be content to stay where they were, playing clubs in Dallas.

One thing all of us had in common was the booking company Southwest Talent Agency. STA consisted of three managers: Johnny Waters, Norm Miller, and Bob Carlson. They played an important role in the whole Dallas club scene, managing or getting bookings for nearly all of us.

A Dallas band that I went to see that would have ramifications in my budding life as a band leader was Pore, Cooke & Neal. They played Sunday and Monday nights at Fannie Ann's on Greenville Avenue in Dallas, an interesting slot because most working musicians played Tuesday through Saturdays and had Sundays and Mondays off. Fannie Ann's was the musician hangout those nights and there was always a good and attentive crowd. Pore, Cooke & Neal began as a trio and then added drummer Steve Mitchell. These guys were doing what we were trying to do. They had a few originals, but mainly played covers that you couldn't hear anywhere else, or creative rearrangements of familiar songs that were pleasant to the ears.

. . .

For many years now, performing artists in clubs and bars have felt obligated to play original music almost exclusively. Playing your own songs is a great goal and should be encouraged. However, looking at it from the audience's point of view, there is a disconnect that many songwriters don't seem to understand. Musicians will say, "I don't want to be in a cover band" and they equate that with performing in some hotel lounge, playing "Pink Pony Club" or oldies. But playing something the crowd is familiar with is a bonding experience for everyone–the audience members who are with one another, and the performer with the audience. What has been lost in this equation is the cleverly conceived and arranged cover song. My son Adrian and his music partner Paige Lewis were playing at a large club in Sacramento with the usual all original set, but they threw a curveball right off the bat and started with a completely re-imagined version of Taylor Swift's "Trouble." It took a second for the crowd to register what song they were hearing, but soon enough everyone stopped talking and paid attention. This seems a lost art. When a songwriter/artist plays a set of completely original songs in front of people who aren't familiar with the songs, they are asking a lot of the audience. First, if lyrics are important to the songwriter, and we know they are, the songwriter is at an immediate disadvantage because the average listener in the audience picks up maybe a third of what the singer is saying, depending on the acoustics of the room (usually poor), the type or lack of a PA system, the noise level of the crowd, and the particular enunciation of the singer. Your heartfelt ode about a lost love or a lost dog may never reach the ears of the intended. On top of that, playing one song after the next that the crowd has never heard before is asking for audience brain fatigue. The brain can handle only so much new information at a time. Unless you are making it uniquely interesting with either visual or special effects, come the third song the crowd will begin to tune out.

Buster Brown playing "Betcha By Golly Wow" is a prime example. In the wrong hands that song could have been a slow form of torture, but those incredibly funky musicians brought the song to a higher, almost spiritual place. True cover bands in the mid-70s played Stevie Wonder's "Superstition" or "Signed Sealed Delivered" (and they still do), but we played deep cuts like "Superwoman," "Tuesday Heartbreak," and "Lookin' for Another Pure Love." Audiences loved when we did that, and it opened the door for them to be receptive to our originals.

There were several bands in Dallas who used this formula to great effect. In fact, it was a Golden Age for that type of group. One of those was Pore, Cooke & Neal, whose broad-chested guitarist, Danny Neal, the same guy who played guitar in my high school jazz band, was fantastic on acoustic guitar. I renewed our acquaintance during set breaks, and it turned out we had a great deal in common both musically and in what we wanted to accomplish. He first asked me to join their band; after one attempt which didn't work out, I asked him if he wanted to start a new band. He said yes, and we took his drummer Steve Mitchell with us. So, along with lead singer Richard Oates, bass player Richard Bannister, and with the addition of saxophonist Steve Gay, we formed Uncle Rainbow. I was sixteen.

Uncle Rainbow rehearsed in the Duchess Trail practice room, and right away we knew we had something special. We had three singers, and took advantage of as much harmony as we could. We also had an unusual skill. I wasn't close to being a lead singer yet, but with my perfect pitch I could match Richard's vocals on the choruses, so we "stacked" vocals, like on all our favorite records. Our setlist was eclectic. We spent a lot of time on song endings for our own amusement and for their shock value. We weren't *as* funky as Buster Brown, but we could funk pretty hard, and we were more musically diverse.

We were the first all-white band to play a Lemmon Avenue nightclub called The Red Noodle Lounge, run by a guy named Snake, a decent man who took a chance with his own clientele by booking us. It was an uncomfortable vibe as we set up, getting the side-eye from the staff, but ten minutes into the first set we had the crowd dancing, and soon enough our skin-tone was forgiven. Snake escorted Richard and me out to our cars with our money each night with a shotgun; for our own protection, he said. A few months later Snake was shot dead in his office.

Uncle Rainbow took over the Sunday-Monday slot at Fannie Ann's from Pore, Cooke & Neal, which proved to be our legacy in the Dallas music scene. Fannie Ann's, owned by Wayne Morgan, was the location of so many fond memories of my time in Dallas. The first that comes to mind is watching my parents, Helen and Harry hold court at their table in the middle of the upstairs seating. Everybody loved Mama and Papa B, largely because Papa B would buy drinks for his many new friends. Fannie Ann's was where we honed our sets. We concentrated on innovative versions of album cuts by popular artists, or unique remakes of popular songs, with an occasional original thrown in. Fannie Ann's was *the* place to be on Sunday and Monday nights.

Steve Mitchell was a "right-note" musician with excellent time. Not a flashy player, he disdained drum solos, and never made any rhythm more complicated than it needed to be. Steve was as good a *fan* as he was a drummer, which made him a great musical mimic. He *loved* music the way I loved baseball when I was nine years old. He could play every Beatle song Ringo Starr ever drummed on and the few he didn't. Because he listened to so much music, he had an intuitive sense of where the drums fit in every type of song. This had little to do with the gymnastic fills and runs that many drummers took great pride in performing, whether the tune called for it or not. Ringo was a "right-note" drummer, too. He hardly ever did anything flashy, he had to be begged to take the solo in "The End" on *Abbey Road* and is usually not mentioned on the Mount Rushmore of greatest drummers. Steve was most like Ringo. Like many musicians of that era, he idolized The Beatles, but he went to great lengths to be at almost every bigtime rock show that came through the Dallas-Fort Worth area, filling us in on all the details if we weren't there.

Paul McCartney's Wings Over America Tour was the biggest concert event happening in 1975. Wings got ready for the tour by practicing for three weeks at their first concert location, Tarrant County Convention Center in Fort Worth, Texas, thirty-five miles west of Dallas. The sound system company hired for the tour was Dallas-based ShowCo. Being local, we knew a fair number of the guys at ShowCo. Steve was the only one in our band who really put the *fanatic* into "fan." While it may have crossed our minds, Steve pounced on the opportunity to use his connections with ShowCo to get himself inside the Tarrant County Convention Center for a Wings rehearsal which, incidentally, was also an Uncle Rainbow rehearsal day and he had neglected to tell us of his plans.

Security was tight at the arena, so there weren't many

spare people around other than the sound engineers and stagehands. Steve, looking like a rocker himself, was able to meander around. He wandered up onto the stage right behind Paul as he sat at the piano sound-checking "Maybe I'm Amazed." When Wings' drummer Joe English was nowhere to be found, Paul, half in jest, half in frustration shouted into his microphone, "Is there a drummer in the house?" This could have been Steve's finest hour, but he modestly neglected to speak up. Nonetheless, after the rehearsal, Steve was given another golden opportunity.

Paul and Linda were connoisseurs of the Herb but couldn't bring any with them, being under scrutiny from the authorities, so they had to bum such things off the locals. Steve was "Stevie-on-the-Spot" and produced the requested reefers from his front shirt pocket. Paul and Linda in return graciously invited Steve to ride in their limo with them all the way back to their hotel in Dallas! Along the way, they asked him what he did for a living, and he told them he played drums. In fact, said Steve, he was playing with his band Uncle Rainbow this Sunday and Monday nights at a place called Fannie Ann's on Greenville Avenue in Dallas. Coincidentally, Paul and Linda were looking to break up the monotony of being sequestered in a hotel for weeks by planning a night out. They took down the info and gave it to their driver. They were coming! Paul had one request: that we don't tell anyone because, {hear Paul's voice} *"well, if word got out it might become, you know, quite the madhouse."*

After Steve got to their hotel and said goodbye, he found a payphone and called my house. Not knowing his *fan*tastical story, we were upset that he hadn't shown up for rehearsal, but once we were filled in with the almost unbelievable details, all was forgiven. Steve reiterated, made us *swear*, that we wouldn't tell anyone, or they might not come in at all. We were so excited we all heartily agreed. Our lips were sealed. Except for maybe *one* other best friend. And our girlfriends, of course, who were *sworn* to secrecy.

That Sunday night outside of Fannie Ann's there was a swarm of about three hundred people spilling out on to Greenville Avenue well above the usual sellout crowd. At about 9:15, a black limo came down Greenville and slowed down almost to a stop in front of the club before picking up speed and moving on. The limo circled the block and did the same thing again, before landing down the block about five hundred yards away at a small, half-empty, honky-tonk dive featuring Delbert McClinton. We had no one to blame but ourselves. Steve was heartbroken. He ended up going down to the dive and saying hello to them on one of our breaks. Of course, he may have told a friend or two, too.

Many different types of musicians sat in with us at Fannie Ann's. Because Sunday and Monday nights were days off for most musicians, they were all available, and many would come and spend their busman's holiday with us. One of the odd places we found available artists on their days off was the Venetian Room at the Fairmont Hotel in downtown Dallas. You might think that someone doing a week or two at the Venetian Room would make for strange bedfellows with young rocker-types like us, but that's not how we thought. Anyone was fair game. Our first ~~victims~~, er-performers were the incredible vocal group The Manhattan Transfer, who were doing a month-long stint at the Venetian. We befriended them and before long they sat in with us at Fannie Ann's. We were agile enough to learn some of their material, and they were talented enough to pick up on ours. Tim Hauser invited us to spend time with them at their hotel, and Laurel Massé ended up singing background on our first single. One night at the Fairmont, I was leaving Tim's suite and almost ran over the tiny Bette Midler. I also befriended the Pointer Sisters, although they never sat in with us, spending an afternoon in their suite at the Fairmont having coffee and croissants, their wigs off, and chatting away for a couple of hours. I learned early on that you could use one name to get you to another. Another obscure artist I befriended from the Venetian was O.C. Smith, who was known then for having the 1968 hit, "Little Green Apples." Sometimes all it takes is one hit, and you can parlay that hit into weeks at places like The Venetian Room. I got in touch with O.C. and he agreed to come down to Fannie Ann's on his night off. Of course, we learned "Little Green Apples," and he performed it in front of an appreciative and amazed audience. Amazed that we had the chutzpah to pull something like that off yet again.

Later that year my friend Ken Murphy and I took a road trip to Los Angeles because neither of us had ever been, and there were whispers that the band might relocate to California. When we arrived in LA, we got in touch with O.C., who was recording his new album *Together*, and he invited us to come to the session. John Guerin, who had played drums on Joni Mitchell's *Court and Spark*, one of the greatest albums of all time, and was currently living with Joni in a house in Topanga Canyon, was producing this batch of songs. After we watched O.C. record some vocals, Guerin invited Ken and me over to his house. I sit here, fifty years later, thinking, *Now why would he do that?* We'd just met him, only barely knew O.C., whom he *didn't* invite, and we had nothing professionally to offer him. But invite us he did, and we found ourselves sitting in his below-ground study, smoking weed. About fifteen minutes after we got there, a beret-wearing Joni glided through the room in a hurry and barely waved a cursory hello. I'm pretty sure I wouldn't have liked having young strangers in the house if I were her.

Back in Dallas, I enrolled for the fall semester at Mountain View Community College for possibly genetic reasons–I think it was so drilled in me that this is what we Bourgeois children did that it made sense to me. I took a piano class, reading Classical music, not a forte of mine. I never learned how to properly sight-read music or read well at all. I could read a chord chart, but I stumbled over Beethoven and Mozart. At the end of the semester, the class had what were called piano juries. I played a selection previously assigned by the professor in front of a three-person panel of fellow professors, who sat with pencil and pad ten feet from the piano. Never have I been so nervous in my life. I have performed in front of 75,000 people more than once, and this was infinitely more stressful. I took my "gentleman's C" and never did it again.

It was at Mountain View that I met the second young woman who would figure prominently in the rest of my time in Dallas. Debbie Lovelace was an attractive, studious and shy college student. I was nowhere near ready in the way she was for a deeper relationship. She was a couple of years older, and considerably wiser and more mature. Debbie and I dated until I moved to California with the band. Who knows what might have happened if we had stayed in Dallas? My parents liked her. She probably would have moved to California if I had asked her to. She came out to visit when we first got there, and when I said goodbye to her at the airport, I don't believe I ever saw her again. I just wasn't ready. Too many seeds were left unsown. She died too young of heart failure several years ago.

I was a teenaged boy, very good at this one thing and immature, even for my age, at most other things. I was selfish, self-centered, and ambitious. *In my defense*, I was thrust into this life before my brain was anywhere near ready to handle it. There is almost nothing that can twist your mind like being a local music hero. I liken it to young sports phenoms. He can shoot the lights out of a basketball gym, but is he ready for the rest of it all? The only governor on me would have been my parents, but they were my biggest supporters. I got away with stuff none of my siblings ever did.

In the mid-1970s, it was hard to find someone doing what we did for a living who was completely clean and sober. That included ninety-five percent of the people who worked in the establishments in which we played, and most of the audience that came to see us. There were a few, but they were rare. I knew a few people who didn't drink (much) but used drugs. And I knew some who drank (a lot) but didn't indulge in most drugs. Guitarist Jimmy Wallace was the one person I knew in those days who was completely clean and sober from the beginning.

It was New Year's Eve 1975, and for some reason Uncle Rainbow was not performing. New Year's Eve was the biggest-paying night of the year, so I don't remember what was going on with that, but the whole band ended up at one of our favorite venues, Sneaky Pete's in Dallas, to watch our good friends Lynx ring in the new year. Lynx featured Jimmy Wallace on guitar and Johnny Marshall on organ, two guys I remain friends with to this day. They were a more rock-oriented band than we were, so we complimented each other nicely. The place was packed, the cigarette smoke so thick it was as if the whole place was enveloped in a fog machine. The waitresses were having an impossible time getting through the crowd to serve drinks.

As the clock closed in on midnight, one of the waitresses passed me and stuck a white wrapper in my hand. "Happy New Year!" she shouted. This was not unusual at that place. The bartenders at Sneaky Pete's would send up shots of the Greek licorice-tasting liqueur Ouzo before each of our four sets. Convinced that I knew what was in this wrapper (cocaine), I went into the men's room and did it all. After all, it was New Year's Eve! It turned out to be something much stronger, and I had just done *way* too much. After a few minutes the room started spinning and I couldn't talk. I staggered over to the bar on which guitarist Danny Neal was leaning, and he knew right away something was wrong. After Danny consulted with Richard Oates, Richard took me outside for fresh air. I was a babbling fool, so he put me in his car with a window rolled down and that's where I spent the rest of the night! I missed the whole celebration, staying in his car until the club closed at 1:30. Everyone then headed over to a friend's apartment to continue partying. Richard walked me in, and I was propped up on a bed in the bedroom, and someone checked on me every so often.

There is a humorous side to this story. Because I had taken this "whatever-it-was" early in the night, I hadn't had a drop of anything to drink except water. Meanwhile, all these folks coming in to check on me were getting more and more drunk as I sobered up. By about five AM, I was the most sober person in the place, and it was funny to see the tables turn. But it was a very foolish thing to do, and I hope this story stands in for all the stupid druggy things that happened in those years.

Richard and I were determined to write original songs for Uncle Rainbow, and after a few false starts, we wrote two songs that the band not only added to our repertoire but recorded as our first single, which I think my father co-financed. "Sail On," and "My Boy" do not stand the test of time. They were corny then although my mother loved them. I also wrote a song on my own called "The Break," which Barry Manilow would have thought too schmaltzy. Mom loved that one, too. "The Break" was my solo singing debut in the band. We weren't off to a flying start as songwriters. I don't think I wrote a decent song with lyrics until I moved to California. We wrote a song called "Indian River" which we turned into a medley with a much better instrumental I wrote called "After the Storm." On that one I called on my jazz piano playing and showed off the fine chops of all the band members.

In the summer of 1976, we booked a month-long trip to beautiful Colorado. Most people, when they hear of Aspen and Vail think of it as a skiing mecca, and it certainly is. I absolutely loved it in the summer, especially to get away from blistering hot Texas in the worst months. Hiking in the mountains, drinking cold fresh water right out of a stream, seeing wild elk and deer amongst the aspens–and then getting paid to play music in ski clubs at night–I never failed to remember how lucky I was to be doing what I was doing for a living.

Even when we played at a place where nobody knew who we were, we always pulled out different cover songs like "Nature Boy," or "God Bless the Child," which Richard sang and I played piano for, or James Taylor's cover of a Bobby Womack song, "Woman's Gotta Have it," or a Beatles medley, or a Steely Dan song that nobody else did. We played songs that we liked, not just songs that were popular. A medley that no band other than us would have dreamed of playing was Frank Zappa's "Village of the Sun" into The Fifth Dimension's version of Laura Nyro's "Stoned Soul Picnic." We played enough funk that people could dance if they wanted, but always tried to stay away from songs other bands played.

In what would be a continuing theme well into the 1980s, we had crowds every night of the week. There were fewer things to distract them from coming out. People drove a lot more before, during and after they'd been drinking. That wasn't a good thing for others on the road, but it sure increased the attendance in clubs. This was just before Cable TV, VHS machines were new, and there were no computer games, no cell phones and no internet. There wasn't as much competing with us. Nowadays, it's a lot harder to get people out of their cocoons. They'll pay $300 or more to see a legacy act, but it's difficult to attract a crowd for a local songwriter show on a Thursday night.

Our saxophone player, Steve Gay, was a quiet, intelligent, talented guy with a wry sense of humor. Lurking beneath the surface was a proud musician who wanted a larger say in the direction of the band. In a group with so many strong personalities, his opinions were often not heard. He made the decision to leave the band. Steve's departure opened the door to a new chapter of the Uncle Rainbow story. It was time for "The Chicken Man."

John Lee Sanders, alias "Little John," alias "The Chicken Man," was a small, slightly built, eccentric, lovable musician with an almost indecipherable Louisiana patois and a one-of-a-kind personality. He was a great saxophonist, a fine Bourbon Street pianist, and possessed a unique vocal quality that spanned races and genres. He also had perfect pitch, which now made two of us in the same band. Hiring John was not without risk, as he had been recently fired by Buster Brown. After his dismissal, John went home to his parent's house in Monroe, Louisiana, and that's where we found him, at a crossroads in his life. He immediately said "yes" to joining Uncle Rainbow, and two weeks later was sleeping on the pullout sofa in the practice room.

John instantly injected a heavy dose of personality into the band. His unpredictable energy made him a must-watch character, giving folks yet another reason to come see Uncle Rainbow. Most importantly, he was a songwriter, and his songs were immediately incorporated into our repertoire, becoming the principal songwriter in the band. He sang some of his songs, and Richard sang the rest. We now had four strong singers and our vocal combinations became that much better. John was also an accomplished manualist–he could play hand farts like nobody we'd ever seen, which of course we slotted into our nightly presentation. He would perform "Happy Birthday" and whatever else we might think of on his hands to the delight of the audience. He went on *The Gong Show* when we were in LA and won with his performance of "Sweet Georgia Brown."

In retrospect, adding John to the band stunted my growth as a songwriter. Once John joined, and we started playing his songs, the pressure was off me and Richard as songwriters. I should have accepted it as a challenge, driving me competitively to match John's creativity, but instead I shrank back into playing keyboards and singing. I coasted for a long time. In my music career, I try not to look back with too many regrets, but I can't help but feel some regret for neglecting a golden opportunity to write more music for a fantastic band when I had the chance.

By 1977, Uncle Rainbow was getting noticed. Everywhere we performed was packed with fans of the band. We played a one-hour concert in the studio of KZEW, the #1 rock station in Dallas. We opened for Al Stewart, Robin Trower and then the

English prog-rock band Gentle Giant in quad! That concert was a moment in rock history when the PA system was set up in every corner of the room and the sound engineer had a joystick that he rotated like a video game and sent the music spinning all around the concert hall. Not great for people whose heads were already spinning.

Richard's cousin, Sharon, married to one of the two Doobie Brothers' drummers, Michael Hossack, came to see us one night at Sneaky Pete's and was so impressed that she called her husband and convinced him to come to Colorado and see us when we played Aspen and Vail in the summer. He drove out from California in his Ferrari and before he left Vail, he had convinced us to move to California! He had ties to a new record company called Riva Records being started by Billy Gaff, Rod Stewart's manager. Gaff's first signee was a young fellow from Indiana named Johnny Cougar. Michael thought, with his help, we could sign a record deal with Riva.

One of his critiques stung us at the core. Hossack felt we needed to improve our rhythm section. That meant drums and bass. Being a drummer, Michael was most adamant about the drum chair. The best drummer any one of us had ever heard, George Lawrence, played in Buster Brown. George was the polar opposite of Steve Mitchell. He was technically brilliant, the kind of player who called attention to his drumming without even trying, took amazing solos, and garnered "oohs" and "ahhs" from the audience. It was a difficult decision to make, as Steve was a great friend and a fine drummer, but we were ambitious and smelled the chance at greater success, so we made the tough choice and asked George to join Uncle Rainbow. It turned out George was ambitious as well, and seeing the opportunity laid out for us, he said yes and prepared to move to California with us. It wouldn't be the last decision like this we would have to make.

By the end of the summer, the band, our crew, and about fifteen other assorted wives, girlfriends, managers, and hangers-on packed up the trucks and vans and moved to the Bay Area. I had just turned nineteen and was moving out on my own.

———

With Richard Bannister

Steve Gay, BB, Richard Oates, Richard Bannister

nclc Rainbow

Danny Neal

John Sanders & Cindy Oates

Little John Sanders

Uncle Rainbow Dallas 1975-1977

Richard Oates

5
MOVIN' ON UP–CALIFORNIA

aifornia, the place to be for up-and-coming rock bands in the '70s, was a lovely mystery to me. There was a conscious feeling that if a band stayed too long in a provincial place, they would grow stale and wither on the vine. Dallas had a vibrant live music scene, but it was off the beaten path for record companies.

It was a great comfort moving to such a far-flung location with a tribe of familiar people. When we were first approached about moving, we weren't sure where we were going in California—we assumed it would be south, to LA. But Michael Hossack and the Doobies lived in the northern part of the state. Michael lived in a beautiful house tucked back in Redwood Estates off Highway 17 near the top of the Santa Cruz Mountains, between Santa Cruz and San Jose. There was a wonderful music scene in the Bay Area as well, so to the North we headed.

We were given various choices of apartments available in the surrounding areas, and each chose according to their needs. Our manager, Norm Miller, and his wife Connie opted for a beautiful Victorian house in Santa Cruz. I settled on an apartment with my friend Ken Murphy off Stevens Creek Road in San Jose. I had never rented an apartment, and I didn't know a good one from a bad one. This was a corporate one. It was San Jose just before the great tech boom, Silicon Valley before silicon.

Before we had even settled into a practice routine at the Hossack house, it was apparent another change was coming. Now that we had one of the world's best drummers in George Lawrence, he was going to need more support at the bass guitar position. It's a lot like when you fix one part of your house, you start noticing the broken-down part next to it. In both cases, bass and drums, there was nothing wrong, per se, with the players we had; Michael was looking for something extraordinary, and once we got George, they both were looking for something additive from the bass chair.

Eric Tagg was a keyboard player and great vocalist in Dallas who wrote and sang the Lee Ritenour hit "Mr. Brief-case." Eric also penned a song called "Kingdom Come," a staple in our repertoire that we almost considered our own. He had an older brother, Larry, who played bass in a Denver-based group called Heaven and Earth. I knew Eric, and I knew *of* Larry, and had heard he was a great bass player, but never met him. Turns out that George played with Larry on brother Eric's solo album, so they had experience together. George and Michael summoned my future partner Larry to the Bay Area to join Uncle Rainbow and a week later he drove up Michael Hossack's driveway in his light-blue Fiat Spider, and the version of Uncle Rainbow familiar to Californians over the next four years was born. I ended up saying goodbye to another friend, Richard Bannister, with whom I had shared many a music memory.

When we moved to California it was under the assumption we were going there to make a record. We had "graduated" from club-band status in our own minds, and recording an album was just the first step to fame and fortune, touring and gold records. We rehearsed with the album solely in mind. Our new drummer, Mr. Lawrence, got mad at us one day for joking around too much. He didn't think we were taking it seriously enough, and I was probably guilty as charged. Michael Hossack was in and out of the rehearsal room, adding little comments and ideas here and there. We put a lot of faith and trust in a guy we hardly knew. He *was* in the Doobie Brothers, and *did* have some connections, but he was also a hot-headed fellow with a heroin problem who owned guns and was at least partially involved with the Hells Angels. This all came dripping out to us bit by bit. We just thought he was moody.

After we rehearsed for about a month, we were itching to play somewhere, anywhere, and Hossack was getting tired of supporting the whole band by himself. Michael had some friends who owned a bar called Mesa's in Los Gatos, a lovely little town on the San Jose side of the mountains, and it was…a biker bar.

In this little place Bay Area legend Captain Whizzo did his psychedelic light show (he called it "Painting with Light") with colored oils in large petri dishes and an overhead projector. I can't tell you how much overkill this light show was for a place of that size, and also how out of place we felt playing in a biker bar. Our repertoire was decidedly un-biker bar-ish. This was our introduction to California and California's introduction to us.

In the end, it went better than expected—for the most part. Picture this: We're playing on a narrow stage, facing the large picture window that fronts the bar. Captain Whizzo is up in a little booth about twenty-five feet away and slightly to our right, flashing his psychedelic bubbles behind us. The bar is to the far left. It's a Thursday night and we're playing, of all things, "Man In The Green Shirt" from Weather Report's 1975 *Tale Spinnin'* album. If that wasn't incongruous enough, we had tucked inside this ten-minute jazz song a round of *The Mary Tyler Moore Show* theme song. Why? It fit perfectly that's why! Just as we reached that part, a fight broke out near the front window. Before we got to the chorus one biker threw another right through the plate glass window and out on to Santa Cruz Avenue. And we're playing *The Mary Tyler Moore Show* theme song in this biker bar with Captain Whizzo doing psychedelic lights behind us. I think we paused for about ten seconds...and then, what the heck! The show must go on, so we picked it back up and kept playing while order was restored.

Among the people who showed up during our run at Mesa's—and we did start attracting a respectable crowd—was a blond young lady named S___. S___ seemed to get a wide berth when she made a path through these tough-looking bikers. Turns out she was nineteen years old and a major cocaine dealer. S___ became a problematic figure in the band's life over the next couple of years. Not too long after we met, Little John and I moved into a three-bedroom house with S___ and she became a dark House Mother to us. It would take me another ten years to finally be free.

Uncle Rainbow started recording in the fall of 1977 at Chateau Recorders in North Hollywood. Michael Hossack was the "producer" in name, but we largely produced ourselves. As with most recording sessions I have ever been a part of, the drums, and everything concerning the sound of the drums were seen as more important than everything else put together. Getting a proper drum sound could take hours, even days. The same holds true for drums in concert venues. The drums get two hours, everyone else gets fifteen minutes. Combined. The mid-to-late '70s were the epitome of the dry drum sound. The rooms were all carpets and thick wood, everything designed to minimize "bleed," or one instrument's sound bleeding into the recording of another. The result, in the wrong hands, could be sterile and lack excitement. In the right hands, it produced landmark sonically pristine albums like Steely Dan's *Aja* and *Gaucho*. Recording in the 1970s, now that there were sixteen tracks, or sometimes even twenty-four, was all about separation between instruments, so that each instrument could be pulled up by the engineer on its own and manipulated without the noise of another instrument bleeding through.

I had an opportunity to crash a Stevie Ray Vaughn recording session in Austin, Texas. On one side of the studio, Stevie erected a complete wall of speakers. Stevie and the band set up on the opposite side and played right into the speakers. He wanted as much "bleed" as he could get, because that's how you replicate the live sound. It was incredibly loud (funnily enough, probably the second loudest music I ever heard) and I never forgot it. After seeing Stevie Ray Vaughn's session, I became a convert of bleed. But this is future-casting from me, because I didn't go to that Stevie Ray session until a few years later.

At this point our young careers, we put our faith in the recording engineer, figuring he knew a lot more than we did about how to get good sounds. The result was sterile and lacked excitement. We did the overdubs in Monterey, California, one of God's beautiful places on earth. These sessions were co-produced by two English gentlemen, Ian Samwell and Jimmy Horowitz. Ian was an original member of British legend Cliff Richard's band and known for producing America's debut album which featured "A Horse With No Name," while Jimmy had produced many English artists including Rod Stewart and Long John Baldry.

If you are looking anywhere in the world for that Uncle

Rainbow album online, in used record shops, in my garage—
you won't find it. It was never released. People come up with
many reasons and excuses why something like this happens,
but Occam's Razor says it just wasn't good enough, and I agree.
It sounded dated before we finished it. The songs were mediocre and the production flat. I'm sure there have been worse
records that went on to some success, but this one wasn't
strong enough for the debut album on a new label. Billy Gaff
was smarter than that. There have been quite a few bands over
the years about which one could say, "they never sounded on
record as good as they did live," and Uncle Rainbow was,
unfortunately, one of those bands.

Tails between our legs, we launched ourselves into the Bay
Area music scene. Bad as the recording went, the club scene
experience was great. We were a well-greased, high-perfor-
mance band playing an enticing collection of covers that no
one else played, plus our own originals, which had more
energy live. We played Steely Dan songs live that no one else
did, not even Steely Dan! We did The Beatles better than
Beatles tribute bands. Tipped off that Stevie Wonder was
debuting his first single from *Songs In the Key of Life* on a
daytime TV show, I taped him singing "I Wish" on a little
cassette recorder and we performed it that night. We played a
12-minute version of Herbie Hancock's "Spank-A-Lee," show-
casing the awesome musicality and talent of the band, especially George and Larry. We performed in a circuit of clubs
from Santa Cruz to Sacramento and the whole Bay Area in
between—five or six nights a week every week. In short order,
we became exactly what we were trying to avoid when we
moved to California. We were named the Bay Area's Best Bar
Band of 1978 by BAM Magazine. Yay.

Playing so many nights a week, we never rehearsed, except occasionally in the afternoon in a club, usually after we set up. We did all our fancy tricks and turns and crazy endings as improvisations night after night and gradually built these into complicated arrangements. We all took performing seriously, and it was very rare that any member of the band was incapacitated to any degree. Most unhealthy things took place after the last set was finished between 1:00 and 1:30AM, depending on the venue. We might have a beer per set, but rarely more than that.

Once cocaine entered the picture, dependency followed. Living with S___ changed the nature of things. S___ would pack John and me off to the gig with our little bottles of white powder like tiny school lunchboxes and I would play a game with myself to see how long I could have it around before the urge would overwhelm me and I'd give in. Just having it in my pocket would sometimes be enough. Once cocaine was present, drinking increased. Rarely too much during the gig, but often way too much afterwards.

The band became very popular, we played almost every night, and I was up until just before dawn on a regular basis. Temptation was around us all the time. There was no one to apply the brakes. There were many locals who loved to hang out with a popular band, including quite a few drug dealers. As a local favorite, I knew a lot of these people well. And having few scruples, like I did, I learned who I could take advantage of (while they used me for proximity to pretty women and prestige.) As long as I did my job well, no one said a word about what I (we) indulged in. We were constantly praised for our musicianship. It was easy to ignore that there was anything wrong.

We started to include Sacramento in our rotation. We settled on The Shire Road Pub as our go-to venue. The Shire

Road Pub was owned by Jerry and Karen Sterchi, but it was Jerry's parents, Mom and Pop Sterchi, who were the geriatric muscle in the club. Pop was over eighty years old, with a strong German accent. He would always complain, "Why ya have to play so GODDAMNED loud?!?" "It's too GODDAMNED loud!" It would be hard not to laugh when he said that. We were in a rock club for chrissakes. We packed the place for five nights about once every six weeks. We became good friends with Jerry and Karen, and they became important figures in my future.

*An aside: It's amazing how smoky these clubs were. There were three hundred-plus people in a venue and at least half of them smoked. The smoke was so thick that you couldn't see the back wall from the stage. All our clothes stunk from smoke. We played for over ten years night after night in these rooms, and the second-hand smoke was awful for everyone. Richard was the only one in the group who had a real cigarette habit. I indulged late at night along with everything else, and then became a vehement non-smoker during the day.

We played close to three hundred nights a year, and settled into a predictable schedule. We took the Sunday-Monday night idea from Fannie Ann's in Dallas to Smokey Mountain in Campbell, near San Jose. It became successful in California for the same reason that it was in Texas. These were the nights that all the other musicians could come and see us. And musicians loved Uncle Rainbow. One Sunday night at Smokey Mountain we were asked if a new band in the Bay Area could open for us, as they were getting ready to go in the studio and record their first album. They had a respectable management company, so we said okay. Huey Lewis and the News played for forty-five minutes that night. They were tight. When they tried to bump us off the schedule a few months later after their hit record came out, Smokey Mountain said no thanks.

We often played on Tuesday nights at The Country Store in Sunnyvale. Wednesday would be our day off. Then we'd move up to Barney Steele's in Redwood City on Thursdays. We kept Friday and Saturday nights available for larger venues like The Catalyst in Santa Cruz, The Keystone in Palo Alto, or a couple of nights at The Boiler Room in Monterey. Some of the Earth Wind & Fire guys, brothers Verdine and Fred White, lived in the Monterey area and would come and sit in with us. It was a thrill to play EWF's "Can't Hide Love," one of our best covers, with them. We reserved one week out of six for Sacramento, and sometimes played a whole week in Monterey.

Wherever we played, people loved to dance. We never thought of ourselves as a dance band, but we played a lot of funky material, both original and covers, and people danced to weird things, like Weather Report. These clubs were always at least full, if not packed. At various times, we added a percussionist to the lineup–first Mingo Lewis, and then our good friend Bongo Bob Smith.

My Volvo was a great car, the first nice car I owned. It had an especially fine stereo. But this Volvo became legendary for the trouble in which it found itself. The first episode happened in Pismo Beach, a beautiful central California seaside town next to San Luis Obispo. We played a week at a club called The Jetty. There was an actual jetty around there and I took my Volvo out to Morro Bay to watch the sunset. Parked on a cliff facing the ocean and a famous rock formation called Morro Rock, I had a splendid view. As I sat with the windows down, the temperature perfect, a cool ocean breeze filtering into the car, I once again pinched myself that I did this for a living. Right after the sun dropped its last rays on the wave-filled horizon, I turned the key to leave, and the car wouldn't start. I had had this problem before–Volvos of that era had a large bellows hose that would come slightly undone and needed securing. I opened the hood and clamped down the bellows hose with a small screwdriver, but left the hood open just to make sure the car would start. I turned the key again and there was a loud pop! like a bottle rocket. I looked up to see the bellows hose flying high in an arc into the ocean. Stunned, I wasn't going anywhere now, it was almost dark, and this was the era before cell phones. I walked about a mile to a pay phone, and someone came and picked me up. The next day I went to a junkyard in San Luis Obispo and luckily found a 1975 Volvo bellows hose!

The most infamous incident with the Volvo happened one evening in Santa Cruz. We were playing at a club called The Albatross, and I was running so late I had to jump out of my car and have our good friend Malcolm park it for me. As I headed through the front door of the club, I heard a horrible *scrrrunnntchhh*. That sound was Malcolm trying to put the car in reverse. Did I mention it was a stick shift? I don't think I did. Malcolm had shredded the reverse gear shaft. From that moment on, the poor car had no reverse. My Volvo became famous for having to "Flintstone" out of every parking situation. It's amazing what a person gets used to. Whenever someone drove anywhere with me, I would stick my left leg out the driver's door, and the passenger would stick their right leg out the passenger door and we would "Flintstone" out of a parking space. As you might imagine, this led to some awkward situations, including some embarrassing dates. One time, in San Francisco, home of the ridiculously steep hills, I was at a light at the bottom of California Street when the car in front of me stalled. Him stalled meant I stalled. I wasn't going anywhere until he got his car moving again, which took over an hour.

My Volvo also had a problem with electrical fires, having a large electrical harness located under and to the left of the steering wheel. There once was a minor electrical fire outside of the Shire Road Pub which fortunately was put out before too much damage occurred, but I was not so lucky the second time. Enjoying a meal at a Mexican restaurant in Sacramento called Rick's Hacienda with my future wife and a couple of buddies, our waiter came rushing in from outside yelling, "Who owns the white sedan in the parking lot?!? It's on fire!!" It took a long second to realize, "ME!!" and we all raced out to see my beautiful white Volvo consumed by flames. Worse than that, my expensive Prophet 5 synthesizer was in its anvil case in the back seat. Throwing caution to the wind (I probably had a couple of beers) I flew open the back door and grabbed the case. I saved the Prophet 5, but the car was a total loss. The good news is that insurance paid out more than the car was worth, and I ended up with a Honda station wagon, a more reliable if less eccentric mode of transportation.

In Santa Cruz, we played the Catalyst when we could, but often settled on the smaller Albatross. Whenever we played The Albatross, the dancefloor was full. It happened in some places more than others. In March of 1979, we played there for a few nights in a row. Each night, two attractive young ladies came in together, talked to no one, danced together near the front of the stage, and as soon as we played our last note, scurried out of the club before anyone could approach them. I saw this happen a few times, and I felt strongly and peculiarly attracted to one of them. She was slight of build, and very cute with long brown hair and freckles. The third night this happened, I ran out the door and followed this young woman to her car. I had never done anything like that before. Surprising her at her car, I said, "Who are you? And why do you two never talk to anyone?" We quickly and awkwardly introduced ourselves, and she, deciding I wasn't a stalker, may have mumbled something in her very young voice about being a student at UC Santa Cruz before she got in her car, closed the door and drove off. Obviously, she left quickly for a reason and the last person she wanted to talk to was a musician in the band.

The next month found us at The Shire Road Pub in Sacramento on Easter weekend. From the stage I looked down and there were the same two girls *again*, dancing together near the stage and talking to no one. This was too much for me. Sacramento is nowhere near Santa Cruz. Now at least I had something to talk to this girl about. "What are you doing *here*?" Her name was Mary Ann, and she was a Sacramento native going to school at UC Santa Cruz and was home on Easter break. What a coincidence! I had done many foolish things concerning young women since I talked to the very first one, but the smartest thing I ever did was get Mary Ann's phone number and promise to call her when she was back at school. I was still living in Los Gatos, just a quick drive down winding Hwy 17 from Santa Cruz.

From the beginning, she wasn't as excited about hanging around with me as I was with her. She and I were on opposite paths; she had had one boyfriend through high school and was thinking of stretching her wings just a little bit, although dating a musician was not in her plans. I, on the other hand, was bouncing along with short-term relationships going nowhere, and frankly was getting sick of myself. Call it intuition, but I knew that this girl was different. She represented integrity and stability. She had an aura of "goodness." Now the problem was getting her to go along with this revelation. She wasn't so keen. I phoned her a couple of times to go out some-where, and she said she'd think about it, or she had other plans. What to do? I knew she didn't really want to go out with a musician, but I played music almost every night of the week.

Finally, one afternoon she suggested roller skating down West Cliff Drive in Santa Cruz, one of the most beautiful places to walk, bike ride, or skate in the United States. I quickly agreed, before remembering that I'd never roller skated. It was the kind of disaster that probably endeared me in an odd way, as I fell on my rear several times. Women love vulnerability in men, and we always get that wrong. I made a point to take her anywhere but to the place Uncle Rainbow was playing, even though she liked the band. I took her to a tennis exhibition match featuring John McEnroe, and then to the Oakland Coliseum to see the Oakland A's and Rickey Henderson play. There was only so long that I could deny what I did, especially because that is how we met. Improbably, I broke her resistance down and we became a couple. She has had second thoughts about it for the last forty-six years. It would take a long time to turn my personal Titanic around, but with Mary Ann's help, I finally did.

It turned out Mary Ann was in the final semester of college, and soon she was looking for a new place to live. Together we moved into a house in San Jose full of crazy Texans who'd come out to California with us, one being the same guy, Malcolm, who'd wrecked the reverse in my Volvo. The rest of the occu-pants were ICU nurses dealing with crises all day and when they got home, they liked to let loose. It was a loud and wild house with a toddler included, but they were good people. Mary Ann had a broken-down Audi that needed a jumpstart every morning, and I had my no-reverse Volvo, so our cars also made a good couple.

. . .

In 1980 addiction to cocaine hit the band hard as drummer George Lawrence, who, when he joined us was the straightest member of the band, succumbed to the drug in a big way. George had some other offers; Bobby Columby, the drummer for Blood, Sweat & Tears, and a producer for Columbia Records, came to see us one night at Smokey Mountain, but he was really there to scout George. George could have played with anybody. He was as good as Jeff Porcaro. But some pissed off dealers started following him around and he left the band under less than honorable circumstances. Everything caught up with him over the next few years including some broken fingers until he went back home to Mississippi and surrendered to rehab. The good news is that it worked, as George carved out a great life for himself owning a drum shop and playing on the road with some top country artists. He joined Uncle Rainbow for a reunion show in 2008.

In the meantime, we had to find another drummer quickly, holding auditions during the day at the clubs where we happened to be playing that night. We quickly found a great drummer (there was no lack of talented musicians in the Bay Area) in San Francisco's David Perper. Tall, with curly long black hair and a great moustache, David immediately fit in both musically and personally, as he and Larry Tagg clicked right away.

Playing around the Bay Area so much brought us to the attention of one of the industry's top producers in Narada Michael Walden. Narada came to hear us at Smokey Mountain with bassist Randy Jackson and both loved what they heard— the combination of superb musicianship and so many fine vocalists. This resulted in Narada offering to produce the band, and a long-term personal friendship and music relationship with Randy Jackson. Narada had just created Aretha Franklin's "Freeway of Love" and was one of the hottest producers in

America at that time after being among the world's best drummers for over a decade. Narada Michael Walden's name on
drums appeared on many of those records I listened to in Bruce
Yamini's car when I was fourteen or fifteen. He had transi-
tioned to producing and had one hit after another. Narada was
a positive, encouraging man who got the best out of the people
he produced.

The first thing he did for us was to bring in a song he
thought was a hit single, the ballad "Safe In My Arms." With
the benefit of all these years of hindsight, I don't think it was a
perfect fit for us, but we were desperate to be signed and this
hit producer was telling us that the song could be a hit. Narada
produced three songs and then presented the band to the
newly formed Geffen Records. Geffen's first signing was super-
star Donna Summer, followed by former Beatle John Lennon.
There was hope that we might be the third.

Geffen Records had co-heads of A&R. Both had to agree on
an artist to sign them. John Kalodner was a legendary A&R
man, working most notably with Aerosmith, Bon Jovi, and
Journey. Narada invited Kalodner, who liked the demo, up to
SIR Studios in San Francisco to see Uncle Rainbow showcase.
Narada set the mood superbly, with flowers, incense, food,
wine, fabulous lighting–everything as nice as it could be. We
played a great set for Kalodner, seated on a couch about
twenty-five feet away. He actually got up and danced around a
bit, and when it was over, John Kalodner said he loved it. We
were obviously thrilled. Kalodner now needed to convince his
co-head of A&R, Carol Childs, to like it as much as he did. Carol
Childs was a close friend of Bob Dylan's, but other than that
we didn't know anything about her. It was Kalodner's job to
get Carol up to SIR to see us do the showcase again.

So, about a ten days later, John Kalodner showed up at SIR
Studios in San Francisco with Ms. Childs in tow, and Narada

put on the flowers, the incense, the food, the wine, and the fabulous light show, and we played the same set that blew Kalodner away. Carol Childs hated it so much she left before we were through, John running out the door after her. Talk about a balloon popping. It was hard for Narada, the consummate optimist, to find anything meaningful to say. We silently packed up our equipment and headed off to another gig, this event representing the fickle nature of the music business in a nutshell.

In 1980, Mary Ann and I decided to ditch suburban San Jose for life in the Big City. Knowing nothing about what we were doing or where we were heading in San Francisco, we rented an apartment near the corner of Polk and Post Streets, or what is still referred to as Polk Gulch. 1980 was the apex of Gay Pride, just pre-AIDS, and Polk Gulch was the nasty stepbrother of the more elegant and artsy Castro district. From our apartment, we could see Sukkers Likkers, and right down the street was the Horny Owl, as well as several Gay bathhouses. Men led other men across the street on leashes attached to dog collars. These were the days of the "Macho Man," buffed men in black leather vests with no shirt and black leather pants with fat moustaches and leather caps. Our front stoop was always filled with "ladies" sitting and gossiping. All that was fine to us, and Mary Ann never felt so safe walking down an urban street at night.

What we totally missed when we signed up for the apartment was the fire station directly across the street. *That* was ridiculous. At all hours of the day *and* night, the alarm went off, the garage door opened, and a couple of engines stormed out, sirens blazing, amplified by the echoes made by the narrow street lined with tall buildings. All conversation had to cease. It got to the point where we could identify the phone call reporting the fire. And sadly (for us), ninety-five percent of the calls were false alarms, so the trucks would be back in five minutes. This and the cockroaches made it almost too much to bear. As there was problematic parking, to put it mildly, I parked my Volvo without reverse up at David Perper's Potrero Hill house and retrieved it only when necessary.

Although I was in love with Mary Ann, and I knew that for many reasons she was the best thing that had happened to me in my young adult life, that young adult had a warped sense of right and wrong and was still in the throes of the madness of addiction. Mary Ann had been very patient with me, but finally had enough and packed up her things and drove her Honda Civic over the Bay Bridge home to Sacramento. I deserved it.

There was so much to unpack there, but the word I kept coming back to was indulgence. The unquenchable desire for more. Here's thing about cocaine: it was never enough. No matter how much I had, or how much there was, there was always the desire to do more. I would take advantage of my position as a local rock musician of some note to badger, pester, bargain, plead, cajole, cozy up to, and make promises I couldn't keep just for more cocaine. I got a lot more free than I ever bought. The circle of people I hung out with as the night got later and later was lower and sleazier. Alcohol was just the wingman, always there, the constant second choice, balancer of the scales, and like a dog, would always be there when you needed it. I could stop drinking when I had to, unless I was full of cocaine. Then I couldn't stop anything. All good intentions went out the window. All promises made earlier in the day or evening were null and void.

· · ·

It was right about this time that I took a trip to New York with bass player Larry Tagg that would change the course of both of our lives. Coral lived in SoHo in New York City and was married to a guy who sent me cassettes containing fascinating new music. Among songs that made an impression were David Bowie's "Yassassin" and "African Night Flight" from the album *Lodger*, and "Wheel Me Out" from Was (Not Was). There were tracks from a band called Talking Heads. This music had the same kind of impact on me that electric jazz did when I first heard it in Bruce Yamini's car. Our trip to NYC included checking out the burgeoning New Wave and punk scenes. We went to Max's Kansas City, and CBGBs, and a couple of other places whose names escape me. The more we saw, the more we realized that Uncle Rainbow had become a musical dinosaur. When we got home, we attempted to create some music in this new vein, but it was like putting on an ill-fitting sweater. There was something pathetic about seeing our band trying to play music that we were not built for. Larry and I played on through 1980 and into 1981 but it was clear that something was going to have to change. This new music unlocked a creative renaissance in me that was going to have to exist outside the frame of Uncle Rainbow.

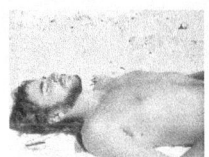
Pismo Beach. Where the Volvo blew its top

George Lawrence

Richard Oates

Little John Sanders

With Richard Oates

Bongo Bob

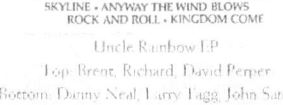
SKYLINE • ANYWAY THE WIND BLOWS
ROCK AND ROLL • KINGDOM COME

Uncle Rainbow EP
Top: Brent, Richard, David Perper
Bottom: Danny Neal, Larry Tagg, John Sanders

Scott Harrison & John Sanders

Narada Michael Walden

Uncle Rainbow in California 1977-1981

6
BOURGEOIS TAGG & HAIRSPRAY: THE MID '80S

Back in the Bay Area, my love life on life support, I moved out of the cockroach-infested fire station loud-speaker San Francisco apartment and took up residence in a Palo Alto house with bandmate John Sanders. We rented two rooms from a female non-drug dealer. This was progress. It would take about another six months, but Larry and I both felt that Uncle Rainbow was a lame-duck band. There were tells that the band had gotten too comfortable with itself. The tempos got faster and faster, and the unpredictable jams got predictable as did Richard's stage patter—we had done it all so many times. Playing five and sometimes six nights a week stunted our growth—there was no time to step back and take stock, listen to other bands, and look at things with a longer lens. Richard, in particular, got very patterned.

There was a guy playing guitar at The Bodega, the place across the street from Smokey Mountain, named Lyle Workman, and Larry and I went over on our breaks and tried to catch a song or two of his band. He had a style that was fresh and unpredictable. We filed him away on the top shelf.

It was at Smokey Mountain, on a Sunday afternoon after setting up for our Sunday/Monday run, that Larry and I gathered everyone into the little dressing room by the side of the stage and told them we were leaving. The balloon just ran out of air. It was nobody's fault, nobody hated anybody else—we just puttered to a stop. Most bands have a shelf life, and Larry and I saw the expiration date before everyone else. We had about two months' worth of obligations to fill and we agreed to honor those gigs.

In the summer of 1981, we played a week up in Sacramento at The Shire Road Pub. Owner Jerry Sterchi had the body of an offensive tackle and the mind of a venture capitalist. Raising Appaloosa horses on his ranch east of Sacramento, now he was in the market for something a little sexier and more exciting to invest in. He had dreams of being a mogul.

On a visit to his ranch, the subject turned to the future of the band we looked to conceive. The main issue confronting us was songs. All else lined up behind songwriting. A continuous hindrance to writing songs was playing music five and six nights a week. The paradox: surrounded by, in and around music all the time, we were unable to find space in our brains to compose new music.

What The Beatles did from 1964 to 1966 was amazing. Somehow, they put out two albums a year, each topping the last one, while they toured constantly, traveling all the time and being cooped up in hotel rooms. If we were going to create enough new music from scratch, we would need freedom from *playing* music every night to give our minds the space to compose. Jerry gave us the opportunity to do just that, offering to rent us a house in Sacramento and pay us a living wage to write music for several months. Coincidentally, the love of my life just happened to be living in Sacramento at that very moment. Hmmm...

Sacramento was never a spot that I looked at on a map and said, "Wow! I really want to live there!" It was just another place we played. Sure, I met a lot of friendly people, but compared to the Bay Area, it seemed like a quiet Midwestern town–too hot in the summer, and too boring the rest of the time. Nice place to raise a family, but...It's funny how those forks in the road go. The opportunity presented to Larry and me was no different than job offers that happen every day. I'm sure my dad didn't look at a map and say, "Wow! Morristown, New Jersey is just the place I want to move my family!" Or Dallas, Texas for that matter. Even as Larry and I moved there, we thought that it would be a short-term residency, and then we'd go back to the Bay Area or move to LA. Yet here I am over forty years later, with one long detour, living in a suburb of Sacramento. I'm sure Larry felt the same way, and he's also lived here ever since.

For many years after we moved to Sacramento, Larry and I worked out at the gym together. Larry was the real pro here, not only at the gym but as a runner, as he qualified for the Boston Marathon. I, on the other hand, had a devil on one shoulder and an angel on the other. The devil was the louder of the two, and won a majority of the arguments, but the angel convinced me that if I went to the gym enough, and even ran three miles several times a week, it might undo some of the late-night damage the devil had wrought. Larry was one of those people who could take or leave drugs and alcohol; the definition of a "normy." He might politely take one sniff, and then the next time around, say, "No thanks! That's enough for me." {What?!?} Same with alcohol. I can remember more than once asking him if he would like to share, say, a bottle of champagne. He would say okay, and then slowly sip one glass while I emptied the bottle, and then asked, "Are you going to finish that?"

Larry and I settled into a nondescript duplex in a nondescript suburb of Sacramento and got to work writing. For the most part, we wrote separately. A song that we did collaborate on was one of mine, "Dying To Be Free," to which Larry provided the perfect "middle eight," or bridge:

If I leave the needle sitting on my favorite song
And I write a note maybe they will turn it on
And dance The Continental
In my memory

Scan me

I had a Tascam 4-track cassette machine, a Roland TR-808 drum machine, and a couple of keyboards. I knew the style I wanted to land in, but it would take several false starts before I got there. The overly melodic sentimental major 7th side of my songwriting was hard to flush. A little bit of that went a long way. I wrote a couple of songs that we demoed but am glad never saw the light of day. Larry wrote a few of those, too. It took us a while to find *it*.

The "Eureka!" moment for me was when I wrote "Changed." It borrowed something from Talking Heads, but it was different. The staccato 16th notes played in fourths like a sequencer but funked up was new. The trick I learned swapping banks in rhythm on the Prophet 5 was definitely new. Maybe most importantly, I found my singing voice.

I used to think I had to toe the line
Stay right in step, everything's fine and I've changed
All these people tell me what to do
They're playing God with me and you
And I've changed, and it's better
Every now and then you wonder
Who is gonna steal your thunder
They're in and out, over and under
But I don't care about that, 'cause I've changed

Scan me

At almost the same time, Larry wrote a fantastic song called "Electric Train," with the great line,

> *"I'll make it again; I've worked out the kinks*
> *You can't win with a train that thinks"*

the philosophy major using a train as a metaphor for the first chapter in Genesis. With these two songs we found our voice.

Some of that voice came out as pure mellifluousness, which, to me, meant, "sounds good coming out of the mouth." The next song I wrote was "The Move Up," an example of lyrics that didn't mean much, but they sang well. "*Yah-ee yah-ee yah hey yah doodoo wop...yeah*" The complicated, tribal rhythm of that song was a serendipitous mistake made on my 808. I tapped out a beat on the sixteen buttons only to realize after the fact I had started a couple of buttons off. The result was a much cooler beat than I intended. Sometimes it's better to be lucky than good.

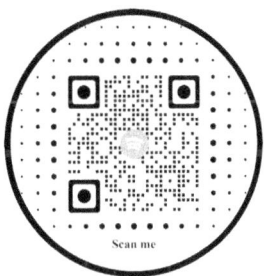

Larry countered with a song called "Zen Physics," with lyrics only a philosophy major could love. I then added the Beatle-esque "Dying To Be Free" (my mom's favorite) about an elderly man making his final preparations for the end of his life.

I mentioned that an ulterior motive for moving to Sacramento was it was the current location of my former sweetheart. Very slowly, phone call by phone call, postcard after postcard, I did my best to woo her back. I was unexpectedly helped by of all people, my mother, who slyly invited Mary Ann to Lake Tahoe on a vacation trip that my parents and I were taking. She reluctantly agreed, and we have never been apart from that time forward.

The English producer Ian Samwell found his way to Sacramento and inserted himself in the day-to-day dealings of our musical lives. With his help we sent our first batch of demos out to a few record company folks and surprisingly got a positive response from one Carol Childs. Oh, the irony. She flew

Larry and me down for a meeting at Geffen in LA. After some pleasantries, we asked if she remembered us. She said she didn't. Hah! We informed her that she walked out of a show-case featuring the last band we were in. She responded evenly that was just the way it went sometimes, and she liked the music we were making now. Fair enough. There was just one thing...she had to get her co-A&R Head John Kalodner to agree. He didn't. This is the kind of experience that would cause reasonable people to question their sanity.

We had gone as far as we could without a band. Most A&R people liked to see a live band so they could gauge how you might do on tour if they signed you. We ran into Randy Jackson at a recording studio in San Francisco and he suggested as much himself. For about three days we called ourselves People To Be, and when Randy heard that, it's all he called us for the rest of our career as a band. We'd see him coming, and he'd shout loudly, "People To Be!!" "People TO BE!!"

We knew who the first "people" was going to "be": guitarist Lyle Workman. It was tricky because Lyle was still in a band. He had *tentatively* agreed to join us at some point, having to fulfill his obligations to his band. In the meantime, we needed a temporary guitar player. It is awkward to ask a musician, "Will you join our band for about two months until the guy we *really* want can join us?" It takes a certain kind of confident musician to say yes. That guy was Sacramento guitarist Lance Taber. Lance was a great player in his own right, and ironically, he became very close personal friends with Lyle Workman. Jazz guitarist Henry Robinett more than ably filled in as well.

Filling the drum position was key, and we kept hearing about this young stud Michael Urbano right there in Sacramento. At the same time, with the music we were writing, we were going to need a second keyboard player. This was the beginning of the synth-filled '80s. We found a science fiction freak named Scott Moon who looked a bit like a mad scientist and owned an Oberheim synthesizer. We set up an audition in Scott's living room in midtown Sacramento and magic happened. Mike Urbano was the perfect fit for the music we had in mind, full of boundless energy, endless optimism and a bit of a swagger. He was a "right-note" player. And something else: I was finally playing with a musician who was younger than me. Scott Moon had the perfect ego for a complementary piece of the puzzle and also was a very good keyboardist. We almost had a band!

There were other musicians and songwriters in Sacramento attempting to do what we were doing, most notably Chuck Ashworth, a.k.a. Charlie Peacock. Charlie's approach was a little more angular, but he fused jazz elements with New Wave–kind of Joe Jackson meets Oingo Boingo, while we were closer to Talking Heads meets Robert Palmer. Charlie had tapped into an idea for a venue that we called a "fern bar." These were medium-sized restaurant/bars that businessmen came into after work, getting their name from the inevitable hanging ferns lined up and down an aisle somewhere in the joint, along with brass railings and no-frills tables and chairs. There wasn't a stage, just a one-step-up seating area, as these places hadn't anticipated hosting live music, except possibly a lonely jazz guitarist in a corner on Friday evenings. Charlie first convinced one place, then another, and then another to open their clubs on the weekends to live music after the businessmen went home to suburbia. These sounded like awful places to play, with no atmosphere, no vibe and no rock aesthetics whatsoever. But a funny thing happened when you crammed two hundred amped-up twenty-somethings in a confined space, turned down the lights, and played loud energetic music: the vibe created itself. Maurice's, which turned into Melarkey's, was first. Then came Harry's Bar & Grill. Then Lord Beaverbrook's. We had an instant scene. The very fact that these places were *not* set up for live music created a just awkward enough setting for fans to be crowded right on top of the bands.

We started playing live as soon as we had enough material for a whole set, padding the originals with some clever covers, but we were masters of that. We played a ska version of The Beatles' "Baby You're a Rich Man." We're the only band I ever knew who played The Stylistics' "People Make the World Go 'Round." We did a tight, hyper version of Robert Palmer's "Lookin' For Clues" and an extra-funky rendition of Talking Heads' "Houses In Motion." There was a tough song by Gang of Four called "What We All Want." We even did a Charlie Peacock song called "Only Love Will Hold Fast," another ska-type tune. But right away we came out playing original music, the sound we always looked for but could never achieve in Uncle Rainbow—modern, futuristic, and edgy, but with enough commercial and melodic elements to appeal to pop fans as well. We drew a crowd as soon as we started performing. We even had a group of regular young female fans called The Tag-Alongs.

One of the Lost Arts of a bygone era was the self-promotional act of putting up flyers. As there was no internet, no cell phones and no social media, it took physical effort and elbow grease to let fans know where you were playing next. Yes, there were the local rags, which might have a small ad paid for by the club where you were appearing, but other than that you and your heavy-chrome stapler were on their own. We got our flyers copied either cheaply or for free by fans who owned copiers. Then we had Flyer Night, when we would fan out to our favorite strategic telephone poles, each of us having specific assignments. It was part art, part science. Flyers went

up over flyers which went up over flyers until the poor telephone poles were in danger of collapsing under the weight of
so many ads for forlorn local bands. But it worked.

Two months after we started performing live, Lyle
Workman finally joined the band. Bourgeois Tagg was born.
Inspired, I was writing like I hadn't...ever. Listening to Nigerian
star Fela Kuti led me to write the song "Perfect Life" which was
the fullest combination of melody, lyrics and rhythm I had
produced thus far, accompanied in the song by the quin-
tessential Lyle Workman guitar solo he was put on this planet
to do.

I also wrote a pair of songs with heavy lyrics inspired by all
the depressing history books I kept by my bedside. "Let the
War Begin" was a slow funky burn with a low menacing
melody. The chorus went:

Let the war begin
Your world ends in violence
Tell the war to come in
Your world ends in silence

"Body Count" was written about the Vietnam War and featured the phrase:

1,2,3,4
Count the children don't make me listen

Happy stuff, for sure.

Mary Ann and I settled into an apartment in Greenhaven, a suburb of Sacramento. Most of our troubles were behind us, but drugs and alcohol would remain an issue for some time to come. Bourgeois Tagg didn't play five and six nights a week, so there weren't as many late nights. But there were enough. Around Christmas 1982, I asked Mary Ann to marry me. I knew she was the only woman for me, and I felt compelled to make it permanent. Taken aback, Mary Ann said she'd consider it, and eventually said yes. The wedding was set for August 6, 1983.

Around this time, my good friend Charlie Peacock concluded that his life had become unmanageable over the same issues that plagued many of us and decided to join a 12-step program. When this happened, a few of us, stuck in our own denial, thought it was a weak move. Charlie just disappeared for a while. When he re-emerged, he and his wife Andi had joined an evangelical church and a Bible study. They convinced Mary Ann to join them, and there was a moment of tension between us all as I had not connected with this newly found faith. It would be another couple of years in the wilderness before I came around.

As Bourgeois Tagg got more and more popular locally, it necessitated doing two shows a night at some of the fern bars. We inserted into our repertoire a powerful rendition of The Beatles' "Tomorrow Never Knows," with an instrumental chorus of "Within You Without You" from *Sgt. Peppers'* in the middle, which always brought the house down. Larry wrote a fantastic new song called "Mutual Surrender," that applied to both lovers and nations. It sounded like we might have a single.

Another Charlie Peacock song was added, the fast-tempo jungle beat sound of "Lie Down in the Grass." Larry wrote a hardcore power-funk song that was reminiscent of Gang of Four called "Heart of Darkness" and featured Lyle at his most awesome.

Larry Tagg and Michael Urbano developed a tight, intuitive musical relationship that grew in intensity every night. Urbano became more and more self-assured as the months went on, emerging as one of the best drummers anywhere. Lyle Workman drew comparisons to Adrian Belew, Robert Fripp, and Pete Townsend. Anchoring it all was Larry's bass, his one bass, coming out of his one amp and his one speaker cabinet that he had played through since before I met him. If it ain't broke...

In the midst of it all, Mary Ann and I got married. Mary Ann came from a Catholic family who had made their home in Sacramento all their lives. Her father was half Filipino, her mother full-on Irish. Our two upbringings couldn't have been more different. While I moved around from state to state, and region to region, Mary Ann's family stayed in the same house her parents had bought in 1951 for $7,000. Her mom, Eileen, worked for the Attorney General's office as a secretary and never learned how to drive on a freeway. Her father Phil was a man of few words who worked the night shift at an air force base in town. They had a mynah bird who would say, "Good morning!" and "Good night" to Mom and Dad as they passed each other in the morning on the way in and out. They went on vacation every summer to Santa Cruz. They had one party in their house during Mary Ann's entire childhood. They imbibed little or no alcohol in their home. I had two brothers and two sisters; Mary Ann had an older brother, Tom, and a sister Kathi who was just fourteen months older. They all spent their youth in Catholic School. It was a happy, content, working-class home. They were as home centered as my family was peripatetic. Mary Ann was a brilliant student, but her parents had a low ceiling as far as ambitions for their children, thinking that the best they could hope to achieve was a state job with benefits and a pension when they retired. That was different from my family as well. Mary Ann broke the mold and finished up her degree at UC Santa Cruz. She was so many things I was not. She came into my life at exactly the right time. In the 1996 movie "Jerry McGuire" one of the most endearing lines is, "You complete me." To this day, I feel this way about Mary Ann.

The wedding was held August 6, 1983, at St. Francis Catholic Church in Midtown Sacramento with over three hundred sweating souls in attendance, temperatures topping out at 108°. My whole family flew in from various points across the country a few days earlier and even the Texans thought it was hot. We held the wedding on that day because it when my sister Coral said she could be there. I never lived that down from either side of the aisle.

Ours being a tennis-mad family, everyone scurried to find the local courts and play. There were five of us—my dad, my older brothers Bruce and Brian, my sister Coral and me. Brian and Coral were the real fanatics, although my dad still held his own in doubles. We drove over to the courts at beautiful McKinley Park. Not only were there no other people on the courts, but there wasn't anyone else in the park, except for a local news crew doing a "It's *so* hot!" feature. They interviewed my family as the only folks crazy enough to be playing tennis in weather like that.

We imported our priest from Dallas and if all Catholic priests were as cool, as well-spoken, as handsome, and as thoughtful as Father Don Fisher, the Catholic religion would be in much better shape today. Father Fisher made a big impression on me as a teenager, and he planted seeds that took a long time to mature, but eventually they did, and for that I have always been grateful. Charlie Peacock's daughter Molly served as the flower girl, while my sister Becky's son Daniel was the ring-bearer. Charlie and Little John Sanders played music during the service, and my brother Brian and Mary Ann's sister Kathi were Best Man and Maid of Honor.

We held the reception in a large hot tent in West Sacramento and we hosted many friends from Dallas, all the Uncle Rainbow band and crew, and all my new bandmates as well. Being from Sacramento, Mary Ann had many old high school friends there. Our first dance was to Al Green's "Let's Stay Together," and I am happy to report forty-two years later we did!

· · ·

We began to extend our reach into the Bay Area and down to Santa Cruz. An A&R rep from Island Records in LA, Ian Matthews, made regular checks of venues in Northern California asking who was popular, who was worth seeing, etc., and the name Bourgeois Tagg came up again and again from club owners and booking agents. Originally from England, Ian had been in the popular vocal group Fairport Convention. He hopped on the quick plane ride, saw us at Harry's Bar & Grill in Sacramento, and was impressed enough to bring Lionel Conway, the head of Island Music Publishing, back to see us a few weeks later.

Lionel, another English ex-pat, was second in command to Island founder Chris Blackwell, who was responsible for introducing reggae music into the consciousness of mainstream Western youth. Island Record's roster featured Robert Palmer, Grace Jones, King Sunny Adé, as well as U2. Conway was so taken by our musicianship and original music that he offered us a publishing contract designed to lead to a record deal with Island. This was a huge step, to pay Larry and me to write music. Lionel came to be our staunchest ally in the music business, a mentor and a true friend. I owe more than I can say to Lionel Conway.

With a publishing deal in place and a possible record deal pending, we needed major-league management to help us navigate through all the coming possibilities. This was a complicated problem that wasn't unique to us, the tricky and unpleasant set of circumstances of disentangling from the very people who helped us get to this place. Jerry Sterchi and Ian Samwell and a few others had supported us up to this point and we were grateful, but to move to the next level, we had to turn ourselves over to a more professional management team.

Bill Graham, the legendary rock promoter, started a Bay Area management company for the sole purpose of managing

Santana, but it had expanded in roster size to include Eddie Money and The Neville Brothers. Bill Graham Management had three fulltime managers: Arnie Pustilnik, Mick Brigden, and Kevin Burns, along with a junior member, Morty Wiggins. It was Arnie and Mick who came to see us.

Arnie was from The Bronx and Mick was from London and they had personalities to match. Arnie would say, "I don't disagree," and that one always puzzled me. They liked what they saw and agreed to take us on. But there was one more layer to go through, and that was the Godfather, Bill Graham. By 1984, Bill had seen it all, and was a tough customer, to say the least. He agreed to come down to Santa Cruz and watch us perform on a Friday night at The Catalyst.

I had recently purchased a futuristic German synthesizer called a PPG Wave. The PPG Wave was rare enough in America, but the company had also made a limited edition of a product called a PRK. This PRK had an ivory-type piano keyboard and a floppy disk drive into which you could program all your patch changes (sounds clicked from one sound bank to another) not only from the PPG Wave, but from all the MIDI keyboards hooked up in a series. These were the days of racks of MIDI sound modules stacked up in anvil carrying cases. This was a game-changer for someone like me with so many different sounds emanating from several different keyboards. It was a first-of-its-kind, and I got the third one shipped to America. This double keyboard system cost a cool $8,000. In about thirty minutes I could program our whole set into the PRK and then I just pushed a number pad above the floppy drive and all the keyboards switched to that song's sounds.

We were excited, a little bit nervous, but confident as we got ready to perform before the great Bill Graham. This was the second gig with my new double-decker PPG/PRK rig, set up front and center on the stage and propped up by a new kind of keyboard stand using wire support. On a 90º angle to my right was my Prophet 5 synthesizer on a stand of its own, and all of this was MIDI'd up to a rack of keyboards behind me. A Euroboom mic stand swung back and forth between keyboard stations as I moved from one to the other. We got to the Catalyst early on that Friday afternoon for a thorough soundcheck. The software in the new keyboard being touchy, I waited until as late as I could to program in the fifteen songs we would be playing that night. All set, we went and had dinner.

The Catalyst was a great room to play. It had a large main floor and a balcony that wrapped around the entire perimeter except for the stage. It always sounded good, and the crowd was loud and energetic–the perfect place to play a gig that mattered. The dressing room was right behind the stage. The adrenaline was flowing as we waited to go on. Like so many bands, we put our hands together in a huddle and went out to our fate.

The crowd greeted us warmly–it felt good right away. We played the first song, "Heart of Darkness," which Larry sang, and I played the Prophet 5, facing him. We went right into the second song, which I was to sing facing forward at the PPG keys. As I swung the mic stand around from right to left, I couldn't see the mic cable getting entangled in the cables supporting the PPG keyboard stand. In maybe the longest six seconds of my life, the whole PPG/PRK rig wobbled right, then left, then right, then finally tipped completely over to the left upside down onto the floor of the stage. The band played on while I stood frozen, unsure of what to do. My mind went through several stages of grief–career over, not just mine, but the band's, shock, shame, anger, embarrassment, laughingstock, blame, panic–as the roadies came out quickly to...what? The giant centerpiece in the middle of the stage suddenly lay upside down like a great dead turtle. There was no sense in trying to put it back up; the stand had broken, and more importantly, the keyboard had shut off, so all the set's programming had been erased.

I looked back at Michael Urbano and mouthed the word, "Sorry!" to him as he and the band continued to riff on the opening of the song. He yelled back, "Just sing!" J-u-s-t s-i-n-g...In a slow-motion fog I grabbed the microphone out of the cradle and did something I had never done before. I had *always* sat or stood behind my keyboard shield whether I was singing or not. I never considered myself a "lead" singer like a Richard Oates or anybody else who stood alone with their whole body exposed. But tonight, necessity provided the impetus. It was sink or swim time. To be honest, it already felt sunk, but there was a certain freedom in knowing that all was lost, and it couldn't get any worse. As the roadies carried the keyboard carcass off the stage, along with its broken stand, I took the mic and stepped into the large space created by its absence and became a lead singer.

I still had my Prophet 5 with limited sounds to use from time to time, but for the most part, I did the whole set as a lead singer, and tried to make the most of it. I was determined to go down honorably with the ship. The band, especially our resourceful keyboardist Scott Moon, covered as best as they could, and we (I) stumbled through the set with a kind of zombie energy. We finished the set and got an encore. After we had taken our bow, we all went back into the dressing room and I sat down, head in my hands close to tears and apologized at least five times. Everybody said the right things, but we all knew it was a disaster. We were just awaiting confirmation.

An interminably long ten minutes later, Bill Graham poked his head through the curtain and came in, slightly out of breath. "Fellas!!" he said, "I've seen Pete Townsend throw his guitar through a stack of Marshall speakers! Keith Moon demolish his drum set! I've seen Jimi Hendrix light his guitar on fire! But I've never seen anyone *destroy* an $8000 keyboard—that was FANTASTIC!!" Wai-wha? What did he say? We all looked up at him stunned. And then we all said, kind of in unison, "Oh yeah, thanks, just like we planned, genius move." We couldn't believe it. I couldn't believe it. He said he wanted to sign us based on what he saw. Bill Graham had seen enough showtime disasters that he was most likely looking at how the band responded to such an unforeseen circumstance. I had picked up the mic and kept singing, the guys more than covering for me.

One of the morals of this story is that nobody cares about something like this happening as much as you do. The crowd was probably surprised and slightly amused when the keyboard fell over but had forgotten about it by the third song. It's like when musicians make a mistake on stage. The worst thing you can do is look at them. Another is that a crisis is a chance to show who you really are. It wasn't the problem, but the reaction to the problem that saved us. In this strange and unique way, I became the lead singer of Bourgeois Tagg. Before that show we had two lead singers, Larry and me. Generally, the person who wrote the song sang the lead. Covers were split up pretty evenly. When Bill Graham Management took over managing us, Mick and Arnie thought it was best to have one principal singer, and from then on, that was me. Larry still got some songs to sing lead, but I started singing some of the songs he wrote, most notably our most commercial song to that point, his "Mutual Surrender."

The other thing this incident forced me to do, with the help of our sound engineer and long-time friend Scott Harrison and his toolbox and a soldering gun, was ditch the tower of keyboards in the middle of the stage. That was over. There would be one keyboard—the Prophet 5. We took a plain two-top bar table with a hollow steel middle and Scott welded four wheels on the bottom of it. Then he made a long snake of all the power, quarter inch and MIDI cords and ran them up inside the hollow round center of the table to the keyboard, while the other end went to a MIDI rack just offstage. A flexible mic boom was attached to the table for one microphone when I was playing and singing, and there was a standard mic stand and another mic for when I sang without playing. The whole thing rolled quite easily–so much so that it became part of the show to see the rig flying on and off the stage, depending on the song.

We now had top-flight management and a publishing deal with a major independent label. With Lionel Conway leading the way, there wasn't much space between us and a record contract with Island Records. These things acquire a momentum of their own; a publishing deal requires a lawyer and both require solid management. Management pushes for a record deal, which requires another lawyer, and soon enough Bourgeois Tagg had in hand what had eluded Uncle Rainbow: a record deal. We now turned our attention to making our first record.

————

1984-85. The music industry was in its peak years and also at the beginning of a revolution in technology, creating the monster that ate the record business. But now, there was excitement about computers, drum machines, sequencers and *samplers*. What was a sampler? Apparently, you could make a digital recording of anything–a sound, a voice, an instrument, a drum–put it in this expensive little machine and then through MIDI play that sound on a keyboard or a midi drum pad in any number of ways. Wow. It's hard now to wrap one's head around how revolutionary that was. In the beginning you couldn't do a whole lot with it because of lack of memory, and it was very costly, but it existed, and we wanted it.

When it came time to choose a producer for our first album, we wanted someone with their fingers on the most advanced technology. We heard an advance copy of Scritti Politti's new album *Cupid & Psyche 85*, featuring sequencers and samples and a terrific modern sound that we were determined to grab for ourselves. In producer/engineer David J. Holman, we found our man. David's latest productions were right up the Scritti Politti alley. When we visited him at his spaceship-style studio next to his home in Laurel Canyon, we knew we had our guy. This oval cave was stacked on every wall and in every nook and cranny with the most analog sound equipment any of us had ever seen. In the middle of it all was a one-of-a-kind sound board handmade specifically for David. To top it off, David had new, rare digital machines, including a *sampler* and a PPG! His was exactly the kind of production canvas we were after. When do we start?!?

All this new technology brought good news and bad news. The downside was the dawn of music on the grid. The advent of drum machines suddenly allowed perfect time to barge into the rhythmic picture. Many years later, things would get sophisticated enough to allow humanizing of the rhythm machines, but in the mid-80s there wasn't the option. It was similar to the autotune phenomenon twenty years later: once perfectly quantized rhythm became *de rigueur* in successful pop music it became hard to do anything else. David Holman told us of a very successful and well-known LA drummer who put his kick drum on a table and pounded out the beats by hand to match up perfectly to the grid.

Using the latest technology came with a price: freedom. We re-encountered some of the same issues that plagued Uncle

Rainbow in the studio. We were a great live band, and it was hard to translate that to this new type of recording. We were at odds with our own objective. The Yes song "Owner of a Lonely Heart" (1983) with Trevor Horn producing and Jon Anderson singing was a fantastic recording, but it didn't sound like a live band. We wanted the elements of that recording at the expense of what got us signed in the first place: we were a compelling live act. But such was the tenor of the times.

When we started recording, the first thing attended to, as always, was the drums. David Holman's studio didn't accommodate live drums, so Bourgeois Tagg's initial recording experience came at Sunset Sound in Hollywood, a well-known recording complex for pop musicians and rock bands. This venerable brick building contained several studios in a square and a courtyard in the middle with a basketball hoop and backboard attached to one of the brick walls of the studio. We were there to record the drums; anything else we got was gravy. The rest of the band set up their instruments and played along with Urbano to give him inspiration, but no one thought their parts were going to count. To record the drums on the whole album took about four days–the first one mainly spent to get sounds. There was quite a lot of free time, especially in the beginning while David Holman tweaked drum sounds with Mike, so the rest of us went outside and shot some hoops. We were all terrible at basketball. It was just something to do.

When we arrived at Sunset Sound, Prince was in a side studio doing overdubs for his *Around the World in a Day* album, the quick follow-up to *Purple Rain*. Everything was purple in his studio, and he had a purple bed in the control room. We were shooting (and missing) baskets when Prince bounded out of his studio and said, "Hey fellas–mind if I play? You guys wanna play H-O-R-S-E?" Of course we said yes. Prince was five foot three on a good day, but he could hoop. He toyed with us for about fifteen minutes–at one point he ran up the wall *behind* the basket and dunked. That was an "R." After winning three straight games, he said, "Thanks a lot gentlemen!" and went back into his Purple Paradise.

We moved into temporary accommodations in LA while we recorded our album. The band was put up at the standard place for musicians recording in LA, the Oakwood Garden Apartments in Toluca Hills off Barham Boulevard. I split a unit with Lyle. It was pure corporate furnished apartment, every one just like the next.

Ours featured a unique element in the young woman next door who kept us entertained with her piano playing when both patio doors were open. She played all the time. She sang, too, but we couldn't hear most of what she was singing so we made up our own melodies and lyrics. It was all major and minor 7ths and 9ths. She played one song over and over and had the same hooky ending, which we could never make out, so we (really it was Lyle) made up our own– "slime-y girl" ...I know, but it just fit the track.

One afternoon six weeks or so into our own recording I was bringing in groceries from my car, and, having two full bags in my hands, kicked the cracked door of the apartment open and quickly threw the bags down on the table before I dropped them. I looked around for Lyle, and instead stood a petite young Black woman with corn rows. Taken aback but chuckling, she said, "Can I help you?" Seeing the piano by the patio door, I realized I had stumbled into the wrong apartment.

"I'm so sorry!" I stammered. "These apartments look exactly alike! We live next door." She took it all calmly and we started talking about why we were both there. I told her we were making an album on Island Records and were almost done. She said she had been holed up in her apartment for the better part of a year, waiting for her producer, Thom Bell, one of the most successful and busiest producers in the world, to finish the projects on his plate and come out from Philadelphia to work on her album. She kept polishing and polishing her songs, but nothing was happening, and she was getting depressed from the waiting and all the delays and broken promises. I, the grizzled veteran, put my hand on her shoulder (pre-#MeToo, we were tight by then) and told her to keep her chin up–it was gonna happen for her, and from what I could hear next door she was going to have a decent record. I felt especially bad that we were zipping through our record while she was still in her apartment playing "Slime-y Girl."

I feel like Paul Harvey saying this, but that forlorn young lady was Anita Baker. The album she was practicing over and over in that apartment was *Rapture*, which eventually won two Grammys and sold eight million copies. Her record company, Elektra, finally gave her full producing control. And if you listen to the record, the hook of fourth song "Been So Long" can be sung as "Slime-y Girl" and it fits perfectly.

I could go through our debut album *Bourgeois Tagg* song by song, but let me say instead that there was fresh, exciting songwriting by Larry and me. Larry's "Mutual Surrender" was a great pop song with a positive message. "Perfect Life" had one of the wackiest guitar solos of that era, courtesy of Mr. Workman, and the overall recording of the song was modern and energetic. The album cover was an inventive painting by my sister Coral that evoked the sound of the record. However, the production of the album suffered from a bad case of the mid-80s. It was as inevitable as LA smog that it turned out like it did. I don't blame David Holman one bit for how this record was produced or how it sounds today: we asked for it and he delivered and more, using every technical arrow in his quiver and inventing new ones on the spot. We had backwards pads, backwards vocals, sound effects, as much sampling as any album made in that year, amazing echoes and reverbs, and the fidelity was top of the line. But if I thought that there was too much separation between instruments on the aborted Uncle Rainbow album, these tracks took that concept to the extreme.

To surround the various sounds–from drums to guitars to synths–with all those wacky effects, they had to be completely separate from each other. For example, Michael's drum parts played at Sunset Sound were full of life and energy–just like Mike. By the time the record was over, his drums sounded like the various parts of a drum machine, which technically, they were. His snare was replaced by a sample, which was then meticulously locked to a grid. The AMS Reverb, a tool that dates certain records as precisely as carbon dating, is all over Mike's drums. In order to get that sound we were after, everything, not just the drums, had to be chopped up into pieces and put back together on the grid, the opposite of the band that we were becoming before we got into the studio. But we didn't understand that. David Holman was just doing what we asked him to do.

There were some good songs in there that we sucked the life out of by better living through technology. We were dazzled by the shiny objects in the storefront window. This was the "modern" 80s. As I listen to this record today, I can't help wailing, "My kingdom for some BLEED!" Everyone played their asses off, particularly Lyle and Mike. The good news, and there was a lot of good news, is that when we went on the road to promote this record, we imported of some of the technology we acquired and combined it with the energy and chaos of our live band sound and the result was better than ever.

Our first single was indeed "Mutual Surrender," an excellent introduction of the band into the pop world. As this was the MTV era, Island Records financed a video made on a soundstage in San Francisco. Our clothes and hairstyles dated our appearance as much as the AMS Reverb dated the music. We were permanently stamped "Mid-80s!"

Scan me

It is speculated that rock bands in the 1980s caused the hole in the ozone layer through the use of Sebastian Shaper hairspray. There were cans of it two feet long. I remember two things about that video. They used my sister's album cover artwork to make sheer hanging strips that we moved through, which was a nice touch. Also, I was getting bloated from drinking and it showed in the video. Bill Graham at one point at a gig even patted my stomach and said, "Getting a little heavy, eh?" We all wore these wide pants at that time, ala Zoot suits, that we got at a Latin clothing store in downtown Sacramento. While they worked on the skinny guys, they just made me look wider.

"Mutual Surrender" came out in the fall of 1985 and did middling well. I remember the first time I heard it on the radio. Years later the movie *That Thing You Do* would encapsulate this moment perfectly. I was in a convenience store near our apartment in Sacramento standing at the counter, paying for a soft drink, and there was a radio on behind the cashier and "Mutual Surrender" was playing! Pointing at the speaker, I shouted, "Hey! That's my song!!" The cashier turned slowly around to listen for a few seconds and then turned back to me and said thoughtfully, "I guess if I had to pick my song, it would be 'My Generation' from The Who," and gave me my change. Deflation.

The album was released in January 1986, and you never know who might be listening. "Mutual Surrender" was a hit on the popular Top 40 station in Seattle. We rushed up there to play a sold-out show at the Moore Theater in front of a thousand screaming young teens. My parents followed us around a bit on the West Coast. My dad gave me some free advice after the show. "Why do you have to play 'Dying to be Free' as loud as you play the other ones? You could use some dynamics." Truer words were never spoken. Dynamics. I just didn't think that thought would come from my dad.

Because of our shared connection with Island Records, we were added in April 1986 onto a national tour with Robert Palmer. Robert, a savvy music-lover, immediately jibed with what he heard from us, particularly "Perfect Life." He was touring with Belinda Carlisle, formerly of the Go-Go's, who ironically would factor a little later in our careers, but for now Robert was so uncomfortable with her music opening his show that he would stay in his trailer until her band's last note was played. He ordered a switch in mid-tour, and it coincided exactly at the time "Addicted to Love" was becoming a huge hit, thanks in large part to its iconic video.

As we were specifically requested by the star, when we joined the tour we were treated with great respect. The Palmer band was superb, with Eddie Martinez on guitar and Dony Wynn playing drums. Robert was handsome and urbane, a musician's version of James Bond, a music historian and collector of World music. We often talked music deep into the night, as he and I had a similar tolerance level and were often the last ones around. Bourgeois Tagg was the perfect complement to Robert Palmer, and I will always be grateful to his organization for the warm way they treated us.

We never had a day off. An opening on the calendar was filled by a club date in either the city we'd just played, the city we were about to play, or a convenient town in between. Those were generally fun gigs. We were comfortable filling the space of a club stage, and in most cases enough people had heard of us to make up a large and appreciative audience.

We played a concert in Sacramento with Julian Lennon, who was supporting his first solo record. He surprised us when we walked in for our soundcheck by having his band play a chorus of our song "Body Count." We've been friends ever since. We played another show in Sacramento with The Fixx, whose big hit was "One Thing Leads To Another."

Being on tour afforded fewer opportunities to get myself into trouble. The infamous myths of the road generally applied to the big-time headline acts. As an opening act, we finished our set, patted each other on the back, changed clothes, said hello to the headliner as they were approaching the stage, and soon enough were back on the bus headed to the next location. There was no cocaine–where were we going to get it? "Partying" was limited to a couple of beers in the dressing room or on the bus after the show. When we played club gigs, the same scenario applied. Being on the road was healthier for an addictive type like me than being in my hometown.

When we got home, we made a video for the song "Perfect Life." I wasn't sure of the purpose, because "Perfect Life" was a cool song, but it wasn't a single. I think the guy who directed it offered us a super-cheap deal because he liked the song. Nevertheless, it was shot with an 8mm camera, and we got to wear florescent paint and use up three two-foot cans of Shaper hairspray. Another artifact, when found in a thousand years, that will point directly at the era it was made.

Scan me

Bill Graham wasn't around a lot, but when he was, he was always a big help. When we played Bay Area shows, if he was present, he introduced us. That alone gave us a prestigious boost. His price was $2. We always had to come up with $2 for him to introduce us. He was of greater help to us in New York City. There were good and bad headline road crews. The English road crews were the worst. We did a two-night set of shows at The Roxy in Manhattan with Madness, whose biggest song to date was "Our House." At soundcheck on the first day, the Madness road crew were rude, arrogant assholes. Many of these types were lower-class English brats and this was the first chance in their lives they ever had to lord it over someone else. They gave us a space the size of a medium welcome mat to set up. Our soundcheck was about five minutes, even though Madness hadn't even shown up to the venue yet because their drugs hadn't arrived. We played the show, hardly able to move, and immediately went to complain to Papa Bill. The next afternoon, we had all the space we needed, got a thorough sound check, and the roadies were pleasant, if not exactly nice. The whole time, Bill leaned over the railing of the balcony, staring down at the proceedings. He didn't say a word.

We encountered more road crew assholiness when we did a West Coast swing with the Norwegian pop group a-ha, who were touring behind their huge MTV hit "Take On Me." The video was something special. The band, not so much. The crew thought they were the roadies for the Rolling Stones, although I imagine that the Stones' road crew are much nicer guys. Again, it was an English crew, and they relished the chance to boss a band like us around. Mick and Arnie did their best Bill Graham imitations, but it wasn't a great experience. We did get to enjoy schadenfreude at the Universal Amphitheater in LA. In front of a celebrity crowd that included Michael Jackson and Elizabeth Taylor, as we watched from the side of the stage, a-ha's lead singer ran to the front, backed up, and fell right over a monitor and landed on his ass. Sorry not sorry.

After the Palmer tour and in between these other shows, my good friend Charlie Peacock asked me to help him produce his self-titled album. The church he was a part of, Warehouse Christian Ministries, was forward-looking musically, and believed in the power of rock music to attract young people, presenting Friday night rock concerts bringing in nationally known Christian artists to play in their modern auditorium. I had attended a few of these shows. The idea of rock concerts in churches started with Chuck Smith and the Calvary Chapel "Jesus people" movement in LA. Texan Louis Neely was the Warehouse's pastor, and his wife Mary was determined to be a player in the music industry. With Charlie and fellow Warehouse band Mike Roe & the 77s, she grabbed her chance, and Exit Records was formed. The church had a 24-track studio tucked in a room off the stage. Charlie engaged Englishman Nigel Gray to engineer the recording. Nigel engineered the successful debut album from The Police and was quite a catch for the church and Charlie. I brought my PPG rig over to the Warehouse, and we started recording.

Some turning points in your life are obvious when they

happen, and others take time to sink in. Recording this album with Charlie was a turning point for me, but I didn't see it right away. When Charlie got clean and sober and joined a church, I didn't think much of it or about it except when he and his wife Andi tried to talk Mary Ann out of marrying me because we were "unevenly yoked." I'm not even going to explain that–you can look it up. She married me anyway, bless her heart, and the whole Peacock family participated in the wedding, so the damage was minimal. Charlie and I remained good friends and kindred spirits. When we met up to do his record it was obvious to me from the first day that he had changed. He almost wasn't the same person, and the changes were good. Whatever he was doing was working.

Whenever you are intimately involved in a recording project, you end up spending a concentrated amount of time with a few people. That is what happened with Charlie, Nigel and me. Nigel and I were still in thrall to the substances that controlled us, while Charlie had reconstructed his life. As we worked on the record, Nigel and I did things in front of Charlie that bother me to this day. It wasn't Nigel's fault–he was a hired gun traveling five thousand miles to work at a church. He was who he was, and Charlie's eyes were wide open about that. But it was selfish of me to not take Charlie's sobriety into consideration. However, it was his *reaction* to the things we did that made a deep impression on me. He had every right to be at least *peeved*, and I'm sure he was, but he never let it show. We ended up traveling to London and Surrey to finish the record and I ended up deeply impressed.

I had been a taker all my life. Even when I was young, I had no clear moral compass–I did the right thing if convenient. I tried almost anything to get a laugh or attract attention. I hung around people I didn't like if they had something I wanted. It's not that I was a *bad* person, it's just that my musical ability had allowed me to function successfully without having to be a particularly *good* person. Watching Charlie transformed, I wanted what he had. I wanted something *good for me* for a change. The seed was planted. It just needed a little time to grow.

———

1st Picture of BT with
Lance Taber

Larry & Brent w/Ian Samwell

Brent w/ Dad and
Jerry Sterchi

1st PR shot

Larry in the studio

1st album/Coral's cover

1st band photo w/Lyle

Mutual Surrender video shoot

Brent & Larry w/ David J. Holman

Early Bourgeois Tagg 1982-1985

We have fans in Seattle!

7

TODD & GOD

O ur self-titled first album sold reasonably well for a debut record–the same numbers today would be a runaway bestseller–and got enough critical acclaim to be considered a success. The main measure of a success in the record business? Island Records picked up our option and gave us the opportunity to make another record. The fact we were racking up insurmountable debt is a footnote. It's not that we had to pay that money back; it's just that we would have to have a success of Swiftian proportions to ever actually *make* any money from royalties.

We met in the offices of Bill Graham to select a producer for our second album. These offices were a visual history of the San Francisco music scene. It was like walking into a museum. Posters and pictures from the Fillmore West and all the amazing concert venues that Bill hosted covered the walls. The Day on the Green, Altamont, early Grateful Dead shows, Janis Joplin, The Rolling Stones, Jimi Hendrix, The Who, Led Zeppelin and Santana all mixed in with psychedelic artwork and photos of Graham with the royalty of rock.

A surprising list of producers was available to us–we honestly didn't have any idea that our name had garnered that much attention. One name stood out above the others–Todd Rundgren. We were all Todd Rundgren fans–I had been since I was fifteen years old. Honestly, we all stopped looking when we saw his name on the list. "We can get him??" someone asked. "Yep" came the reply. *Sold*!

There was a brief negotiation with lawyers and managers from both sides and Todd became our new producer. He had just finished up an album from another favorite of ours, XTC– an album that would create controversy before we ever started recording. Todd, a Philadelphia native living in Woodstock, New York, had recently established a second residence in Sausalito, just on the other side of the Golden Gate Bridge. He came to meet us at Bill's office. We tried to be cool in front our musical idol, but we were fanboys. What was the allure for Todd? He came up to Sacramento to hear us play and I think he was impressed by the musicianship, especially Lyle, Larry and Mike. As a multi-instrumentalist, it stoked his interest to work with such a talented group of players. He talked about the *music* in our original songs but didn't say a word about our lyrics. That shoe would drop shortly.

We began the writing process for album number two (eventually titled *Yoyo)* with the confidence that came from a national tour and some critical success. Lyle Workman hadn't written anything on the first album, but he was a creative guy, and it was only a matter of time before we felt his composing influence. Lyle showed up at my apartment one afternoon with a cassette. He had written a track on Side A that he wanted me to listen to for a possible co-write, and as he was about to leave, he said, "You might want to check out the little thing on Side B if you have time." We said our goodbyes, and I went into our spare room with my Tascam 4-track and the cassette. I honestly do not remember Side A, as it didn't make an impression, so I flipped the tape over. Side B contained a lovely acoustic guitar pattern that I immediately fell in love with. Kismet. In the few times I have been inspired like that, words and melodies come tumbling out and I am just a channel. I think I wrote the whole song, "I Don't Mind At All," in an hour.

The time for talking's over now I guess it's time to let you go
But I don't mind at all
It's getting so you never know when things are better left alone
But I don't, no I don't mind at all
It's important to me that I don't see you laughing at me
But I'm smart enough to know
That I have to let you go
But I don't mind at all

Sentimental tears may get you far as you might think they will
But I don't mind at all
Misery loves company but she will never foot the bill
But I don't, no I don't mind at all
It's important to me that I don't see you laughing at me
But I'm smart enough to know
That I have to let you go
But I don't, No I don't mind at all

Scan me

Larry and I went to Todd's house in Sausalito to play him some of the demos we had been recording. He had no problem with the music–he never really did–his focus was on what we were saying, and as we found out, his criticism could be brutal. Both of us, but especially Larry, the philosophy major, were influenced to a great degree by the "observational" style lyrics of someone like David Byrne. "Look over there! Isn't that interesting!" To Todd, this was heartless. He listened to song after song, with no comments about the music, only criticism over our callous use of the English language. "Listen," he said, "you have forty-five minutes on the psychologist's couch. This is a forum not available to most humans. You have to use this to say something meaningful worth listening to. Use more heart, less head." I'm paraphrasing. The way he said it cut like a knife.

I'm not sure about Larry, but I walked out of there defeated, embarrassed, and not a little angry. I went home and spilled it out to Mary Ann. She suggested if I was going to spill, spill on the piano. Taking her advice, I sat down and came up with this:

What the hell do you what from me?
You say all you want is the best from me,
Well I believe you, how I want to believe
You know I used to be a local hero
But I'm sure that that means not much more than zero
To someone like you
Look at me!
I'm tough and I'm strong and I don't care if you like this song but
When the light goes off
I cry like a baby

Scan me

"Cry Like A Baby" was the direct visceral response to Todd's criticisms. A couple of days later, I played it for him, and in true Todd fashion, although it was directed at him, he said I was finally on the right track! He also liked "I Don't Mind At All" so we were headed in a positive direction.

Another one I wrote, "Out of My Mind," was a funky song in the mold of Squeeze's "Tempted." But it was also influenced by Todd himself. It was hard not to be influenced in the presence of someone I had used as a songwriting model in the past:

How many times must I keep moving on when I already was there?
How many years must I live alone, tie me on your bed of nails (and)

Hit me over the head! Spit in my face! Bang on the drum!
I must be blind, I must be blind
Hit me over the head! Step on my feet! Make me feel numb
I must be blind, I must be going out of my mind... And it's
worrying me

Scan me

He had that effect on all of us.

Larry got into the flow with the beautiful and emotional "What's Wrong With This Picture." He wrote another catchy pop song "Best of All Possible Worlds" which ended up being not only the album's opener but our future set starter as well.

Charlie Peacock brought over an idea that I ended up finishing as the song "Stress," which is about nothing but emotion.

I'm fighting tooth and nail
Right down to the last detail
I would call this a critical time
There's a meltdown in my mind
Stress... Somebody take the weight off of me
Stress... And off the woman and her family
Stress... When it all comes tumbling down
Stress... I'll remember that the world doesn't end here

Scan me

And finally, I wrote "Coma," a song that may or may not have been about me:

Hey and what's all this stuff about moderation?
If the spaceship's there I'm gonna fly it
I'll travel far beyond the dotted line
With an invitation to come to coma

That "moment of clarity" was coming sooner rather than later.

We entered into rehearsals for the record. But first, Larry had a bachelor bowling party, as he was getting married to his girl-friend Tracy. Todd came and we all had a great time. He left his polka-dot shirt in my car, and there's a picture of me in the same shirt three days later at a gig.

Todd's biggest arrangement contribution may have come on Larry's "Waiting for the Worm to Turn." Larry's home demo was a mid-tempo, quasi-funky ballad. It was a good song but needed juice. Todd, with Lyle's help, took the chorus vocal line and turned it into a chiming guitar figure that I supported on keys, giving it a poppy sound that transformed the character of the song and made it exciting to play. One thing was for sure—this was not going to be a grid-based, sequencer-type record. Todd was out to capture the sound of the band.

It was the end of spring, and the weather was nice as we commenced recording at Todd's studio on Mink Hollow Road in beautiful rural Woodstock. We stayed in an old farmhouse owned by Todd. Up the hill about a hundred yards away was his recording studio with a brick fireplace in the middle, and a couple of hundred yards further up the hill was Todd's home, which he shared with his girlfriend and future wife Michele. Like every studio session in history, the first day Todd and Mike worked on drum sounds. Lyle and I took that opportunity to get some exercise playing racquetball. About twenty minutes into our first game, Lyle sprained his ankle, and it swelled up like a grapefruit. He ended up on crutches throughout the recording.

The first song we recorded was "Waiting for the Worm to Turn." Todd turned the drum set into a junkyard kit by adding a host of percussion instruments tied around the set. It was an inspired choice and got us off to a great start.

Scan me

Todd's control room was up a steep flight of stairs and felt like an attic with a window out to the studio. It was in many ways the opposite setup of David Holman's. He had some outboard gear, but overall, he relied on a few key things, like twenty-four separate EQ units, one for each channel, lined up right over his head. It all felt lived-in and old-school, and we immediately felt like he was capturing *the band*.

Back in the old farmhouse, Todd told the story of *Skylarking,* the XTC record he had just finished. It wasn't a pleasant experience for XTC founder Andy Partridge, who was braying loudly in media interviews. XTC had picked Todd because their English record company was imposing upon them an American producer and his was the only name they recognized. On and on Partridge went, slagging the album, which we thought was brilliant. Why was Andy so angry? He had run smack into his American doppelganger. Andy was the British Todd Rundgren. Both are witty, sarcastic, opinionated, and don't suffer fools well–Andy had met his match and then some with Todd. At one point, Andy and Colin Moulding, his partner-in-crime, were fiddling around for hours with a drum machine part. An exasperated Todd, who had brought in drummer Prairie Prince for the recording, said to them, "When you finish dicking around with that thing and realize I'm *right*, come and get me. I'll be up at the house." We got to hear the XTC songs Todd *didn't* use on *Skylarking*. They sounded like the old XTC–clever, complicated, a lot of things a musician would like, but difficult for the average listener. Todd chose the most melodic songs and put them in an order before Andy and Colin even arrived– an act of producer tyranny that clearly rubbed Andy the wrong way. How dare he?!? The result was the best and most popular XTC album ever and it paved the way for a couple of more in the same vein, though without Todd. It was interesting getting the inside scoop from Todd, who chose not to fight it out in the press.

Todd was not an easy guy to record with. If you were looking for encouragement, or warm, fuzzy pats on the back, he was not your man. He could be cutting and sarcastic. He was wickedly funny when the humor wasn't aimed at you. At a lunch with the Island Records team in Woodstock, someone ordered a whole fish. Todd spent the entire meal making an elaborate sculpture out of the fish parts. After one vocal, he caustically informed me it sounded "like an Ohio Players' B side." He told Michael Urbano to "stop playing those numb-skull fills." His classic line that I still repeat to this day came at the end of what I thought was my best vocal take on the whole record, the lead on "Cry Like a Baby." I finished, slightly out of breath, looking like a gymnast after an Olympic vault, and there was silence...and a little more silence. Finally, I said, "Well?" He slow—ly looked up from the computer manual he was reading and leaning over painfully, pressed the talkback button and said, "Well...what?" Exasperated, I asked, "Did you like it??" He took a deep breath, like I had interrupted something important, and said, "Well...it didn't bother me." That was Todd. It didn't bother him.

We adjusted to this reductive "praise." A "not bad" or "that'll do" was great. "We might be able to work with that" was all Michael Urbano needed to hear. Todd actually liked Lyle's guitar playing, and Lyle ended up in his band for several years, as did Mike and Larry. Lyle provided the usual atomic fireworks on guitar, especially on "Stress." That song benefitted from Todd's studio wizardry.

The recording moved to the West Coast for more overdubs, landing in both The Record Plant and Studio D in Sausalito. Studio D was another well-known recording hangout, hosting Fleetwood Mac in their prime, and The Record Plant, among other things, known for Sly Stone, who had his "Pit" carved out with the console in the middle of the small studio and windshields providing some minor soundproofing so he could wheel around and direct the band. (He was into bleed, and I loved it!)

It was here the idea of a string quartet for "I Don't Mind at All" took shape. Todd instructed Lyle and me to write the chart for the quartet even though neither of us had ever composed such a thing before. So, we put on our George Martin hats, sat on Todd's patio, and worked bit by bit, tossing notes on a page. Hearing the string quartet play this music was a "pinch yourself" moment. Combined with Lyle's virtuoso guitar, the song blossomed into something special. Island Records made it our first single, a risky choice because it didn't sound like anything else on the record, or anything on our first record either. But it was magical.

We finished overdubbing in late spring 1987. We also, for grins, recorded a version of the Beatles' "Tomorrow Never Knows" to possibly use as a B side or a CD extra.

On one of the last nights of recording, Todd, Larry and I went around the corner to get some sushi. Todd and I split several pints of sake, nothing out of the ordinary for me or him. The band shared a rental apartment while we were recording in Sausalito, and Larry took off for that house while I volunteered to drive Todd on the ten-minute ride back to his home. About halfway there, red-and-blue lights flashed behind my green Honda station wagon. The policeman submitted me to a field sobriety test. With Todd laughing at me from the passenger seat, I failed, was handcuffed, and taken to the Marin County jail. Todd drove my car to his house. Lionel Conway, our publisher, happened to be in town to listen to some final mixes, and had to be awakened to bail me out in the early morning.

By the time I got to the drunk tank, I was almost sober. I sat in a chastened silence on a cement bench in a bleak, tile-filled room with one drunk on the other side, head between his knees. For me, this was it. I had several hours to review the mess I had made of my life right at the very moment of its greatest possible success. In my mind, it wasn't about alcohol, although my views on that would revise over time. Cocaine was the source of my problems and my addiction. Although I hadn't used any that night, it continued to be the master of my mind. There's a phrase, "I wasn't doing it; it was doing me." Cocaine told me where I was going and when to go home. It told me whose house to visit and how long to stay. It brought me into lower and lower company, and completely controlled my sleeping patterns.

Two events spoke to me the most. The first was a big deal. We played a showcase event at the Wiltern Theater in LA with Robert Palmer. He had just released his album with "Addicted To Love" on it and there was a lot of press covering the show. As we got ready to go on, everyone in the band was climbing the walls with nervous energy. Everyone except me. All I could think about was the after-party. Now *that* was going to be cool. I was sure there would be cocaine and champagne and I couldn't wait. In a moment of clarity, I stepped out of my body and said, "Look who you've become. You are a slave." We played a great show, despite my thoughts, but I remembered.

The other event was so small that I otherwise would have forgotten it. One afternoon, in the middle of a normal week at home in Sacramento, I decided to see a movie. Cocaine said I couldn't go to the movie without it. So, I called up my least favorite dealer, and embarrassingly met him at a park on the way to get a little bit to take me through the movie. That was the last time. I was so disgusted with myself that I knew it was all coming to an end.

As I sat in jail, I thought about how this *thing* had a hold of me. I never cheated on my wife as a married man. I was hardly ever with females at night. My life revolved around a group of men who desperately enjoyed each other's company until the drugs ran out, and then we raced to beat the sun home.

One sad sack story that's funny now: I was sleeping in at about 10:30-11:00 in the morning, probably in my fourth hour of rest (it took time to get to sleep when you were full of cocaine, no matter how much you drank) when outside my window I heard the horrible sound of *leaf blowers*! I flew into a rage, indignation pouring through my veins, grabbed my robe

and stalked outside screaming, "Do you know what *time* it is?!?
It's eleven o'clock in the f'ing morning!!"

Sitting in jail I kept remembering time after time I was
going out to some club, and promising myself it would be two
drinks only tonight. Two drinks were exactly what it took to
weaken my resistance enough to get on the pay phone and call
a cocaine dealer. And once that happened, all bets were off. I
had seen what happened to Charlie Peacock; how his life
completely turned around. I had had enough. I was "sick and
tired of being sick and tired."

Lionel Conway bailed me out of jail and took me to Todd's
house to get my car. Lionel, one of Rod Stewart's best mates,
had seen it all. He was a complete gentleman and tried to give
me confidence at a dark hour.

A few days later manager Mick Brigden set me up with an
attorney. A DUI in California was a serious thing. Mick's wife
Julia was sitting in the lawyer's office when I arrived, which
was unusual. The lawyer's name was Maureen Kallins.
Maureen was friends with Julia. After exchanging a few pleas-
antries, Maureen asked, "Do you think you have a problem–"
Before she could get the rest of the words out, I said, "YES! I
have a problem!" I feel like I said, "I do I do I do!" She was, of
course, referring to alcohol; after all, I was in her office for a
DUI. But I was talking about cocaine. *That* was *my* problem.
Alcohol was the wingman. Maureen and Julia knew better than
I what my problem was. Call it addiction. Call it alcoholism.
The nomenclature doesn't matter. Maureen suggested a
meeting of Alcoholics Anonymous, and I said, "Where and
when?" That sneaky bastard manager of mine had gotten me
an AA attorney!

I didn't know the first thing about AA except that Charlie
had gone to it and, well, look at him now. There were a couple
of reasons for AA and not NA, or Narcotics Anonymous. AA was

more popular and offered far more meetings. And besides, the only way I could stop doing cocaine was if I stopped drinking. That was undeniable. I hadn't ever considered myself an alcoholic. To me, the term conjured up images that didn't fit; people like some of my dad's pot-bellied friends, slobbering over the piano with a cocktail in one hand and a cigarette in the other, slurring while requesting some stupid song. Or scruffy, smelly old guys stumbling down a city street begging for money. Sure, I drank a *lot*, but much of the time it was to balance out the drug, or to help me come down to sleep. But it didn't matter what you call it or how I parsed it, I was done.

One of the driving forces to get sober right then was that Mary Ann and I were expecting a baby in September. I had to stop what I was doing now. Mary Ann had suffered long enough. There was simply no way I was going to stay up until almost dawn, and then hope against hope to be a functioning father. If I needed any extra incentive, I had it. As we prepared the house for a child, Mary Ann walked me to my first AA meeting about five hundred yards down the street. I went in with no preconceptions. I remember two things from that first meeting. On a smoke break (a *smoke* break!) I got to talking to two women a little younger than me. One had sixty days of sobriety, which seemed like a *long* time, and the other had nine months, which seemed incomprehensible. They were old-timers to me. The other thing I heard was a reference to "clean house." It was a metaphor, but I took it seriously, and when I got home, I was digging in our bedroom closet, pulling old things out, when Mary Ann said, "What are you doing?" "I'm cleaning house," I replied.

I had just turned twenty-nine and was no longer the youngest musician around, even in my own group. I was married for

over three years and had a child on the way. I was raised
Catholic, married in the Catholic church, but had no religion
per se, although I had begun to sniff around Warehouse Christian Ministries. Politically, I was a nominal Democrat, but my
views were superficial. I think I even voted for Reagan in 1980.
I was all for certain liberal social ideas but put no effort into
any of them. I had few convictions of which to be courageous.
My life revolved around whatever was happening next in my
career. My friends were either musicians or, preferably, musicians who liked drugs. I liked physical activity, from softball, to
the gym, to running, and occasionally tennis or racquetball. I
was selfish and self-centered. And then that person, metaphorically speaking, died.

Life, sober or not, went on, and Bourgeois Tagg performed at
the Bammies, or Bay Area Music Awards, as a nominee for
Band of the Year. We did our version of "Tomorrow Never
Knows" with Todd sitting in on guitar. We had several other
gigs scheduled, but they were complicated by Mary Ann's
pregnancy. We turned down a three-day mini tour in the
Pacific Northwest because it fell inside the two-week delivery
window. Of course, the baby, like many first babies, was late.
Because it was a three-hour drive from Sacramento, and I
figured I could get back in time if needed, we decided to play a
night in Fresno at the Wild Blue Yonder, a club owned by the
members of a band of the same name. I always thought "I Was
In Fresno When the Water Broke" would make a great country
title, and that is indeed what happened. Fortunately, we
finished the gig, and I hurried back to Sacramento in plenty of
time to welcome a baby boy, whom we named Adrian. I was
allowed in the delivery room, and just as the baby was pushing
out, my wife in extreme discomfort, the delivering doctor

noticed my Robert Palmer tour shirt, and started talking to me about seeing him in concert. I couldn't believe it.

"I Don't Mind At All" was the surprise pick for the first single, and to publicize it, Bill Graham invited the press and selected notables up to his house for a release party, which included a live mini-concert by our band. This was a special treat and an honor– one of the many ways that Bill went the extra mile for us. Much of Bay Area royalty was there as well as selected members of the LA press corp.

We chose an up-and-coming young director named David Fincher to direct the video. Fincher had developed a new technique: transparent glass blocks floating and turning upon which videos of each person could be imposed. We liked the concept, and he was hired. Another guy I patted on the head and said, "Keep on doing this, kid, and I'm sure something good will happen for you." We're kind of proud to say we gave the now renowned film director his start in the music video arena. It was a beautiful video that stands up well today and was played often on MTV.

Scan me

Doing press for *Yoyo* was a learning experience, to put it mildly. I absorbed a painful lesson I've never forgotten. Larry and I were in LA being interviewed by one of the evening newscasts. All the local LA news stations had entertainment sections just like sports and the weather. The young woman with enough hairspray to match ours started the interview by asking us about our new *ballad*. The word "ballad" never sat well with me–it was a trigger–and I answered, "Well, it's not a 'ballad' like one of those corny Lionel Ritchie ballads, etc, etc, etc." Insert foot in mouth. Poor Larry, innocently sitting there. Unbeknownst to us, at that exact moment, our friend and former producer Narada Michael Walden was at Lionel Ritchie's house writing for Lionel's new album. When they took a break and turned on the TV, it happened to be on this very station. We came on, and Narada told Lionel about us, as they played the "I Don't Mind At All" video on the broadcast. Lionel, listening attentively, said, "I'd like to write with those guys." Seconds later I blurted, "those corny Lionel Ritchie ballads." I owe Larry a house worth of songwriting royalties he'll never see. Narada called up Bill Graham Management and, as politely as he could, said, "That idiot just insulted Lionel Ritchie while we were watching! And right after Lionel had complimented them!" I spent the next week writing apology letters to Ritchie, his management company, his lawyers, his publishing company, and his dog. He declined to offer us a writing session.

Nancy Wilson, the guitar-playing Wilson sister in Heart, heard "I Don't Mind At All" on the radio and requested an advance copy of the *Yoyo* album. The Wilson sisters then asked the band to open on the 1987 Bad Animals tour.

There were a lot of "firsts" when we went on this sixty-three-date North American tour with Heart. First time on a tour bus (rule #1: no #2). First time playing arenas, including Madison Square Garden. First time in many of the cities the tour landed in, including Canada. Being an opening band for a headline tour like this (and we became experts) depends greatly on the largesse of the headliner. If the headliner chose you, which Heart did, then you could expect to be treated with

respect and given many little things that can make the difference between enjoying the tour and dreading the next stop. It's
not the headliner that makes the difference; it is, more importantly, their crew. Because we were chosen specifically by the
Wilson sisters, we were treated quite nicely by all involved.
There are a thousand little ways a headliner's crew can either
help or hinder the opening act. Getting an adequate amount of
space to set up in front of their backline. Getting an adequate
amount of time to soundcheck. Being able, or not able to use x,
y, or z, which could be anything from an extra cable to the
lower set of PA speakers.

   The band was friendly and helpful to each of us in our own
stations, and Ann and Nancy couldn't have been nicer.
Watching Heart, we all came away with much admiration for
Ann Wilson's heroic voice. She had amazing pipes. Cameron
Crowe, *Rolling Stone* writer and creator of the 1982 classic film
Fast Times at Ridgemont High and later *Almost Famous* was often
on the tour, as he and Nancy were a couple and soon to be
married.

   Being an opening act was a mixed proposition. Interaction
with the public was limited to a meet-and-greet before the
show. We got the opportunity every night to play in front of
large audiences most of whom never heard of us before. Our
job was to win a certain percentage of them over, which could
be tough. As a concertgoer, the opening act's set, especially if
the opening act is one you've never heard of, is the time to get a
beer, something to eat, browse the headliner's merch, or
allows you to be late to the show. Audience members walk
around, talking to friends before the main act, and many view
the first strains of the opening act's initial song as an imposition. The audience for Heart, being led by two beautiful female
artists, was skewed heavily male. As in many concert situations, the more vocal and fanatic crowd members cram up

front. Those often-shirtless guys wanted no part of Bourgeois Tagg–they just wanted to watch Nancy play guitar and hear Ann sing "Barracuda." Dangerous things were thrown at us. Nonetheless, there were small victories, especially as the tour went on and "I Don't Mind At All" gained traction. We were an exciting band, after all, and by the end of our set we won over even some of the more obstinate crowd members. But I will admit to some scary moments looking down into the eyes of frenzied fans standing in front of the stage.

To promote *Yoyo,* we were booked on a couple of tours of Europe, going back and forth several times. That was good news, because it meant "I Don't Mind At All" and its video were doing well. At any other time, I would have looked forward to this as an exciting opportunity but having a new baby and being freshly sober made it a challenge. It didn't feel right leaving Mary Ann and Adrian so soon.

We played several dates in Germany with the English band T'Pau, featuring the red-headed powerhouse singer Carol Decker. T'Pau was touring behind their hit single "Heart and Soul." We played Hamburg, Hanover and Stuttgart, all cities with British and American Army bases. British soldiers, or "squaddies," made the British roadies seem like gentlemen. They loved to get completely hammered and yell lewd remarks at Carol. This happened first in Hamburg, but when we got to Hanover, Carol had had enough. As soon as one little squaddie started yelling obscene things at her she jumped down off the stage and beat this guy over the head with her mic stand while two other squaddies held him down. We were all kind of proud of her.

When we got to Germany, we landed right in the middle of Octoberfest. It was Beer Porn. Our German record company reps took us to a celebration right out of a movie, with long tables and hundreds of people sitting around them, all quaffing steins of lager the size of small garbage cans. As I sat there and steins were filled like Jesus at the wedding party, one of the German record company people took me by the scruff of the neck and said, "What's the matter with you? You don't have a beer!" I said meekly, "I don't drink." He replied loudly, "Oh, komm schon, Mann!! You may not drink in America, but you are drinking HERE!" And he shoved a gargantuan stein in front of me. I said to myself, not for the last time, *I hate being sober, and I hate not being sober!!* I was uncomfortable in my own skin much of the time.

Wherever we went, we were known, if at all, by one song, "I Don't Mind At All." We weren't sure where to put it in the set. As an opening act, if we put it at the end, that was too late. If we started with it, we had nowhere left to go. So, we decided to put it at the beginning *and* the end, starting with a snippet, "The time for talking's over now and *we're the guys who do this song...*" and then we'd launch into "Best of All Possible Worlds." And we'd do the rest of the set, and end with a full rendition of "I Don't Mind At All."

We drove across Europe in a Mercedes van, driven by our road manager, an English guy named Nigel Paul. Nigel was a wonderful man, well-dressed, calm, funny, and organized–all the things we were not, except the funny part. We put a lot of miles on that van. We drove from Frankfurt, Germany to Reims, France in one trip, and it was beautiful, historic, and sad. I read a great deal of WWI and WWII history, and every village and town name we passed had meaning for me, some battle fought, many young men dead. As it was the early evening and we were hungry, we stopped at nice-looking restaurant in Metz, France. Nigel was the only one of us who even spoke passable French. I tried to revive my high school

French before the trip and could read a menu but speaking French to French people was two steps too hard.

Nigel, being the driver, and this being before GPS, wanted to know how far we had to go before we made it to our destination, Reims*, one of the most iconic French towns, known for the largest cathedral in a country full of grand cathedrals. After ordering our food, Nigel asked the waiter, "*À quelle distance se trouve Reims?*" "How far is it to Reims?" Even I knew that one. The waiter looked at Nigel like he'd asked him how far it was to Timbuktu. "*Reims??*" the waiter replied. "*Oui, Reims.*" The waiter looked around the room as if he was looking for a lifeline. He started asking people at the bar, asking other customers, and soon the whole place was buzzing with "Reims? Reims? Reims?" This was ridiculous, because it was like asking someone in Baltimore where Washington DC was, or asking someone in Cleveland where Akron was. Nigel, who was seldom flustered, got out a napkin and a Sharpie and wrote R-E-I-M-S and underlined and spelled it out as he showed the waiter. "*Reims!!*" The waiter picked up the napkin, looked at it for a second and started laughing. "*Ohhhh Rrhh-haahhhnnnn! Rrhhhaahhhnnnn!!!*" and he waved the napkin all over the restaurant saying, "*Rrhhhaahhhnnnn!!*" and the rest of the customers replied, "*Rrhhhaahhhnnnn!*" and everyone had a good laugh because it was right down the road. *(Not to be confused with Rouen, the capital of Normandy, pronounced *O-whannn*)

We spent a lot of time in the British Isles. Our song was doing well there, and we were invited to play it on the venerable show *Top of the Pops*. This was a real honor, and we were provided a string quartet. We shared the bill with Australian singer Kylie Minogue and were presented as an American group re-importing the Beatles sound back to England. Next, we played *The Terry Wogan Show*, England's answer to Johnny Carson. It was Super Bowl week, so they booked an American football player, Brian "The Boz" Bosworth. I remember him rifling through the Green Room complaining loudly that the damn beer wasn't cold enough.

We were also unexpectedly asked by the British Island Records team to make a music video while in London. Unexpected because we hadn't talked about it with management, or even decided what the next single would be. But apparently the home office thought it was a good idea for us to shoot "Waiting For the Worm To Turn" while we were there. It was a catchy song, no doubt. We gathered inside a huge soundstage having no idea what to expect. Fifty yards in front of us stood a large stone-like faux mountain. Next to it was a smaller set of rocks onto which we were deposited. It took us a while to figure out that the director's vision was to have all kinds of people of all different ages jumping off this mountain, gleefully plunging in slow-motion to their...I don't know–it wasn't entirely clear. It was almost cult-like. We never saw the finished product and the song didn't really catch on in Britain, so the video was buried. It surfaced about thirty years later on YouTube and remains a weird idea for a video.

Scan me

The band took a tour of Liverpool on the Magical Mystery

Tour Bus because our song was a Beatle-y sensation. We passed John's Aunt Mimi's house, saw where Ringo was born and the Art School they attended, went down Penny Lane and saw the barbershop, and stopped at both Strawberry Fields and the Cavern Club. Larry and I did a morning radio show in Liverpool with Paul McCartney on another line from wherever he was listening to our song to get his reaction, which was, "It's quite lovely!" (British people love the word "lovely.")

Larry and I made several press trips on our own because it was easier to move the two of us around than take the whole band. When it was just us two, we were treated like rock stars; when it was the whole band, we slept in hostels and took vans. Because of Europe's compact size, we flew to an interview in one country in the afternoon and played a gig in another that night, which made for some amusing scenarios. One afternoon, we were interviewed in Brussels, and both given fancy hotel rooms even though we were only going to be there for about an hour. Larry naively used the hotel room phone to call his wife Tracy in Sacramento. Ruh-roh. That 15-minute call cost him over two hundred and fifty 1987 dollars. Overseas calls from hotels were extremely expensive.

We flew to Stockholm to do an interview on a major Swedish radio program, mainly because of this lyric from Larry's "Pencil & Paper":

A man whose father beat him, he's a poet on a folk guitar
A nice girl from Sweden, she's a thief in Zanzibar
One man is poor while his brother is well to do
It's my conclusion that you can't figure people without some
confusion

The interviewer was quite impressed that the name of their country was mentioned, and he began by asking Larry all about it. What Larry couldn't honestly say was that "nice girl from Sweden" rhymed with "man whose father beat him" and that was the end of it, but Larry twisted his verbiage into a pretzel and made the entire country feel good about themselves. We stayed overnight on this trip, and our hosts put us up in *twin* presidential suites at an amazing hotel with balconies overlooking the whole of Stockholm. The rooms could have each accommodated fifty people. Unfortunately, neither of us knew a soul in Stockholm, so we both sat in our oversized suites reading books, sipping on Diet Cokes.

Larry and I, along with Mick and Lionel went to Paris to meet our French record company. There I endured the five-hour dinner from Hell. It was slow water torture. There was wine before the meal, lots of wine, and then there was more wine with each course, which lasted an hour apiece. There was at least one champagne toast somewhere along the way. I loved champagne. Then some sweet wine with dessert and brandy or cognac to top it all off. I was miserable. It was the kind of event in which I formerly excelled (in my own head.) At least maybe until dessert. Then my head might have fallen into the tiramisu.

We played at an Island Records anniversary gala while in Paris and then traveled to Zurich, Switzerland where another surprise awaited us. During the day, we were ushered to a soundstage elaborately set up to make a video for "Out of My Mind." We had no inkling this was going to happen, no warning. The set-up had us traveling in a slow-moving vehicle on a rail while different scenes passed by, one with firefighters, another with religious types, a war scene, and a half-dozen more. The amount of work put into this production was incredible. We did our bit and then went to our regularly scheduled gig. We never even saw a rough cut of the video, and it has never surfaced.

The greatest story from our time in Europe came when Larry and I were invited by Island head Chris Blackwell to be his guests at the Princess's Trust Auction for Charity Luncheon in London. A star-studded rostrum included Peter Gabriel, Phil Collins, George Michael, Annie Lennox, Elton John and more I can't remember. The headliner was Princess Diana, who auctioned off things from her *toilet* or her boudoir. Larry and I sat at a large round table with Mick, Lionel and Blackwell and another new Island band, the Jamaican reggae group Aswad, four nervous young men who sat quietly, almost certainly stoned out of their gourds.

The auction began with bids for all kinds of small but valuable royal tchotchkes, pieces of jewelry, tea sets, and even vacations. Bidding steadily increased as time went on, and soon we were watching bids for ten or twenty thousand pounds. At our table, we sat on our hands; between Larry and me and the four Aswad guys, we didn't have ten pounds, much less ten thousand. So, we just watched, mouths agape. For the *pièce de resistance*, Princess Diana came out to present a small, beautiful music box, lovingly enameled and jeweled. As she slowly glided around the room, holding it up, the bidding started at ten thousand pounds, and quickly escalated to twenty, then twenty-five, thirty, thirty-five, forty, forty-five...going once...then forty-six, forty-seven...going once, going twice...as the auctioneer raised the gavel to close the deal, the lead singer of Aswad, Brinsley "Dan" Forde, stood up and yelled, "Fifty thousand pounds!!" SOLD!! We, along with everyone in the room were dumbfounded. This fellow didn't have 50p on him. But moments later, here he was, with his band, crowded around Princess Diana looking like the cat that swallowed the canary, getting their pictures taken with the most famous woman in the world by every press outlet in the UK. Larry, Mick and I looked at Chris Blackwell, expecting him to be livid, annoyed, or perturbed at the very least, but he was grinning. "I couldn't have gotten that amount of press for three times the cost of that bloody music box," he chuckled. I never found out if he put them up to it.

Being on tour five thousand miles from home and a new baby was hard. I felt guilty not being there, especially because we were in all these cool places and Mary Ann was tied down at in Sacramento. She did, thank God, have the help of her mother and sister. I was a real pain to the record company people in every country, employing my well-honed skills of persuasion for them to let me use office phones for trans-Atlantic calls. I called every chance I got, and then I'd have to tone it down to, "Yeah, we saw a lot of old stuff today. The Cathedral at Cologne is really dirty on the outside" or, "The Eiffel Tower isn't all it's cracked up to be."

We went back and forth to Europe several times—one morning we flew from Hamburg, Germany to Orlando, Florida and played a gig at Disney World that midnight. By a quirk of nature, it was colder in Orlando than it had been in Hamburg. My fingers, along with everyone else's, were frozen during that show. The last time we flew to England, I finally got to take Mary Ann and six-month-old Adrian with me. We spent time in Cornwall, at the southern tip of England with friend Nigel Gray and his wife and three boys.

As a kid, I watched *American Bandstand* on TV almost every Saturday afternoon, so I was thrilled when we were asked to appear on the show. Arriving at the studio in LA, we were treated to a homemade fried chicken lunch by Dick Clark's wife Kari, who served us outside behind the soundstage on picnic tables with white and red checked tablecloths, like something out of the 1950s. I'm not sure what we expected, but it wasn't that. It felt like going over to the Clark's house for a picnic. We performed "I Don't Mind" and "Cry Like A Baby." After we played, Dick Clark interviewed us. It was surreal.

Scan me

We also appeared on the American version of Top of the Pops, recorded in LA. Once again, we were afforded a string quartet, and it was one of our best performances, sounding just like the record.

Scan me

"I Don't Mind At All" achieved an almost unparalleled success, rising in 1987 to #2 on the AC (Adult Contemporary) chart at the same time it was #3 on the AOR (Album Oriented Rock) chart, a feat only accomplished by Eric Clapton's "Tears In Heaven." On the pop charts it reached the mid-30s, and it seemed like it was being heard all the time, with all the different formats playing it, plus the video in heavy rotation on MTV.

The culmination of the *Yoyo* experience was being asked to perform "I Don't Mind At All" on *The Tonight Show with Johnny Carson*. In the late '80s, his was still the only late-night television talk show, with nightly ratings higher than all the present-day shows combined. He didn't generally have "rock" bands on. The only reason we were accepted was because of the style of the song. You know what I was thinking? This was just the first time. Alas, it would be the only time as a performer.

We walked into *The Tonight Show* Burbank studio at about one o'clock in the afternoon. The crew was gracious as we ran through our soundcheck. We rehearsed two songs; we would play "Cry Like a Baby" at the end of the show if there was time. The other guests were Harvey Korman and Cathy Guisewhite, the originator of the *Cathy* cartoon. Johnny Carson said hello to us in our dressing room, as did Ed McMahon, both more loquacious than they had to be.

A couple of things got our attention. We watched Doc Severinsen pre-tape an Alpo commercial with a dog. They kept making the dog throw up to get it to do take after take. We weren't impressed with that. The other was that with all the joking about Ed McMahon's drinking, and the guys in the band sneaking around the corner for a drink, Ed actually ran a fully stocked bar right behind the set where he sat. It looked like something out of a saloon.

Taping began at five-thirty Pacific time. We went on second. Standing at our places during the commercial break, I was nervous, being under the impression that despite the early recording time, what we were performing was going to go out live, sink or swim. They came out of the break with the Tonight Show band playing just to our left, and Johnny held up the album and got the name of the band right, which was the hard part, but then flubbed the album title, saying, "Yoko, er, Yoyo-gentleman!" and he pointed with his arm to the left. I do a quick "4" with a finger snap to cue Lyle because it's a cold opening without rhythm. I sing "The" and he comes in on "time." It's kind of tricky, but we had done it enough that it was no biggie now. So, I said "4" and "The" and Lyle stepped forward to play his first chord and his acoustic guitar came unplugged. There was nothing. But me. Standing there. In front of millions of people. Career over. Again. A new blooper reel. Remember that band with the funny name that gakked on *The Tonight Show*? Anyway, another of the six longest seconds of my life passed before the producer said, "Cut!" and we got to do it again. Neither Larry nor I knew until that moment that we were allowed a do-over. The second time was the charm, and we went back into our dressing room to find out if we were going to be summoned to play "Cry Like A Baby." But Cathy Guisewhite ran long, and the show ran out.

Scan me

There was no time to rest on our laurels because we had a show to play that night at The Coach House in San Juan Capis-trano, a large funky club in lower Orange County with long picnic benches seating about eight hundred people. We drove down the 405 floating about a foot off the ground and did our soundcheck. When it was time to do the show, there were *maybe* a hundred hearty souls in the building including the staff and crew. Everyone crowded to the picnic tables up front. How quickly this business reminds you where you really stand. We played an energetic set but stopped in the middle of a song because there were TV monitors mounted up high in several places on the walls, and guess what was on while we were playing? *The Tonight Show* with special guests, Harvey Korman, Cathy Guisewhite and Bourgeois Tagg. We had everybody in the club turn around and watch us play "I Don't Mind At All" before playing it live.

We had one more tour to do to complete the *Yoyo* cycle, and that was with Belinda Carlisle. It was ironic, given what Robert Palmer thought of her music. Belinda, the former lead singer of The Go-Go's, was riding a hit solo album produced by Rick Nowels. She was a sweet young woman who knew she was fortunate to be in her current position. She had loads of personality to go with a so-so singing voice and was propped up vocally by a gaggle of female singers in her band, notably Bekka Bramlett and Suzie Davis, who impressed me in particular, and I filed her away as someone we might want to consider for our band. The tour was fun, everyone got along, and at the end of it our band dressed up like theirs and surprised them on stage. As Belinda Carlisle, I made my first appearance in drag.

I went home to Sacramento and started to focus on the real things important to me, my sobriety and my family.

———

Scott Moon & Lyle Workman   Michael Urbano   Larry Tagg video shoot   Lyle & Timi

"I Don't Mind At All" video shoot

"Perfect Life" video

David Fincher, Lyle, Mick Brigden
"I Don't Mind At All" video shoot

Todd's polkadot shirt

Brent stole Todd's polkadot shirt

Condom-Mania

Bourgeois Tagg "Yoyo"

Ian Samwell & Arnie Pustilnik

Lionel Conway & Mick Brigden

Bill Graham

Bourgeois Tagg "Yoyo"

Touring Liverpool

Catchin' some shuteye

At the German office

On tour in Europe

Breakfast at my home in Dallas

Four hour French dinner

Lyle taken hostage

With Belinda Carlisle

Forever

At the German office

With Lionel Conway in Paris

With Suzie Davis

Euro TV show

Bourgeois Tagg On Tour 1986-1988

8

SOLO: THE REAL THINGS

L ike the all or nothing addict I am, I dove headfirst into
AA with the same zeal that I formerly felt for a bottle
of champagne. While there were those who went in
and out before they were finally beaten down enough to
surrender, I surprised myself by taking to it right away. I
desperately wanted for once to do something good for myself
and my family. Sleep-training a baby requires two adults on
duty, and I was now able to function as a normal father and
partner. I found my East Sacramento tribe, even if some of the
old-timers thought it was first-world problems to be
describing my angst over long French dinners.

I never stopped believing in God. God just got pushed
farther and farther into the background. When desperate, I
relied on what is known as a "foxhole God," as in, "God, if you
just let me fall asleep this *one* time, I promise I'll be good
tomorrow." I wasn't an atheist; God was just another entity in
whom I had no conviction. AA wants us to find a Higher
Power–the founders were smart enough at the beginning to
avoid insisting on only the Christian version, although it must

have been tempting in mid-1930s Ohio. Being raised a Catholic, I had no problems with Jesus. In fact, I liked Jesus considerably more than I liked the people who followed Him in His name. I felt the same as Gandhi: "*I like your Christ. I do not like your Christians. Your Christians are so unlike your Christ.*" So, the thing that hung up so many AA'ers was not a problem for me. I started attending Warehouse Christian Ministries services with Mary Ann, following again in my friend Charlie's steps. I wasn't ready to completely commit, but I couldn't deny there was something going on inside me.

Another thing that occupied the space between my ears was writing songs for my publishing contract. This didn't just mean songs for Bourgeois Tagg; I was also required to write a set number of songs to be pitched to other artists. Lionel Conway was paying Larry and me a living wage to create songs for others. I never felt I was good at doing this, and my lack of successful credits showed it.

Mary Ann, baby Adrian, and I moved into a classic 1930s-style house, porch swing and all, in East Sacramento, turning a tiny room off the kitchen into a budding studio. I bought a mixing console, an 8-track reel-to-reel tape recorder, and most importantly, through Todd Rundgren, I was able to snag a developer deal on an Apple II Macintosh for under $10,000 (!) that was expandable to 8MB of RAM! I used MOTU's MIDI sequencer called Performer. Late

'80s cutting edge home studio. One of the first things we recorded in this studio was a suite of songs—one by Larry, one by me, and one by Lyle. Mine was called, "My Little Island," an odd little piece of Beatle-esque-ness.

I know you worshipped me
You said you did when we first made love

You quoted Blake
You said you saw the heavens open up above
The phone now sits in silence
Everybody kicks you when you're down
Another solitary Sunday morning comes
My little island

Scan me

The heavens were opening up all around me. I had a second composing awakening now that the cobwebs were beginning to clear from my brain. The first song to come out of recovery would be one of my best, "The Real Things," built around a figure on the Fender Rhodes that I thought was a hook in and of itself.

I want to know about the real things, important to me
Like beauty and love and family
I carry the words upon my knee
And execute the letter of it faithfully

When I think about getting out of my head
I pick up a book and I get on back to bed
Now we old boys, we had our fun
Attempted the setting of the rising sun
But hey, boys, it's time to go on home

Scan me

Todd talked about writing from the heart, and this was directly from my core. The chorus became a mantra to me. Beauty and love and family. I felt like I was going to write my 4th Step as a whole album of songs. A confessional. I began writing songs for the third Bourgeois Tagg record but something was different.

I piled up songs in my studio. Peter Gabriel's *So* was released and was a big influence on me (and everybody else.) "Evil Run Riot," a desperate plea for help, wrapped itself in a Gabriel-esque track.

It hurts down to the bone
It hurts to be alone
Oh I was hurting
I should have sounded the alarm
I could have bought the farm
Oh I was hurting so bad, baby
Just one more for the road
One more claim upon my soul
Get the monkey off my back
And the albatross from around my neck
If it comes to war, then it comes to war
'Cause I can't take any more of this
Evil run riot

"Scene of the Crime" emerged from a valley of emotions, as I struggled to come up with the reasons why I acted the way I had for so long. Again, the rhythm track exuded a Gabriel-esque vibe:

I humble myself at the altar of my God
I'm just feeling happy to be any place at all
It's a miracle that anyone survived that year
I just want to know what on earth am I still doing here?
And I go back to the place where it all began
The place that I thought that I became a man
But it doesn't mean what I thought it did then
There at the scene of the crime
And it's time to let go of those years and move on ahead
'Cause the answer lies with the living and not the dead
I'm so much more at peace than I ever was then
There at the scene of the crime

If this sounded like the makings of a solo record, that wouldn't be wrong, but I didn't know that. Yet.

As we began preparations for our third album, after having a nice run on the second, it felt like the pressure was on for a commercial success—the third album was the make-or-break record for recording artists in that era. Nowadays we're so used to one shot—one single, one video—that we forget there was more leeway given to artists in the '70s and '80s. We felt good about our prospects. Bourgeois Tagg was in that up-and-coming basket of groups from Britain and America destined to take the next step forward. Our management pushed us to consider Austrian producer Peter Wolf, who had a string of hits from the Starship to Heart, to, more important to us, Big Country and Wang Chung, two artists in our class having great success, especially at MTV. This appealed to us, and we arranged for a meeting in Sacramento.

Peter was a handsome blonde man with a big smile and a strong German accent. Everything was "wonderful," "brilliant," and "amazing" to the optimistic Wolf. He saw us play at Melarkey's in Sacramento and gushed with compliments. We agreed to record four songs with him at his studio in LA and if everyone liked the results, continue with the rest of the record.

Lyle, in the meantime, had handed me a beautiful guitar track needing a melody and lyrics. It gave me another opportunity to tear open my own scars.

Sooner or later
I gotta get out of this chair
And dance with the demons
That brought me here
Still I can't feel the pain
I can't feel anything at all
But I know I never ever

Want to pass this way again
Can't you see the madness
That's been going on?
'Cause you don't have to move a mountain
Or swim a sea to be free

This was the basis of "Can't Feel the Pain." One of the things that may have been incongruous to the other members of the band was that on the surface, I was doing okay. I never deviated much from the superficial "business as usual" attitude during the day, and the "last man standing–where's everybody going?" posture late at night. You didn't look at me and say, "There is a drowning man," but for years, I was in an increasingly leaky boat. I was turning thirty and realized I had cruised through the last ten years like Mr. Magoo, the extremely short-sighted cartoon character who stumbled and bumbled his way through one dangerous scenario after another, coming out unscathed while things around him fell apart. As I looked at my former self, I saw a guy in a bulldozer marauding through life without much thought of anyone else. I had a lot of amends to make, especially to my wife. This was my frame of mind as we assembled for the sessions with Peter.

Royalties had been kind to Mr. Wolf. He had an eight thousand square foot house in LA equipped with a custom recording studio. The jewel in his crown was his Synclavier, an uber-sampler capable of Herculean feats that later became commonplace, but in 1988 was unique, powerful and extremely expensive. I arrived with about a dozen songs while Larry had three, the first inkling that something didn't feel right. Nonetheless, we started with two of Larry's, one of mine, and one that had been co-written by Larry, Lyle and me, a ballad called "We Are Home."

Peter Wolf was the kind of guy who could make you feel

good about a toothache. In many ways he was the anti-Todd. Michael Urbano set up his drums in Peter's studio, and as usual, the first thing they did was get drum sounds. As Mike was hitting each drum, Peter said, "Michael, your drums sound great! Amazing! However, I have this other kit over here that I would just love for you to try, and if you don't like it, we'll go back to yours, ok?" Mike, wanting to please, agreed and began playing the other kit. "Oh Michael! *Those* drums sound even better than before because you are playing them! I've never heard them sound so good!" Mike now played Peter's drums on the recording.

When it came time for Larry to get bass sounds, the same thing happened. Larry had only used one bass sound since the bass guitar was invented, and it remained a great one. Peter Wolf listened to Larry's bass, and said, "Larry, your bass sound is fantastic! I'm wondering, just for grins, if you would like to try this incredible bass guitar I have over here in the other room?" Larry, to be polite, agreed. As he was playing the new bass, Peter exclaimed, "What an amazing bass sound! You are making that thing really sing!" Larry now used Peter Wolf's bass.

When it came to Lyle, Peter had met his match. Lyle had a large General Electric refrigerator full of pedals, amps, modular dinghies, and a guitar for every season. Still, Peter, while pouring on the praise, convinced Lyle to at least try some of his guitars and amps and I think he might have gotten Lyle to use one.

Of course, it went without saying anything we were going to play on keyboards could be better done on the Synclavier. I was kind of bowled over by the thing. What none of us knew but soon found out is all the sounds we were getting, everything we were recording was going to be dumped into the Synclavier to be locked up, synced up, enhanced and dehumanized. We recorded Larry's song "½ Yes & ½ No", a musical sequel to "15 Minutes in the Sun" from *Yoyo*. Then we launched into the ballad "We Are Home." I was not happy–it sounded so generic. When I realized that the third song of Larry's was not new, but a ten-year-old Uncle Rainbow staple called "Christopher Columbus," I almost left then and there. I had the better part of an album written and we were doing Uncle Rainbow! How was this "moving forward"?

The last straw came when I was driving back on the 101 freeway to where we were staying in North Hollywood. I was flipping through the FM stations when Wang Chung's hit, "Everybody Wang Chung Tonight" came on. The drum sound was *exactly* the same as the drums Urbano was now recording with.

That night back at our residence, Lyle left an acoustic guitar on a bed tuned to D A D A B E. I don't play guitar, at least not well enough to claim that I play guitar. I regret that I didn't learn it along with the piano when I was young. But I picked up that guitar and even I could make it sound good, finding if I moved my fingers together on the lower two strings, I could create all kinds of relative chords. I fiddled with it until I had the musical outline of the song "Compromise," which Larry always thought I wrote about him but was really about the whole situation.

I won't roll over and play your dead dog
I have traveled down that road too long
I never want to play another song
That I can't feel just a little
And you might have a better way to do things
That's okay, I might as well be wrong
'Cause I could walk away from you tomorrow
with nothing lost and nothing left to borrow

Maybe we'll meet in the middle?
I like what you do
It's important to you
But there's no room in me left
For compromise

Scan me

We went home to Sacramento after inputting our four songs into Peter's Synclavier. I was at a crossroads. The band was desperate for a hit single, and I understood that. They were ready to go to any lengths to get it, even at the expense of compromising all their own sounds and recording a ballad that was no different from the song Uncle Rainbow did with Narada Michael Walden ten years previously. I couldn't have been in a more different place. Emotionally, I was turning inward and writing more personal songs, while the band was doing "1/2 Yes & 1/2 No" and "Christopher Columbus." I felt removed from the whole process.

Leaving the band now would be insane. We were on our way *up*. But I looked at all the songs I was writing and every one of them was about recovery; introspective, solo-artist type of compositions. I didn't feel comfortable singing or even bringing them into the band. It sure didn't seem like the kind of record we were making, either. On the other hand, Peter and the band was a bird in hand, and leaving would be a step into the giant unknown. What was I to do?

I decided to confide in Mick and Arnie. Surely our managers would talk me out of leaving. Surely, they would side with the even-handed, logical thing to do. *"Keep your solo songs in your pocket and at least stay through this album cycle."* Only they didn't. Neither of them was pleased with Peter's production, which they viewed as a step backwards after Todd Rundgren. They both said they would back me in whatever I decided to do. I asked them to suss out my solo prospects as I had the better part of an album already written.

While they looked for that answer, I talked to Lionel Conway, the closest person in the music business to me. He had a lot at stake with Bourgeois Tagg but had seen the changes in me and had heard and approved of the introspective music I was writing. His words were, "You're leading with your heart." My heart was working overtime at that moment. He thought it would be throwing good money after bad to keep going with a project that one of the leaders wasn't happy with. He asked me to think about it for another week. Mary Ann questioned the financial implications, and I reminded her that most of the money I made came from my publishing advance, same with Larry, and that soon the money would begin to come in for my part of "I Don't Mind At All." The band was somewhere around a million dollars in the hole with Island Records by the time we had finished four songs with Peter Wolf. We had never made money from the albums and probably never would.

During the *Yoyo* cycle, the two Island Records employees most responsible for the success of "I Don't Mind At All," Head of Radio Promotion Bob Catania and Marketing and Promotions guru Phil Quartararo, or Phil Q as he was known, departed for the startup record company Virgin America. Mick and Arnie didn't have to look far to find a couple of important folks who had positive feelings for me. They arranged a meeting with Jordan Harris and Jeff Ayeroff, the co-heads of Virgin, and Bob and Phil. I told them I had most of an album written along with a great idea for a cover of "Time of the Season," the 1968 Zombies hit. They were as encouraging as they could be. I think it was another case of Mr. Magoo stumbling into a good situation at the right time. Based on the meeting, I made the difficult decision to leave the band. My eyes were wide open as to the effect my decision would have on the other four members of the band, especially Larry. I certainly didn't expect him to understand. And he didn't. It took them all completely by surprise.

As unhappy as the other members of Bourgeois Tagg were with me, all five of us appeared together on Todd Rundgren's *Nearly Human* live-in-the-studio album just a few weeks later. The atmosphere was frosty within the band, but that was to be expected, as Todd gathered up to seventeen musicians on every track to record in one fell swoop all the parts that would normally be overdubs and background vocals. In the morning, he would bring a song in on his Akai digital 12-track recorder, we'd spend an hour or two learning it, and then we'd start rehearsing. By around five o'clock in the afternoon, we were ready to record. I played keyboards on some of the songs and sang background vocals on others. These are still some of my favorite Todd songs of all time. I was grateful to be a part of eight of the ten songs.

On "The Waiting Game" I was assigned his double vocal, or his alt lead. On "Fidelity," still one of my Todd faves, I had the main opening keyboard part that played through the whole song. Same with "Parallel Lines." Todd wanted them just like he had demoed them, and there were no fixes, except occasionally on his lead vocals; by the time five o'clock rolled around each day his voice was battered and bruised. I played the synth vibes on "Hawking," a beautiful song in any era. Todd, the cynic, can also be one of the most eloquently compassionate songwriters. With "Hawking" he topped himself. "The Want of a Nail" was perhaps the most fun, as he welcomed R&B legend Bobby Womack in for a duet. I sang background vocals, and got to know singer and percussionist Vicki Randle, who soon came back into my life in a bigger way.

Within a couple of weeks, I was looking for a producer for my solo album. I felt I connected with Danny "Kootch" Kortchmar, the longtime guitar player for James Taylor, Carole King and recent producer of two of Don Henley's hit albums *Building the Perfect Beast,* featuring "Boys of Summer," and *End of the Innocence.* His resume spoke for itself. At the same time, I was still fond of David Holman, and thought highly of the vocal sound he had gotten on our first album. After meeting with both, we decided to split the record between them, with Kortchmar getting five songs, and David getting the other six.

A constant during these years were my flailing attempts to write songs for other artists as part of my publishing deal. I made a few writing trips to LA, but I generally struck out on these. On one trip, though, I met a guy named Peter Beckett, songwriter and guitarist in the group Player, who had the 1977 hit single "Baby Come Back." Together, we wrote a song called "Wild Child," which ended up in the 1989 movie *Big Man On Campus.* Kortchmar liked it and wanted us to record it for my record as well.

I wrote quite a few forgettable songs in my home studio for "other people," but one stood out. I was convinced my blue-eyed soul tune, "Dare To Fall In Love" might be a hit for somebody. Somebody other than me. It was a good song, and might make me some money, but it wasn't in the style I wanted to present as a solo artist. When I sent my demos for my solo album to Virgin Records, I made sure "Dare To Fall In Love" *wasn't* on any of the tapes, because I knew that somebody might get the bright idea to suggest it for my album. But despite my best efforts, some well-meaning creature at Island Publishing sent it to Virgin and sure enough, they wanted it on the record, thinking it could be the first single. This was hypocritical of me to consider. After the stance I had taken on the Peter Wolf recordings, I should have said no. But Virgin was a new relationship, and this was their only request. They otherwise had accepted all my material. And I wasn't sure I had a single on this record, based on the demos, and neither were they until they heard "Dare To Fall In Love."

Scan me

Before I could start my record, I needed minor surgery on a deviated septum, the result of too much cocaine use. I sat recuperating in an LA apartment, getting ready to watch Game 3 of the 1989 World Series between the San Francisco Giants and the Oakland A's when a giant earthquake hit the Bay Area minutes before the game was set to begin. It was surreal looking at the broken Bay Bridge I had travelled across so many times, and the pancaked MacArthur Overpass in Oakland. I apparently over excited myself because some packing came loose from my nose, and blood spurted out like a horror movie. I laughed until it wasn't funny anymore–I was losing a lot of blood. Beginning to panic, I called Danny Kortchmar, who came right over with his wife, Maggie, and drove me to an emergency room. In the ER, a male nurse took one look at me and brought out something that looked like a large, inflated condom filled with white gloppy goo attached to a glue gun. I asked him what it was, and he answered, "pure cocaine." I immediately said, "No no! I can't do that! That's what got me in this shape to begin with! I cannot do that!" He said, "Son, you're gonna do this or you might die. You've already lost a tremendous amount of blood." He didn't wait for my answer— he just shot the balloon up my nostril and it was the most painful thing I ever experienced, nothing ever coming close. But it stopped the bleeding, exactly what the drug was intended to do.

I started recording my album at George Massenburg's The Complex in West LA. The rhythm section was a Dream Team of Steve Jordan on drums, Randy Jackson on bass, and Danny Kortchmar on guitar. Young Ross Hogarth was the engineer. Steve was the drummer in Dave Letterman's band and had just finished playing on Keith Richard's first solo album, *Talk Is Cheap*, with his side band The X-pensive Winos. He was a bundle of energy, a music historian and had a fetish-like love for playing the guitar, most notably with a wah-wah pedal. He carried a Stratocaster strapped around his neck, ready for action at all times. He recorded a punch-in "fix" on drums with the guitar strapped on. We ended up giving him the chance, under the name 'Fo, which was short for Mofo, which was short for...I gave him a thrill later in the process when I booked him to come to David Holman's studio and do his first paid session on guitar.

Steve was a walking music encyclopedia. John Fogarty, the legendary founder of Creedence Clearwater Revival, came to the Complex to rehearse in a separate studio for a rare benefit performance with Randy and Steve as his rhythm section. Fogarty didn't play CCR tunes in public because of a long-standing dispute with his record company, but he was making an exception in this case. He was a bit rusty, but Steve had his back. I watched as Steve led the rehearsal, stopping Fogarty several times to remind him of his own parts on guitar.

Randy was all positive vibes. He still yelled "People To Be!" whenever he saw me coming. He had just gotten off the road with Bob Dylan, and I could only imagine those two polar opposite personalities. He said Bob wore a hooded sweatshirt the entire time and never removed the hood from his head. Randy added to his own legend on my song "Shit Out of Luck" by giving it a unique iconic intro and then carrying the rest practically on his own.

Danny had a quiet authority. He didn't say a lot, but every suggestion he made came from years of experience and was almost always the right thing to do. His guitar-playing had the same kind of right-note command. I simply felt in good hands.

Ross, our engineer, is someone whose friendship I've carried forward to the present day. We discovered many years later that he met his wife Kristin, who was working as a cock-tail waitress at The Albatross in Santa Cruz, on the same fateful night I met Mary Ann.

The first song we recorded at the Complex was "The Real Things." It held a special place for me because it was the first song I wrote in sobriety. Danny replaced my Rhodes piano figure with an eighth-note guitar figure of his own on the upbeats. I had enlisted percussionist and singer Vicki Randle to pull double-duty on this album, and she made an appearance on Track One. It also marks the first appearance of the myste-rious 'Fo on wah-wah guitar.

The five songs recorded with this cast and crew were, "The

Real Things," "Can't Feel the Pain," "Dare To Fall In Love," "Wild Child," and "Time of the Season." At the same time, down the hall, Fleetwood Mac were mixing a couple of songs from *Behind the Mask*. It was amazing watching the progression of the two sessions. Fleetwood Mac had earned the right to take as long as they wanted. They had five 24-track reel-to-reel tape recorders synced together, one for each member of the band to have taken home and filled up with their own overdubs. I had never seen anything like it before. Mick Fleetwood alone had dozens of tracks of various African percussion instruments. The band spent most of their time at the Complex sitting in their lounge waiting for the call to comment on a mix. We took advantage of their inactivity and began to recruit them to play on my record. They seemed happy to do it, if only to do *something*. Guitarist Rick Vito was first, playing slide guitar and dobro on "Wild Child."

One day, I had my sister Coral bring her jewelry from her company *Art For Ears* to the studio and set up a table in the hallway between our studio and theirs. Coral brought earrings, bracelets, pins, and hair clasps, all in the style of our first album cover. It was like leading bears to honey. Christine McVie and Stevie Nicks bought a couple of hundred dollars' worth, followed soon by the men in the group for their ladies.

Much later one evening, as we closed our session, Mick Fleetwood prowled the hall, looking for...me, it turned out. Not exactly *me*, per se, but for virgin ears. "Come into this studio," he said, beckoning me into a small editing room. "I have something I'd love to play for you." Not wishing to turn down a request from Mick Fleetwood, I said sure. On the desk in the editing suite next to the tape machines was a tower of DATs (digital audio tapes), each capable of holding ninety minutes of recording. "Sit down," he said, and I sat down, apprehensively. After all, he had been to Africa and had released a solo album in 1981 called *The Visitor* that I liked a lot. Still, that pile…I was quickly trying to do the math in my head of ninety minutes times…fifteen? twenty? I was going to be there all night. The bottle of coke around his neck was not encouraging, either.

"My father was a World War Two fighter pilot for the RAF," he began. "He flew many dangerous missions over Germany and Romania and his plane was hit multiple times. {Sniff} {Sniff} My father was also a poet, and this is some of his poetry set to my percussion accompaniment." Before I could open my mouth, Mick was inserting the first tape into the DAT player. The sound of a rain stick and shakers fluttered for a few long seconds until Major Fleetwood interjected with his deep, sonorous British voice,

"The wind beat against the damaged jet…I felt my heart beat against my damaged chest…the flak! Oh, the flak!"

At that moment two assistant engineers walked by, peeked in behind Mick and started pointing and laughing at me, as if to say, "I can't believe he got *you*!" As the conga drum wailed and the tambourines flailed, Major Fleetwood bravely continued:

"The moon beckoned with its sallow face—wouldst I see again this hallowed place, or vanish darkly with ne'er a trace, deign I never conceive of such a race while the clouds deny the flak! Oh, the flak!" And another diving kettle drum into a crash cymbal…this was the first few minutes of the first DAT, and there was a mountain more. I was sure I would die before the brave RAF pilot.

"Through cloud after cloud the engines roared…and as I betook my shield and sword…for to die in service to the King and my Lord"
——

I raised my hands up in a major stretch and yawn and I said to Mick, "This is so compelling. I would love to listen to it all night, but I have to sing early tomorrow, and I have sworn myself to get an adequate amount of sleep. Will you forgive me?" Mick, disappointed, said something about it just getting to a good part, but his mouth was blocked by the coke bottle as he took a couple of more snorts. I was standing by this point and had put on my jacket. He turned off the DAT player and accompanied me out the door, down the hall, and to my car. I really don't think he had anything better to do. "Tomorrow then?" I said as a goodbye. "Tomorrow again," he replied, a bit forlornly. I thought of the two young engineers as I drove away, wondering if I was the last person standing he could snare into listening to the poetic adventures of Major Fleetwood, RAF.

"Can't Feel the Pain" was another started by a Lyle Workman guitar track, and rather than try and re-create it, we asked Lyle to send us his original 16-track recording, a flawless, beautiful rendition of his main guitar part. Michael Urbano had also contributed a drum machine part to this demo, and we kept that as well. Rick Vito lent his superb musicianship again on dobro and slide.

Unbeknownst to me, Ross had been on the crew of Christine McVie's recent solo tour, and he invited Christine to come down and take a listen. She poked her head in while we were playing back "Can't Feel the Pain" and inquired, "What is that? It's lovely." There have been two times in my music career when an odd wish has become a reality. When I wrote "Can't Feel the Pain," on my demo I tried to sing the harmony parts like Christine McVie. She was who I had in mind and now she was standing at the control room door, complimenting the song. I replied sheepishly, "I wrote it with you in mind" and it was true. I asked her if she would like to sing on it and she said,

"Sure, I'd love to." This was literally a dream come true. When Christine sang,

When it comes down to you, love
I just don't know how to feel love
But I know I'm never ever gonna pass this way again
it was perfect in a way that happened twice in my life.

Scan me

"Dare To Fall In Love" and "Time of the Season" were both arranged and produced as singles. In "Time of the Season's" case it may have been overdone. Sometimes, more is just more, and that song used a lot of bullets. "Dare To Fall In Love," on the other hand, was just what I thought it might be, a blue-eyed soul song in the manner of Bobby Caldwell's "What You Won't Do For Love." It was well-produced and sounded radio ready, but I was afraid it would overshadow the message of the rest of the record.

As we were recording, change was afoot inside Virgin America. Phil Q was being recruited as a record company president by several of Virgin's rivals. To keep Phil in the fold, Richard Branson offered him the opportunity to pilot the revival of its Charisma label in the US. Charisma was the UK home of Genesis, Peter Gabriel, Julian Lennon, and Monty Python, among others.

I was summoned into the Virgin offices and entered a room

with Jordan Harris, Jeff Ayeroff, Phil Q, and my manager Mick. They asked if I would like to join Phil and become the first artist on Charisma Records USA. It seemed like a no-brainer, as Phil Q was the top promotion guy in the country, and being the first release would get all kinds of extra publicity. I think Mick and I said yes before the words had floated to the ground.

First things first; I still had another half of an album to do.

One of the songs I wrote for this album with an interesting story is "A Long Way From Home." Mary Ann and I saturated Adrian with music from his earliest days. Mary Ann went more for the children's tapes, while I started him off with Beatles songs with funny titles and subjects like "Yellow Submarine" and "Octopus's Garden." My good friend Steve Mitchell was responsible for Adrian's life-long obsession with the Beach Boys, while my brother Bruce sent him tapes of rock'n'roll from the '50s and early '60s.

One of the sets of music Adrian received, probably as a Christmas gift, was a cassette of cowboy songs accompanying a Pecos Bill book about the Old West. This music sounded staged around the campfire. Many were old Irish pub songs, which incidentally also made for fine worship music with a few lyric changes. One of the songs that caught my attention was a "ballad" in a different sense, in that it read as almost an epic traveling song. I tried my hand at it, and "A Long Way From Home" was born. These are among my favorite lyrics, as close to real poetry as I'll get:

> As the last burst of sunlight peeked over the sea
> And the wind and the cold water purified me
> A cleansing of body as old ocean rolls
> Though I can't say the same for my poor wretched soul
>
> Well it's been seven years since I first left my girl

I've wandered and traveled all over the world
But I still haven't found one as perfect as she
I don't know what the devil has come over me

Now if I had a nickel for every time that I
said, "I'm coming home soon" well I could retire
With pride in my pocket I lay down and pray
For the spirits and demons to be swept away

Now be still for a moment so I can explain
I'm a drifter of oceans, a runaway train
It would ne'er do your heart well to tangle with me
Alone I arrived here, alone I shall leave

I'm a long way from home
But home is where my heart is telling me to go
I'm a long way from home

At the first ray of sunlight I'm back on my feet
It's good to move early in the tropical heat
A prodigal son with the whole world to roam
Yet she will always remind me I'm a long way from home

Scan me

Within David Holman's magic trunk of amazing gear was a Neuman U47 that I loved called a "Church" mic because it had been modified by Stanley Church, an engineer at MGM Studios in the late 1950s. Every mic is different on every singer's voice, and this one sounded great on mine. Although a handful of expensive microphones rise above the pack, there is no consensus "best" microphone because each one behaves differently on every individual voice. For years, Mick Jagger used a mic that you could buy down at Guitar Center. Enya, the angelic Irish vocalist with the million-dollar sound, used a hundred-dollar microphone to make her recordings. On the other hand, there are tube mics made in the 1940s costing tens of thousands of dollars, and the sound is worth every penny. The Church mic was an expensive and extremely rare one that happened to sound perfect on the individual qualities of my voice. And on no song did it sound as good as on "A Long Way From Home."

The songs recorded at David Holman's were, with one exception, the introspective ones. For the most part, we used drum machine, with some programmed by Urbano. I also did some auxiliary recording in Sacramento at David Houston's Moon Studio. David was a longtime Sacramento musician, recording engineer and producer, and a good friend. I had done my fair share of demo recording at Moon Studio and was part of a locally infamous Christmas album there on which I did my impression of Elvis. For my solo record, I wrangled performances on guitar and dobro from Sacramento musicians Ray Elzey and Tom Philips. Lyle Workman made an appearance at Moon playing the three-part eBow solo on "My Little Island."

Recording at David Holman's studio felt like a warm, comfortable winter coat. Some of it had to do with the hospitality of David's wife Laura, and some with the familiarity of having recorded there before. These were songs with emotional impact, and it was important to feel comfortable in my own skin to sing them. David still had all the innovative tools at his disposal, but for my record, we went for a more organic feel.

One song that stood out from all the others was "Shit Out of Luck." I don't know where this lyric came from, but it seemed to be pulled from someone's backside. There were several opportunities for the grownups in the room to say yeah...no. I thought it was funny, but I still had the sense of humor of an eighth grader, still the guy singing "Slime-y girl" to Anita Baker's heartfelt piano in the next room. Randy Jackson understood the comical aspect right away. Randy, who would go on to greater fame as a panelist on American Idol, was one of the most optimistic guys you could ever meet. He was still a large man back then, but humble and self-effacing. He came over to the studio and laid down an iconic bass part with its own sense of humor. This song also contains the most "PPG" of all PPG synth lines–the melody that ends the choruses.

Scan me

In the least surprising move, Phil Quartararo and his Charisma team chose "Dare To Fall In Love" as the first single not only from my album, but to launch the Charisma label as its initial release. And at the height of the MTV era, a top-notch video was a must. Jeff Ayeroff was Virgin's visual guru, and he started taking ideas from the best video directors. I was soon called into a meeting with David Fincher, who had skyrocketed to stardom with several iconic Madonna videos. Fincher came into the meeting with a detailed storyboard.

I was still in the early stages of sobriety and had started going to church at Warehouse Ministries. The pendulum had swung to the side of doing what I thought to be the right thing, trying to be a present and loving husband and father, making up for lost time, and even the beginnings of a life inside the scope of Christianity. I was in the process of rejecting much of the person I had been for the last fifteen years. I wrote "Dare To Fall In Love" as an exercise in craft to fulfill a publishing contractual obligation with no intent of doing the song myself. Though I had written more than my fair share of mediocre songs as part of that obligation, this just happened to be a good one. I knew if the record company heard this song, especially given the nature of the rest of the album, they would pick it for the single. And now I was about to fully understand why I didn't want "Dare To Fall In Love" to represent the album.

Fincher presented his concept, highlighting all too clearly the line, "One kiss is a dangerous drug." His idea involved me and a female model in many compromising situations–making out in a car, in bed, and in varying stages of undress. Just about anything the mind could imagine, all expensively and fashionably presented. Everyone around the table listened intently and approvingly; after all, Fincher was on the roll of all rolls, and he was telling a hot story. Everyone turned to me, "What do you think?"

What I thought was: *I can't do this. I can't make a video like this and face my wife who has put up with so much already. I can't let my son watch this when he is old enough to understand.* I looked at Mick, stammered and spluttered, and said, "I can't do it." This is when I lost the room. To them, I wasn't prepared to do all I could do–the hell with my integrity. They had gifted me with a David Fincher video that would cost a quarter of a million dollars as the initial presentation of a new record label. And I said no?!? Fincher left the room and with him went the goodwill of Virgin/Charisma Records.

Despite my rejection of the Fincher idea, there was still a video to do, so Mick and I powered through a couple of dozen director's reels. Unlike music producers, choosing a video director became the last creative decision you made regarding your video. After that, you were at the mercy of the director's vision. We settled on a French fashion photographer who had made a beautiful video for The Innocence Mission, like an Impressionist painting, and more in line with my sensibilities. In the meantime, I did a photo shoot for the album and the image chosen for the cover was a serious, somber picture of me looking almost angry. Todd later called it the green Don Johnson.

The good news was that the video would be shot in Paris. The bad news was that the video would be shot in Paris. Traveling to Paris was never a bad thing, unless you were newly sober and fearful of four-hour dinners. Being so far away also meant that we would be beyond the control of the record company until the video was in the can. The director, whose name I cannot remember, had given us little indication of what he had in mind. After the Fincher rejection, I wasn't in any position to be difficult. We had pinned our hopes on our impression of one video we liked by this man.

Mick and I flew to Paris and before shooting began, met for dinner with the director, who spoke broken English. Mick and I only spoke enough French to order dinner. His explanation of his vision for the video was hard to visualize, like looking through a foggy window, or a glass brick. The next day I went with the clothing designer to buy an outfit for the video, an ensemble that made me look like a country-rock musician from Austin, Texas. Video production was starting the next day and I had to admit I was excited.

I showed up early the next morning to a large soundstage on the outskirts of Paris, where a crew of about forty men and women, every last one of them smoking, busily moved sets around, hammered large props into place, and tested lights and camera angles, all very exciting. In the green room, I met five beautiful young models who were going to be in my video. Hmmm...ok. A few minutes later, I opened a huge, heavy iron door, and hit the hipbone of one of the models coming the other way. There was nothing there but bone. She ended up with an ugly purple bruise the size of a softball. Next, I went to hair and makeup. A middle-aged woman sat me down in a barber's chair and started working. Like most of the employees I met that day, she spoke a quasi-passable form of English. As I took a deep breath and looked at myself in the mirror, I reflected on where I was and how far I'd come. I was in Paris doing an expensive music video for my debut solo record. All these people were here at this soundstage for me, and I was sober and present for it all.

As I gazed in the mirror my eyes landed behind the stylist on a clothing rack up against the far wall full of bondage and stripper clothing, made of wildly colorful plastics and rubber. I was in a large complex. Who knew what went on before and after my video? Pointing to the clothing rack, I joked to the stylist, "That must have been some shoot." The stylist didn't understand, so I said, "Those costumes. That must have been a crazy movie!" She looked behind her at the rack and chuckled, saying, "Oh non, monsieur, those are for your video." Thinking she didn't understand. I said, a little slower and louder, and pointing directly at the clothing rack, "Those costumes behind us. What were they here for?" "Those *are* the costumes for *your* video," she said loudly and slowly. Wai-wha?? "MICK!!" I cried.

As he came rushing in, I quickly pointed the rack out to him. "Those are costumes for *my* video!" He looked at them and laughed. "Surely there is some mistake," he chuckled, "those couldn't be..." Mick ran off to get the director.

Thus began a "you couldn't make this up" hour-long debate with a famous French fashion photographer over what was "sexy." For all my newfound values, I wasn't a prude, and certainly Mick wasn't. We knew there were going to be sensuous scenes, and meeting the young models made that certain. But bondage and stripper outfits? This was a debate we weren't going to win. In the end, we got some concessions over the worst of it, but the result was a comically over-the-top sexy video. At one point, a camera fell from the ceiling directly into the cleavage of a spinning nun. The main concession I won was that I wouldn't have to touch or be touched by any of the women in the video. It's still, to this day, a funny clip, though it wasn't intended to be.

Richard Branson and I appeared at a press conference in New York to announce the first single release on the new Charisma US record label. The video did well on MTV and "Dare To Fall In Love" made it to #17 on Casey Kasem's Top 40 radio show. We did a subsequent video for "Can't Feel the Pain" featuring Vicki Randle that was beautiful and exactly on point. Everyone should have a slow-motion movie of themselves walking along a railroad track at dawn with a train approaching slowly behind them.

Scan me

I learned from this experience that it was better to be the second release on a new label. Half of the radio promotions team wasn't even in place when my single came out. Maxi Priest was Charisma's second artist, and he had a #1 single with "Don't Turn Around." Nevertheless, my album brought relief and solace to many people in various stages of recovery, especially those who were considering it but needed a final burst of inspiration. I received many messages from people about listening to it in dark times and finding it of tremendous comfort. I was just paying it forward.

———

Ross Hogarth

Danny Kortchmar

With Steve Jordan
I'm the cool one on the left

Arnie, Phil Q & Jordan Harris

David J. Holman

Ross, Hogarth, Steve Jordan, "Kootch", & Randy Jackson

With Christine McVie

Vicki Randle

Randy Jackson

Mick Fleetwood

"Can't Feel the Pain"

Solo

Solo 1989-1991

9
THE FIRST AND THE LAST

While I was making my first self-titled solo album, I learned that Charlie Peacock had moved to Nashville to pursue a career in Christian music. I didn't know much about Christian music, but what I knew, I didn't care for. Just as we'd done with our move from Dallas, Charlie brought several families along with him to Nashville. He left some breadcrumbs...

I was at home in Sacramento one day when I received a surprising call.

"Hi Brent? This is Jimmy Iovine. I'm sitting here with a lovely singer-songwriter named Maria McKee and we just saw your song 'I Don't Mind At All' on MTV and we both love it and were wondering if you would like to try a co-write with Maria?"

"Ummm, sure," I stammered. Jimmy is the legendary producer and founder of Interscope Records. To say I was shocked to hear his voice on the other end of the line would be an understatement.

"What would you like to do," Iovine continued, "come down here or her come to you?"

Considering my low batting average at this kind of thing, I thought it might work better if she came to my more familiar surroundings. Meet the wife. See the Capitol.

"If she wanted to come up here that would be great."

"Alright, great, we'll be in touch."

Maria had gotten a lot of publicity for her debut album with Lone Justice, and now she was making a solo album with Jimmy Iovine. I wish I could tell you this ended well, but Maria McKee flew to Sacramento for two days to...co-write? We didn't. Why? Because I just wasn't good at it back then—I never became very good at this kind of co-writing made so popular in Nashville. Two songwriters meet in a room at a set time and just start riffing on ideas back and forth. I felt lost in that situation from the start, just too self-conscious. For me, co-writing means *they* start something, hand it to me like Lyle did, so *I* could finish it. Maria didn't have anything started, at least nothing she wanted to play me, so I had her record some songs I had already written. She was very nice and compliant and sounded good singing the songs, but after she flew back to LA, I never heard from her or Jimmy Iovine again.

Things went better the next time I tried it. The actress Katey Sagal, famous for playing Peg Bundy for years on *Married With Children*, was also a fine singer. She had sung backup for Bette Midler as one of her Harlettes. Unlike Maria, Katey was looking for songs, not necessarily to co-write. Katey had an interesting problem. She was a good singer, and wanted to make a serious, heartfelt album. Her fans thought of her as Peg Bundy and expected anything she sang would be light and quasi-comical.

She was trying to break out of the sitcom mold she had lived in for so long and chose a song that I had co-written (finished) with my longtime friend, percussionist and producer Bongo Bob Smith called "All Is Well." And then I finished a song with songwriter John Shanks and Katey called "Act of Faith." Neither had anything to do with Peg Bundy. They spotlighted a committed, mature singer named Katey Sagal who sang the heck out of both. Unfortunately, people wouldn't let her out of her box.

On June 1st, 1991, Mary Ann and I welcomed our second child, Delaney McDowell Bourgeois into our family. Her middle name is a combination of her grandmothers' last names, McMahon and Dowling.

Adrian was already showing a special talent for music. At the age of four he appeared as a drummer for a band in Skip's Music's Stairway To Stardom in Sacramento, a competition for young musicians, and he was already banging away at the piano as well. We didn't know what to make of his curious habit of putting his two little record players side-by side and finding skips on records and playing the skips simultaneously over and over again. A budding DJ?

I continued to write songs for my publishing deal–after all, this was my main source of income. Lionel Conway was extremely patient with me. My best songs were for and about me; the songs I wrote for "others" I considered mediocre. After the success of "Dare To Fall In Love" though, I was afraid this was the kind of song my record company would be looking for more of, and I was right.

Much of what I have written is derivative of artists I listen to and admire. All artists, not just musicians, are guilty of that to some degree. We learn by copying. I am guilty of amounting to the sum of my many musical influences, which you can hear throughout my songwriting. There is almost a straight line from The Beatles to Sly Stone and Stevie Wonder to jazz musicians like Weather Report and Herbie Hancock to Todd Rundgren to Peter Gabriel. There are pieces of Talking Heads, Joni Mitchell, James Taylor, and African artists in there, too. You can add the many hundreds of 45s we listened to in our homes in New Jersey and Dallas. My hope is that no matter how derivative a song starts out, by the end, it has been subsumed enough into my own personality to stand on its own.

My record option was picked up, which was good, but to be honest, I didn't feel a whole lot of support from Charisma. The David Fincher refusal didn't help. I also think Charisma Records USA had not gotten off to the kind of start they had hoped for. I did no public performing for the first record, which was odd. No touring, no special performances, nothing. They had spent all their promotion dollars on the video.

There was one event worth mentioning for how bizarre it was. I was asked to be the third wheel at an event featuring the comebacks of two child stars who each had new records to promote, David Cassidy and Donny Osmond. They were both appearing at a large club in Rockford, Illinois, and somehow, I got added to this bill. I flew to Chicago, rented a car and drove to Rockford. In the hotel, I met Donny, and he couldn't have been nicer. Apparently, David and Donny were feuding over the timing of their new releases, though the bad feelings were all on David's side. David refused to drive in the same limo with Donny, so I took his place. We arrived at the venue as a line of middle-aged women wound its way around the block. I performed first, obviously, and sang to the track of "Dare To Fall In Love," which was received politely. I don't remember, but I probably did a couple more songs. I was followed by Donny, then David who each received screaming adulation.

The performances over, the three of us adjourned to an upstairs hallway, where three separate merch tables were set up for autographs. The women lined up again, wrapped around the entire space inside the building. My table was first, followed by Donny's and then David's. For the next hour or so, hundreds of women handed me their instant cameras and asked me to take their pictures with Donny or David. Several times Donny sheepishly apologized for the imposition, but I thought it was funny. I don't think David noticed or gave it a second thought.

Another odd promotion that came through Charisma was a softball tournament in Redding, California. Slow-pitch softball was a game in which I excelled. I had even started an AA team called the Highballers, and we won more than we lost in a tough league. I was a good hitter, and I took it seriously. I was going to be playing in this tournament with the local pop radio station team, which was co-ed. Immediately, my snobbery kicked in. A radio station team? Coed? I had played coed softball informally, and the girls weren't good. This tournament was one of the few promotional events offered to me, so I buckled up and drove to Redding with low expectations. Little did I suspect that this was a serious endeavor, and the radio station was thinking the same thing about me! *We have to stick this recording artist in our lineup in a tournament? Give up a spot to some bonehead musician?* Before long we realized we had seriously misjudged each other. The team was *really* good, and the co-eds were fantastic high school and college softball players. So now it was on me to prove I belonged. They batted me last in the first game and I hit three home runs. I ended up with five on the day, and we won the tournament.

· · ·

In October of 1991, we were stunned by the terrible news that Bill Graham had died in a helicopter crash, along with his girl-friend Melissa Gold and pilot Steve "Killer" Kahn. I had flown in a small plane several times with Killer. It was a terrible loss, truly the end of an era. Bill Graham was a one-of-a-kind human being, and a part of rock'n'roll died with him.

Around then, Robert Palmer invited me to spend a week in Lugano, Switzerland to hang out and do some songwriting. A lot had changed since the last time I saw him. Most notably, I had gotten sober. Robert was living with his long-time mistress Mary Ambrose, with whom he was madly in love. Despite my anxiety about co-writing, this was an opportunity I could not refuse. Robert and Mary picked me up at the small local airport in Lugano.

They lived in an old mill converted into a lovely, rustic home, with books and albums climbing up the walls and stair-case. He couldn't wait to play me old Brazilian and rare African records. He was a creative man–music was always on his mind–what is referred to as a "muso." He brought a guitar in the back of the car whenever we went to dinner. He also drank more than anyone I ever knew. It didn't seem to affect him at all. He would drink from ten o'clock in the morning when he emerged, until well after midnight, and only then did he appear a bit slurry. He was very interested in, and a bit put off by my declaration of sobriety. The Brent he had expected was a solid drinking buddy. The first night I was there he started questioning me and we spent hours talking about it. He even-tually asked me if I thought he was an alcoholic. Not wanting to blow the whole trip, I mumbled that I had no idea and thought he held his liquor quite well, which was true. He listened to selections from my solo album and didn't care for it all that much; he thought I had gone soft. After all, his favorite song of mine, and probably the reason I was sitting in front of him was the track "Perfect Life" from the *Bourgeois Tagg* album.

The next morning, before he got up, I joined Mary sitting by the pool, and she brought up the subject of sobriety. They must have talked about it the night before. "Do you think Robert's an alcoholic?" she asked, "I think he drinks too much and I'm worried." Again, I was not about to get in the middle of this. Not for the last time, I wished I wasn't sober, or at least could have had a hall pass for the week. I don't remember exactly what I said, but it was some fast double-talking. Eventually between long dinners and visits from friends, we wrote a couple songs, one which went on a later album of his, and "I'm Down With You," which was one of the songs on my next record, *A Matter of Feel.*

After four or five days in their home, the party had swelled to six or seven people hanging out at his house, including his keyboard player, Alan, from Australia, and his girlfriend. We ate at expensive restaurants twice a day, and my meals were all paid for. Before I left, I knew that for propriety's sake, as well as my own dignity, I was going to have to treat the others to one meal. I had seen a "homestyle" restaurant, a mom-and-pop establishment several times along the way to fancier places, and Robert and Mary always raved about it. I thought, *Maybe I can take them all here and get out a little cheaper.* So, we went to lunch there on my penultimate day, and true enough, "Mom" met us at the door. We ate at picnic-style tables with red-and-white checked tablecloths and paper menus and dined on Wiener schnitzel and sauerkraut and several bottles of wine. "Pop" handed me a bill for almost two thousand dollars. {*Gulp.*} That was the "cheap" meal.

During this time domestic concerns rivaled anything to do

with music. As our new daughter Delaney approached her first birthday, we saw signs that all wasn't well. She hadn't hit the markers babies hit at eight months, ten months and a year. She didn't roll over, didn't crawl on time, didn't pull up, and was using her hand to propel her lips to babble. We put her in physical therapy, where the diagnosis was hypotonia, or low-toned muscles. At one point, doctors advised us that she might not walk. Through a great deal of hard work and ther-apy, Delaney walked by fourteen months. I was happy to be home and fully present for the many doctor's visits and therapies.

In what was becoming a successful yearly collaboration, Lyle Workman sent me a guitar track hoping it would inspire me yet again. This one had a complicated verse, which we opened into a Beatle-y "Don't Let Me Down" chorus. I loved it and wrote maybe my most intimate lyric:

> *Something's happening inside my body*
> *That lovely feeling's leaving me*
> *My head is pounding, my hands are shaking*
> *I'm in trouble deep I know too well*
>
> *I love you madly, can't live without you*
> *Why is this feeling haunting me?*
> *Moments of magic, comic to tragic*
> *Live forevermore under your spell*
>
> *Ooh, don't cry, it's over*
> *No tears for me, it's over*
> *I thought you were my friend*
> *But you let me down again*

This lousy feeling is disappearing
I think I'm heading back for more
My Cinderella, I'm a lucky fella
I'm still hanging 'round her front door

No tears for me, it's over
I'm finally free, it's over
I thought you were my friend
But you let me down again

Oh, alcohol
You let me down again
So for now, this is the end
Oh, alcohol

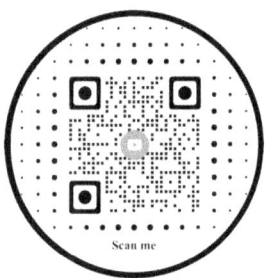

Scan me

So, for now, this is the end. So true. Every song I had written with Lyle, I counted as one of my best. I could co-write–with Lyle.

I wrote a song that was unique for me, in that it was written and sung from a woman's perspective. It was called "A Matter of Feel" and I first demoed it with a languid, rhythm-less feel, featuring a long, melodic outro figure that ran off into the sunset. I sang the whole thing in a falsetto I didn't know I had. Honestly, I was channeling Christine McVie again. Then I heard the DNA remix of Suzanne Vega's "Tom's Diner" and fell hard for the rhythm. I could sing "A Matter of Feel" right along with it. When I tried a similar rhythm, I liked it.

Woman to woman
There is a freedom
Free to bare your soul
But man is a silent one
He keeps himself hidden
Deep inside his heart of
Heart of stone
Only you know what you wish to do
But careful what you wish
'Cause it might come true
A puff of smoke and I might disappear
It's a matter of feel
Not a measure of time
Just a matter of feel
Not a grand design
If that's how you feel
I can't hope to change your mind

Scan me

I was hiding in plain sight as I wrote the song "One Foot in the Water":

He has one foot in the water

And one foot in the sand
And one eye toward the heavens
As he's sinking into the land
But I'll be strong, and I, ooh
I'll be strong just as long as I can
'Cause he has one foot in the water
And one hand ahold of my hand
Don't pull away

I always liked the melody and chord changes in this song. It has a classic radio sound. It's major 7th, minor 7th without being too sappy. I was beginning to see my way to another album.

I wrote a song about suicide. It wasn't about me–it was about trying to love someone through the terrible thoughts that can lead to self-destruction, a tough love approach. I went into Stevie Wonder mode with clavinet and Moog bass:

I can't be your silent partner
I won't watch your suicide
No plans to be in mourning
I got no plans to be by your side
Oh, I thought love counted just a little bit
I thought we were right in the thick of it
But I won't be your silent partner

I won't sit here and watch you die

But if you're looking for help
If you need a hand
If you wanna get better
Then talk to me
If you need a reason
To keep on living
If you just can't handle it
Please talk to me
Oh, baby, please talk to me
Oh, talk to me

I couldn't shake the Todd influence from my writing, either, and found out I never would. I only hoped to contain it and bring out his best with my best. I put on my Todd sweater and beanie and wrote "Girl Don't Let Me Down." I go through periods where it's easy to tell what I've been listening to. With regards to Todd, there was an era of his music that he discontinued, and I missed hearing it, so I made some of my own. Call it a tribute. An homage. It wouldn't be the last. I still like this song.

Scan me

Thus ends the half of the album eventually titled *A Matter of Feel* that I liked. If it had been an EP, I would be proud of it to this day. But there were six more songs to go. "Funky Little Nothing", a tongue-in-cheek retro pop song with the same sentiment as "Silly Love Songs" by Paul McCartney led off the album, but the production missed the mark. Four other titles were songs I had written for my publishing contract and shouldn't have been on an album of mine. "Rise Up" was a nice "get-up-and-do-something" blue-eyed soul piece of 90s fluff. "What's She Gonna Do" was another retro pop song that was meant for someone else. "Haunted By Your Tears" was a publishing co-write with a great keyboardist named Jeff Bova meant for someone else. And then there was "Staggered," about which I have mixed emotions. It was a Boz Scaggs-y velvet blues song, the kind that needs an orchestra behind it. I probably would have appreciated it more if someone like Boz Scaggs had recorded it, but I just didn't think I had the resume to sing it. It didn't really fit on an album of mine. That one was a toss-up.

With the help of Mick and Arnie, I found a co-producer for *A Matter of Feel*. It made sense to find an engineer who also had production experience. More than one trusted person recommended Glenn Rosenstein, a New York engineer/producer living in Nashville who had worked with the Talking Heads and had produced the most current Ziggy Marley album. Glenn was a bear of a man with dark curly hair. I liked his knowledge, his musicality, and his sense of humor.

A good sense of humor is an unheralded quality when you are considering whom to spend a couple of months cooped up with. For example, there are ten thousand guitar players in Nashville. A thousand of them could play many of the parts required on most sessions. A hundred of them are among the best players in the world. But only a few out of those are great people to spend several hours a day with. We'll meet a few of those soon.

I made a significant decision as we prepared to go into the studio to make *A Matter of Feel*. Glenn knew a young bass player and budding Nashville arranger named Tommy Sims, and he proposed that Tommy become part of the team to help "modernize" the sound of the record. Tommy became a world-renowned producer, songwriter and artist in his own right, as well as the finest bass player I know. In 1991, he was in the Christian rock group Whiteheart and beginning to make his name in production. I thought his participation would help me in an area, sampling and programming, that I was lacking so I agreed to bring him on. I was impressed with his beats, the sounds he got from his newly acquired Roland 750 sampler, and how hard he worked. He was a great guy to collaborate with and his bass chops were off the charts. But I gave away the arrangements to him. It wasn't his fault; I freely let him take the reins. He did a fine job, but it was no longer my record. To this day, I feel removed from the final product. I sang on it, and I wrote most of it, but Tommy Sims played it.

To be sure, there were some highlights. Robert Palmer came to San Francisco, for a duet of "I'm Down With You," the song we had written together. I did my best "Robert Palmer" to his Robert Palmer. It was a thrill.

Scan me

I spent more than a few days in Nashville for the first time. I had been there on tour, but never for more than a day. It was wintertime, and with snow on the ground, Glenn took me to a Christmas party in Brentwood where I met Chris Rodriguez and Wayne Kirkpatrick, who would figure prominently in my life a few years later. I still try to figure out who was at that party as many of the folks in the Christian music industry that I subsequently knew were probably there.

While in Nashville, Glenn received a package consisting of two Sennheiser 409 tom mics, decent, utilitarian microphones, about $180 each at the time, generally used as part of a drum setup or on guitar amps. Fast forward a couple of weeks and we were back in the Bay Area getting ready to record vocals. I reached out to David Holman about the possibility of ~~using,~~ ~~borrowing~~ his Church mic. David was understandably reluctant to let that mic out of his studio; after all, such a rare mic was a feature of his production portfolio. He finally agreed to rent it to me for a price that included him flying it up and handing it off in person. It was like renting his child. Thus armed, we decided to do a mic shootout in which we lined up every decent microphone in the studio's locker– Neumann U67 and 87, Telefunken U47, Sony 800, AKG C12 and 414, and other assorted mics you might not immediately consider like a Shure SM58, and did a blind test. Altogether, the price of these microphones was well over $75,000. Add in the Church mic, and we had one of the best selections of microphones in the world. Glenn also set up one of the Sennheiser tom mics just to hear if it worked. I sang a verse of something in each mic and listened back not knowing which mic I was hearing or in what order. We performed the test twice, and each time the Church mic came in second. In both tests the Sennheiser 409 tom mic won. I asked for a recount. How could this be? Something within me always wants to be using the more expensive gear, wearing the more expensive clothes, driving the more expensive car. It was a great lesson. Again. My voice is unique. The mic that sounds good for me might only sound good for me. I have never heard of anyone else using a Sennheiser 409 for vocals. I ended up buying one for my home studio.

I wanted to fill this album with vocal harmonies and was afforded the luxury of hiring four of my favorite singers. I reunited with my old bandmate and best buddy Richard Oates with whom I hadn't worked in ten years. He sounded better than ever. I also brought back Vicki Randle, who performed so well on my first album, and added Jennifer Caryn Gross, who sang many demos for me. Jennifer had a great blend and melted into each track. Rounding out the group was Vince Ebo, a powerhouse singer and personality who had sung with Charlie Peacock.

Unfortunately, *A Matter of Feel* arrived stillborn at the Charisma offices. I did like the cover photo. Shot in Soho, New York with the young daughter of some friends of my sister Coral, it showed a softer side of me. As it turned out, while we were making the record, the decision was made to unwind the label. Some Charisma artists were folded into Virgin Records, but I was not one of them. Even if I had been, it would have been uncomfortable dumping an album not made by Virgin onto their staff, who had enough trouble promoting their own artists. They made a half-hearted effort to get the album out to a couple of markets, but it was over before it began. I was the first release on Charisma Records, and, sadly, the last. Sometime in the Spring of 1992, I was released by Virgin Records. I was thirty-three and didn't have a clue what I was going to do.

———

Mary Ann and I were about to welcome our third child into the world, and it was difficult to concentrate at home with Adrian banging on anything he could find, so I moved my studio out of the house in an effort to "go to work" each day. I rented a room at my friend and recording engineer Ralph Stover's APG Studio, which would become my music home for the next year-and-a-half. Mary Ann and I had also bought our first home, that of another good friend, singer-songwriter Bob Cheevers, who'd relocated to Nashville. I still had my publishing contract with the indefatigable Lionel Conway and hunkered down to write songs for other artists.

February 20, 1993 brought us our second daughter, Corey. Unfortunately, I was not present at the hospital at the birth as I was at home in bed with a 104° fever courtesy of chickenpox that Adrian had brought home from school and quickly passed on to Delaney. Chickenpox is not something a mother about to have a baby should be anywhere near, so Mary Ann went over to her mother's house. I was pretty sure I'd already had chickenpox, or was it the mumps, or was it the measles? I called my mother–she'd know. What I didn't know was that my mom was in the early stages of Alzheimer's dementia. She sounded outwardly okay, but her memory was going. "Oh yeah, you all had chickenpox," she confidently stated. Or was it the measles? It must've been something else because I came down with a terrible case of adult chickenpox. My sister Becky traveled from Orange County to help with the kids. Mary Ann went into the hospital where she and our unborn baby received a major prenatal chickenpox vaccine. After the birth the hospital quickly kicked Mary Ann and Corey out. I wasn't allowed to see Corey for two weeks except through the living room window at Mary Ann's mother's house. She got over it.

Charlie started sending me tapes of stuff he was producing in Nashville. He also sent me a monthly Top 40-style Christian music radio show. What he was producing sounded as good as anything I was doing. He was planting a seed. "You should come down here! You should make a record. I have more producing work than I can handle, and I could give you some of it and you could hit the ground running!" My publishing contract was on life support. If I lost that, I would lose my only source of income. Without a record deal, the bet was on me writing music for others, which I wasn't good at. Something had to give.

With Robert Palmer

With Richard Oates, Vince Ebo, Vicki Randle & Jennifer Gross

Vicki Randle & Richard Oates

"A Matter of Feel"

Lyle Workman

With Tommy Sims & Glenn Rosenstein

With Mick Brigden

Solo

"A Matter of Feel 1991"

10

NASHVILLE: THROUGH
THE BACK DOOR

It was the best of times. It was the worst of times.
–Charles Dickens, A Tale of Two Cities

My back was against the wall. Record companies, as with the rest of society, follow winners. I was an almost thirty-five-year-old orphaned artist. I woke up one morning, and not only was I not the youngest guy in the room anymore, but I was on the verge of being too old.

I was still going dutifully to church, reading the Bible, and trying to find the secret sauce. Given a beautiful leather King James Bible as a gift, I was determined to read it cover to cover. There was a lot of elegant poetry inside, though most of it remained a mystery to me.

Charlie was sending me a lifeline. There was work to be had in the Christian music arena. Nashville and Christian music were two ideas I hadn't even considered. If I stumbled onto the only Christian music station on my car radio, I joked that I could always immediately identify it by "God's favorite piano sound," the sparkling Yamaha DX7 electric piano. It was out of a sense of desperation and failure at the job I was supposed to be doing that I started writing Christian music. I was getting nowhere writing for my publishing contract. That was undeniable. If I understood Charlie correctly, despite my low opinion of what I heard on the radio, there were few restrictions on what Christian music could *sound* like; it was much more important what one was saying. I took the bait and started writing.

There were two ways through the door of the Christian music world, which I will now refer to by its nickname, CCM (Contemporary Christian Music.) The first, and by far the most popular, was to be born and raised in it. These were largely, but not entirely southern-born folks from Southern Baptist congregations, people who went to Christian colleges, many sons and daughters of preachers, those who had been indoctrinated into the language of what we not-so-delicately referred to as "Christianese." There was, indeed, a language, and certain words and phrases were almost required in CCM songs. Many of these folks had only listened to Christian music growing up and were only dimly aware of the majority of mainstream pop music. Most CCM artists went through the front door, including a few from California and the "Jesus Movement" started by Chuck Smith and his Calvary Chapel in LA. Things had remained static until in 1977, when a teen-aged girl named Amy Grant took the CCM world by storm, causing a series of domino-like reactions that would center the Christian music world in Nashville.

The other way of entry into the CCM world was through the back door. This entrance was reserved for the born-again misfits: the reformed drinkers and druggies, the former rockers with wild tales of misery and woe who had seen The Light.

This was the door Charlie went through–the Rich Mullins gate. There was a small, brown-bag section in Christian music stores reserved for this group of artists. The problem for the current CCM? These were the artists that were most likely to put the "contemporary" into Contemporary Christian Music. It was a sad saying inside the industry that Christian music was about seven years behind mainstream pop, which was generally true, and Charlie was one of a few hired to help the industry play catch-up. He, in turn, flashed the Bat Signal to me.

No matter what the situation looked like to me, I wasn't making this complicated decision alone. Mary Ann was deeply rooted in Sacramento; her family lived nearby and was a tremendous help to us in rearing our now three kids. Mary Ann's family had always lived in Sacramento. The idea of moving twenty-five hundred miles away to the South couldn't have been more foreign to them. I could have said Poland and gotten a similar response. From the beginning, the choice was fraught with problems. On top of that was Mary Ann's aversion to flying, which made going back and forth from Tennessee to California even more difficult.

With this as a backdrop, I started writing music with Christ-centered lyrics. I was a quick study, so I incorporated the "ese" into the faith-styled songs. The first, "One Love," came out like this:

Whoa, I love You, Lord
With all my heart
All my soul, all my mind
I dedicate my life to You
Do anything You want me to
Pay any price, sacrifice
'Til the sun comes shining into my life

'Cause no one else can comfort me
Whoa, the way that You do
Come on, hear me, Lord

That was pretty darn Christian. I paired it with a Maxi Priest beat and was on my way.

Next was a Phil Collins-type track that featured a cool melody and some slightly more introspective lyrics:

Okay, so I'm not at the place
That I thought I should be
I could talk about it, fret about it
But maybe it's exactly the place
That I need to be right now
The funny thing is life goes by
So quickly, slowly, that
I can't see the changes in me
I take for granted the healing
That You've done inside of me
I can't love like You, I can't forgive like You
I can't do all the things that You want me to
Or is it all in my head?
Is it something that I thought You said?

We all must strive

In the struggle to survive
There is One we can rely on
While we keep His love alive
And be a little more like Jesus
Taught us to be

Scan me

"A Little More Like Jesus" was a good song, regardless of genre. Then again, there was always the thought in the back of my mind that I was a fraud. I was going to church and reading the Bible but how much of this was authentic and how much was opportunity-seeking?

I never went long without writing a Todd track, and "Total Surrender" was probably my favorite song in the whole sequence.

This empty room
Full of warm memories and tender feelings
Has come to be
A cold battleground, a disenchanted love affair
(No happy ending)
In my mind's eye
I can picture the way things used to be
When there was no strain
When the rhythm of life
Went dancing on without a care

Nothing compares
The facts have been laid bare
That the secret of love is total surrender
The path that leads to true fidelity
Requires nothing less than total surrender

Scan me

This was as good a song as I had written. The melody was complicated but easy on the ears, while the lyrics were certainly not the rank-and-file Christian fare. If this was acceptable, which I didn't yet know, I was going to love doing this.

The next song, "Restored," had a more distinct Christian lyric built on a Brazilian-style track with a Paul Simon-like cadence to the vocal.

Where do I go what do I do
When I can't get myself back to You, O Lord
I fall down to my knees once again
Wondering how in the world You let me in, O Lord
I lay down my arms and surrender
'Cause I don't want to fight anymore
I feel an incredible freedom

I am restored
To the purity of a child

I am restored
To the condition I was in
When I was born again
I am restored
Before the world got ahold of me
And I ahold of the world

Scan me

I was beginning to see my way to an album. I've always been a writer who gets on rolls. When it's going well, I can't turn it off if I tried. When it's not, I cannot imagine how I ever wrote a single song. I was on a roll.

Then I wrote an even better song with a Roxy Music *Avalon* kind of feel. I hadn't written any good songs in a long time, and I had begun to doubt if I ever would again. "Perfect Harmony" was everything I wanted my songwriting to be, and it was happening from a Christian perspective:

It's down to the hour, the minute and the day
Each breath of life is precious in its own way
Over the years, I've come to understand
My endless search for truth
Has led me to Your hands
Change my heart in a positive way
I see a picture of a love so real
That I can't look away

There's only one song I can sing
One gift to the world that I can bring
Joyfully bound in rhythm
With You in perfect harmony
There's only one place I can be
One vision so clearly I can see
I want to be with You in perfect harmony

Scan me

Who was this guy writing these words? What had he done with the old me? There was something emancipating about this new way of writing, as if by adhering to a lyrical template, the music was allowed total freedom. I don't know how I knew that, or even if it was right, because I was writing in a vacuum. No one had yet heard any of these songs.

Lyle Workman contributed his most complicated, intensely beautiful guitar track. The trick with his tracks was to avoid the temptation to force the melody to go along with the track. I had to find the counterpoint. In "Let His Love Into Your Heart" I found the sweet spot.

Nobody knows you from your inside out
You keep a tight rein on your heartstrings
Watching the world turn in front of you
Don't you let down once in a while?
Tell me your story, we've got time to burn

I'd love to climb inside your head
You look so lonely against the fire
Don't you get hungry for a friend?

Pray you will, find the Truth
In your heart and your head
Only one can be lonely
I know it's not easy
To trust, to believe
In Someone you can't see
But tonight, take the first step
To let His love into your heart

Scan me

Then I decided to break the mold and go for broke. Since no one was telling me I couldn't, I wrote an Indian raga complete with a time-change in the middle called "God Is Not Dead" which was wacky in any genre. If the CCM establishment and fans would accept this, they would accept anything. This was also the most direct version of my personality intersecting with the Christian milieu:

God is not dead, you must be dreaming
He never tires from playing Father to the world
The little babies never learn
It might be time for thrash 'n' burn

And when it comes down to your turn
A trip to heaven can't be earned

God answers prayers, sometimes unfortunately
The answer may not be exactly as you've planned
It wasn't God who moved a million miles away
It wasn't God who had nothing good to say
It wasn't God who never taught your child to pray

God is not dead, your eyes are blinded
To all the wonders He has given to the world
He let mankind drink from his cup
So what if humans screwed it up
And turned His garden into muck?
The universe is more than dumb luck

Why consider a deathbed conversion?
What is needed is total immersion
But you've never been that kind of person
You found your own version
And now you're afraid that you were wrong

God is not dead, you are mistaken
He is the living, breathing Savior of the world
There is no fence in this debate
Come down on one side of the gate
Or face the twists and turns of fate
No one to shield you from the hate

Come join the living world
Join us in the living world

Scan me

The song that I thought would be the centerpiece of this album-in-the-making was a Peter Gabriel-style track called "Come Home To Me." Lyrically, it expressed how I felt without being preachy, and featured a grand, anthemic chorus.

Neither man nor a woman
Not a white guy with a black beard
Not a pop star in a satin suit
Neither speck of dust nor big galoot
Not a weatherman to stop the rain
Not responsible for sinners' pain
Simply I am and I'll be
Here to set you free
Don't believe what you've heard
Just read the Word
And come home to Me
Whoa, come home to Me
And I'll offer you Heaven
At the end of the world
Come home

No Santa Claus for Jesus freaks
No political evangelist
And no wizard with a magic wand
And neither black nor brown

Nor stunning blonde
Not for Romeos in hot pursuit
No dispenser of the Fountain of Youth
Simply I am and I'll be
Here to set you free
Don't believe what you've heard
Just read the Word
And come home to Me

Scan me

I had no idea if these songs would be accepted in the Christian music world. Charlie held out the opportunity for productions. That would be my fallback if things didn't work out for me as an artist.

As my management team's involvement expired with the Charisma record contract, I sent the tracks to Charlie, as he would carry the ball for me in Nashville. He was as good as his word and proposed me as producer for a new artist on Star-Song Records named Tony Vincent. I had a job before I even moved to Nashville.

The response to my demo was more positive than I could have imagined. I flew to Nashville to start producing Tony Vincent while meeting with A&R people at several labels. Tony's voice had a George Michael quality. I was allowed to play in the sandbox and come up with any arrangements I wanted if the lyrics conformed to the CCM standard. I had my first experience working with Charlie's engineer Craig Hansen, one of the most talented and funniest guys I met during my time in Nashville. His mixes still sound good thirty years later.

While still in the process of figuring out whether we were moving to Music City, I received a letter from a young woman in Nashville offering her services as a background singer for free until I could hear how good she was. This was cold calling at its finest. Molly Felder turned out to be pure gold with a voice that blended perfectly into every song on which I tried her. We worked together for many years on several projects, starting with that Tony Vincent album. This is a great lesson to anyone to stick their neck out and take a chance. I'm sure she was throwing darts against the wall, and it worked.

Mary Ann stuck her own neck out and visited Nashville while I was working with Tony, and although the trip was a portent of not-so-great things to come, she decided to support my future and move our family to Nashville. It was the most difficult decision of her life.

Though I had interest from all four of the major Christian labels, I narrowed my choice of record companies down to two: Word Records and John Mays, or Reunion Records and Don Donahue. Don Donahue was Reunion's young A&R manager, and we hit it off right away. Reunion Records was run by Michael Blanton and Dan Harrell, Amy Grant's management team, though Amy was on Myrrh Records, a subsidiary of Word. If that sounds confusing, I don't think you could be the manager of an artist at the same label that you ran. Reunion's big artist was Michael W. Smith, whom I would have much to do with later. I chose Reunion Records and was on my way to making my third solo album.

· · ·

In late spring 1994, Mary Ann and the three kids went for a final trip to Disneyland with her family before flying to Nashville. We hadn't picked out a house to buy there yet, as we were in the process of selling the one in Sacramento. In an act of gracious hospitality, Rob and Mary Grace Burkhead, two people we didn't know, offered to put us up in their furnished basement in Bellevue. Rob worked at Reunion Records, and we met him as we pulled up in front of his house.

A funny thing happened while unloading the truck. Charlie had arranged for a flock of teens and young twenty-somethings from his church to help us. Mary Ann and I had separated our stuff from the kid's in marked the boxes. There were kid's toys, kid's books, kid's videos, dishes, sports equipment, and adult books and adult videos. We had a lot of videos, as these were the days of the VHS tape, and we had several boxes marked "Adult Videos" to take inside. It didn't occur to us until that moment how it must have looked to these church kids.

We were originally going to split my record up as a co-production. I'd work on five with Charlie and five with Wayne Kirkpatrick. However, Wayne's time constraints allowed him to do only two.

Charlie and his wife Andi lived in a white clapboard church right out of a Grant Wood painting. He built a studio where the garage once was, which was where we got together to pick musicians for the album. We talked first about guitar players. Charlie recommended Jerry McPherson. I knew Jerry's name and reputation as a great studio player and a member of Amy Grant's band. However, the snob in me wanted something different.

"I know Jerry's great and all, and he's on all the CCM

records, but I want something edgier, more unpredictable, a little dangerous," I told Charlie.

"Edgier? Hmmm," Charlie replied, thinking for a moment. "Lemme look." He rifled through a drawer of DATs until he found what he was looking for. "I think I might know just the guy." He put the DAT on, and a monstrous cacophony of mind-numbing, cutting-edge guitar burst from the speakers.

"Yes!!" I cried, "This is the guy! Let's get him!!"

"That's Jerry McPherson," said Charlie calmly.

Drummer Steve Brewster was a seminal member of Charlie's house band, and for good reason. He was as solid as they came. I was fine with Steve, and he has been a trusted source of exceptional drumming for me for thirty years.

A funny note about Steve: We were recording drums on one of my songs on June 17, 1994 (the day after my 36th birthday) and Steve was in the drum room while Craig Hansen, Charlie Peacock and I were in the control room. Like many studios in that era, a TV monitor was set up above the sound board and was mindlessly left on all day and night. This was at the peak of the O.J. Simpson drama. As Steve was drumming, the slow-motion white Bronco chase was happening on live TV. Craig, Charlie and I sat transfixed by this real-life spectacle. Steve finished the take, and...no reaction. Nothing. We had completely abandoned our responsibilities. He, annoyed, finally shouted, "Hey! What's going on??" We just told him he ought to come into the control room for a couple of minutes. We were done for that day.

I already knew who I wanted on bass–Tommy Sims. My demos were good, and we used them as templates for the record. Of all the things I did on those demos, the bass was probably what I was most proud of, and therefore most sensitive about keeping the parts. Yet on every song, Tommy Sims would listen to the demo, nod his head, say, "Yeah, dig," and then completely rework the bass part to a much better place, whereas Jerry McPherson would start playing something while he was warming up, and we'd all scramble to turn on the tape machine, because he wouldn't remember it five minutes later. On "Job (Blessed Be the Name)," he immediately played something fantastic without even thinking and we had to get it right that second, because we knew it could disappear as fast as it came in. When Jerry plugged his guitar in and started playing with an echo/looper, that was it.

"Stop right there. What was that?"

"I dunno, I was just foolin' around, gettin' a sound," replied Jerry.

"Well, do that again!"

"Do what? I don't remember what I did."

"Job" is one song I didn't preview. Writing a song with lyrics taken directly from the Bible started as an exercise and turned into an epic. I won't reprint the lyrics here, as you can find where I got them in the King James version of the book of Job. It was interesting trying to make a lyric out of Bible verse. It needed to rhyme, because it's a Western pop song, but at the same time it must maintain the integrity of the sacred text. "Job" became an album favorite.

Scan me

And then there was "All Is Well," the co-write with my friend Bongo Bob Smith that I had pitched to Amy Grant and received the curious response from one of her publishing or management people that "It sounds too much like Amy Grant." I never figured that one out.

I recorded the other two songs, "Come Home To Me" and "Let His Love Into Your Heart" at Wayne Kirkpatrick's studio inside his beautiful Brentwood home. Once again, we let Lyle's guitar speak for itself, as we asked him to send us his demo of the guitar part. "Let His Love Into Your Heart" benefitted from Wayne's velvet touch, especially the luscious vocal ending he constructed. "Come Home To Me" never reached the *bang! Zoom!* I originally intended, but instead, became a softer, more beautiful piece.

The sessions for this album, eventually titled *Come Join the Living World*, were a great introduction to the Nashville music community. A song like "Perfect Harmony" couldn't have come out any better. The background vocals were stellar. There were two sets of vocalists–Chris Rodriguez, Wendy Moten, and Vicki Hampton in one group, and Christine Dente, Molly Felder and Wayne Kirkpatrick in the other. They all appeared together on "Restored" and "Job." I was captivated by Christine's vocals on "Total Surrender," as she took my falsetto and made it soar. Tommy went over the top on his bass part on "God Is Not Dead." Who knew that the title of my Christian album would come from the outro of an Indian raga? If someone asks me today which of the albums I created is my favorite, I will say *Come Join the Living World*. I think it is the best combination of songwriting, production, and musicianship. The Christian content may be challenging for some people, but most of it is written in a poetic, non-direct way. I wasn't sure whether the rank-and-file Christians from the South or the Midwest would accept it, but it was the best we all had to offer, a real group effort.

. . .

My first appearance as a Christian artist was at Music in the Rockies, an annual gathering of the industry in Estes Park, Colorado. Meetings and seminars were held in the daytime, and concerts happened at night. I was asked to join Michael W. Smith and a bevy of other artists onstage for a culmination of one of the night's events. Michael had just introduced me, and I had taken my seat at the piano when a rack of hanging lights fell from above, narrowly missing the two of us. Welcome to CCM!

Mary Ann and I found a house in Franklin, a popular suburb fifteen miles south of Nashville. The lots in some parts of town were considerably larger than the postage stamp-size yards in California. A 1.25-acre yard surrounded our modest-sized home. Most people in that area had riding mowers. I didn't. It would take me three-and-a-half hours to mow that yard IF I did it every six days. If not, I could barely get the lawnmower through the thick, damp grass. Our big black Newfoundland, Tillie, appreciated it. With her bad hips, she couldn't even make it to the end of the property. She looked like a bear sitting at the front of the house. The UPS delivery guy would throw packages out of his truck rather than confront her on the front porch. Our three young children saw snow for the first time. A slithery green snake dropped from a tree in our yard onto Adrian's head. We also arrived in time for one of the bizarre cicada cycles. These particular cicadas bury themselves in the ground, one set for thirteen years, the other for seventeen. They break out in the millions in their appointed year and live only long enough to mate and die, leaving millions of carcasses everywhere. The noise is intense, and for a while, these harmless creatures are everywhere. All of this was culture shock to my family, especially Mary Ann.

Adrian started second grade at the public elementary
school nearby. On the first day of school, he bragged to the kid
next to him, "My daddy is a singer making a record!" "Oh
yeah," the kid replied, "My daddy is Alan Jackson!" The first
time I visited rustic Franklin before our move, I found a cozy
little "meat'n three" diner, decidedly not fancy. From my seat,
looking to my right I saw George Lindsey, "Goober" on The
Andy Griffith Show, sitting in the booth across from me. This
was a classic Franklin vignette. It was Mayberry meets Hollywood. Many country and Christian music stars lived in this
small town that featured a traffic circle, a cannon and a
Confederate soldier. We would confront this dichotomy for the
entire nine years we lived there.

Mary Ann struggled to acclimate to Tennessee. She had
lived in one climate and one culture her whole life and was
very attached to her family. While I worked among people
from all over the country, and encountered the occasional
southern accent, Mary Ann was dealing day-to-day with the
schoolteachers, the grocery clerks, the next-door neighbors
and the natives who, for the most part, were very southern,
very religious, and very conservative. We were living two
different realities. She did not have her mother and her sister
to lean on for support. The onus was on me to be her confi-
dante, her confessor, her shoulder, in essence, her everything. I
was not worthy of the responsibility. I was a good, conscientious father, but I just wasn't the husband my wife needed at
that critical moment in her life. I was carving out a new life of
my own with a new tribe, making my way in an unfamiliar
environment. And I dove into it with the energy that only an
addictive-type can muster.

I also felt some growing pains while I adapted to the world
of Christian music. "Christian" audiences were defined as
evangelical, and mainly Southern Baptist-based. Catholics

were considered something else altogether, distant cousins. The "high" church denominations, Episcopal, United Methodists, and Lutherans, had little representation in the industry. This took some getting used to. My first phone interview with a Christian radio station did not go well. It was a heppy peppy morning show, a "Bob and Phil in the Morning!" high energy caffeinated romper room. This would be the first of many interviews that stoked an almost morbid fascination with a former alcoholic/addict from the "mainstream" who had descended upon the Christian music scene. "Bob" started by asking, "Now that you're a Christian, what would you say to Madonna if you had her cornered in a room?" {*Wha...?*} "Well," I uneasily replied, scrambling for an answer, "I wouldn't beat her over the head with a Bible...though she might actually like that...Hello?" {*Click*} The phone line went dead.

I went on The 700 Club with Pat Robertson, which, I found out, was a rite of passage for all Christian artists, a kind of tithe one had to pay, akin to "making ones' bones" in the Mafia. I was advised to say as little as possible. While I was backstage in the green room, Pat ran a feature called "Where Do You Fall on the Political Spectrum?" He used a graphic of an arrow pointing in a straight line in opposite directions. He asked everyone, guests and crew, where they belonged on this arrow. *Oh shit. What if he asks me?* According to the trend that day, I was to the left of Ché Guevara. Luckily, I wasn't asked. But again, I was questioned with grisly interest about my past. "How far down in the gutter did you go? Were you beyond the depths of despair?" "Were you drowning in your own puke?" I faced this angle over and over again.

I had gone to Tennessee fully intending to continue my 12-Step journey. I was seven years sober when I arrived and immersed in the program. It wasn't hard to find meetings around where we lived; they were everywhere. I wasn't, however, prepared for *these* meetings. Culturally, Tennessee was about a decade behind California. The first big difference was smoking. They still allowed smoking in restaurants; there would be a non-smoking section and a smoking section, usually separated by a thin aisle. Because in AA, a higher percentage of participants were smokers than in the general public, all AA meetings in Nashville were smoking meetings. They provided a tiny non-smoking section, usually just a couple of chairs, near a door or window. I was immediately asphyxiated and couldn't stand it. They also used some funny phrases. After hearing the term "har par" repeated several times, I leaned over to the guy next to me and whispered, "What's a har par?" The guy looked at me like I was crazy and said, "You know *har par*! The man upstairs!" I turned it over in my mind and it finally came to me in a burst of inspiration: *Higher Power!* One of the downfalls of many recovering alcoholics is moving away somewhere and discovering "they don't do it like we did," noticing the differences instead of the similarities. That's what I did. Combined with my immersion into the Christian world, I gradually slipped away from AA over a period of several years.

We discovered a small church in Franklin full of expat Californians. It was a storefront Calvary Chapel of about seventy-five congregants. I will interject here that in our early days of marriage Mary Ann and I had gotten hooked on the long-running soap opera *Days of Our Lives*. I think it may have started when Mary Ann was a captive audience while nursing Adrian. My sister Coral watched *All My Children* for over twenty years. Crazy things happen. Anyway, one gets to know the characters very well.

One Sunday morning at our modest new church, in walked a young attractive dirty blonde...*Melissa*? "Mary Ann!" I loudly whispered as I poked her in the ribs. "That's Melissa!" from

Days of Our Lives. She was with a handsome blond man who looked like he was right out of a soap opera as well. "But it can't be," Mary Ann replied. "What would she be doing here?" "Melissa" sat down right next to Mary Ann. Neither of us could concentrate for the rest of the service. When it was over, the woman introduced herself as Lisa Wysocki, and she was indeed "Melissa" from *Days of Our Lives,* although she had been recently written out of the show. Her husband David had been a regular cast member on *General Hospital.* They had just moved with their three young children to Franklin. We became good friends and our kids played often with theirs. We went to the zoo together and middle-aged women ran across a hundred-yard field to get "Melissa's" autograph. Later Lisa was at our house after she had appeared on a customary soap opera reunion wedding episode, and we watched her together on *Days of Our Lives.* A surreal moment.

There are several unique features living in Nashville, nicknamed Music City. In ninety-nine percent of the evangelical churches around the country their worship band will consist of one reasonably talented person who becomes the Worship Leader, plus anybody of even marginable ability— cousins, brothers-in-law, coerced friends, sons, daughters, or even pastors, make up the best band that money can't buy. The results are predictable. In Nashville, the average worship band in the smallest church is often filled with studio musicians, singers with recording contracts, or soon-to-be discovered talent. After the service, the parking lots teem with music biz conversations.

Nashville banks are unique, too. If you walked into a bank where I came from in Northern California and told them your occupation was "musician," they asked you what you did for a living. In Nashville, banks have special music departments, and, like every other institution there, have gold records and signed headshots of country and Christian stars on the walls. You are assigned a "music" banker, whom you will often see at a gig, and who very well might be a songwriter or guitar picker.

In most other places, a school fundraiser would consist of a food night, raffle, dunk tank, talent show, or a simple athletic contest. At Adrian's school of one hundred fifty students, the school fundraising event was held at Green's Grocer, a small music venue out in the boonies. There a few parents did an "In the Round"–a venerable Nashville tradition in which four singer-songwriters trade songs one at a time and play and sing on each other's songs. At this "In the Round" were parents Michael McDonald, Kim Carnes, John Hiatt, and me, with A-list studio guitarist Brent Mason playing along. This was the available parent roster at one small school. Almost any other school in Nashville could put on an event with a similar cast list. ("Oh yeah? My daddy's Alan Jackson!")

After several months of recording Reunion Records was happy with my album and pushed it out to Christian radio. The first four singles promoted by Radio Promotion Head Michelle Fink went to #1: "One Love," "A Little More Like Jesus," "Restored," and "Perfect Harmony." That was nice, but the album wasn't a big seller. Why? I learned later what I didn't know then. I was an outsider. I did not use Christian catchphrases in my interviews, and I seemed suspicious to owners of Christian bookstores, where the CDs were sold. I didn't perform much, but when I did, I didn't use the lingo that Christian artists who were brought up in the "bubble" spoke instinctively. Why then did it do so well on Christian radio? The DJs were music fans–

some had come from the secular world, others fancied themselves forward thinkers. As a rule, they were a couple of steps
ahead of the average Christian bookstore seller. And the bookstores were the gatekeepers of that world. I still consider it the
best piece of music I ever made.

I did one tour with a trio from Minneapolis called PFR, or
Pray For Rain. We had a common arrangement: I would back
them up on keyboards, and they would sit in as my band. They
were great guys and were a tight band. Also on the bill and
opening the show was a young, raw acoustic group called Jars
of Clay, who were on the tour because they'd agreed to unload,
load, and set up all the equipment. We started in February in
Minnesota. Brutal. At the beginning of the tour, we all had
singles out. Halfway through the tour, Jars of Clay's "Flood"
became a runaway hit and more people were coming to see
them than either PFR or me. Suddenly, they became a little less
enthusiastic about being our roadies.

Strengthening my own vow to be both an artist and
producer, I produced a couple of tracks on a Petra tribute
album at the invitation of StarSong president Darrell Harris. It
was to be a reimagining of Petra songs by younger "indie"-style
groups. Petra was a venerable Christian rock band who had
won numerous Grammys in the "Gospel" category, mainly
because after they won their first one, Grammy voters, most of
whom knew nothing about Christian music, voted for the only
name they recognized from the previous year's ballot.

I was given my choice of bands and chose Jars of Clay and
Sixpence None the Richer, both wise choices. Jars of Clay,
known for being strictly an acoustic band, picked up electric
instruments and did a rocking odd-meter version of "Rose
Colored Stained Glass Windows." Sixpence, featuring singer
Leigh Nash, did a knockdown version of "Road to Zion" that
guitarist Matt Slocum wailed on in the outro. Coincidentally, it

turns out that I lived two doors down from Petra founder Bob Hartman and never knew it until later.

Mary Ann instigated a tradition of visiting her family with the kids for the whole summer. Given the awful, humid Tennessee summers, one could hardly blame her. I spent the summer wondering which side of me was going to emerge the winner–the artist or the producer. I had a feeling it couldn't be both.

1st Nashville House

With Will Owsley & Chris Rodriguez

Jerry McPherson

Reunion Publicity Shot

Charlie Peacock

Brent Milligan, Steve Brewster, me, Craig Hansen, & Tony Vincent

Art House Studio

Steve Brewster

Come Join the Living World

Early Nashville Music 1994-1996

11
PLATE SPINNING

Cindy Morgan was one of three inseparable friends, along with Leslie Burbridge, the marketing and promotions person at Word Records, and Michelle Fink, from Reunion. Cindy was a native Tennessean from the "holler" and spoke with a strong southern accent. She had won the Dove Award for Best New Artist for her debut album on Word Records. Ironically, for her, this was a problem. Or *the* problem. Cindy's first album was the poppy, R&B-lite record of an artist who went on stage with a headphone microphone and danced around. She had unconsciously channeled Anita Baker's voice. This in and of itself was not unusual in the Christian market; when I got there, many secular artists had their "Christian" *doppelganger*. Anita Baker was popular at that time, so it kind of made sense. But trapped inside this singing pseudo-dancer was a serious songwriter bursting to be musically born again. She had released two more albums on Word, each one bringing her closer to her goal of liberation, but the success of the first weighed heavily against her chances. Word wanted a repeat of the success of her debut album, and the further she strayed from that, the fewer records she sold. By the time I met her, she was ready to explode with creative energy.

I invited her to my little den studio inside our house in Franklin. She sat down at the piano and pounded out twenty-two original songs. I think she was just getting warmed up. She brought tapes filled with even more. I was suitably blown away. Keeping my cool, I asked her whether she wanted to make a true singer/songwriter album, instead of a label-oriented one. What I heard was a real artist dying to be set free. She answered a hundred percent in the affirmative, and a lasting relationship was born. There was so much material to choose from, it boggled the mind. She had come to the right guy from an artist's perspective; considering the crass commercial decisions that a record company has to make, there might have been a safer choice. But Cindy was done with all that.

My first thought was to make an album you wanted to listen to from start to finish, *not* a collection of singles, and then take it a step further and connect the songs into a suite-like format. For this, I would need some musical superglue, in the form of an ace orchestrator. I knew just who that was: another California transplant named Tom Howard.

Tom was a soft-spoken man whose string arrangements were powerfully unique. When I let him in on the idea, he absorbed it right away and became a key member of the team. I secured a commitment from engineer Craig Hansen, and we were on our way. To his credit, Word A&R Director Lynn Keesecker generously allowed Cindy the leeway to further unlock her potential. While creating this album, Cindy found her own beautiful, resonant voice and a songwriting style that would not only propel her on to even greater musical triumphs but make her a first call writer in both the country and Christian markets.

To cast the album, I was pleased to call on another California transplant and a good friend of mine, drummer Aaron Smith. Aaron was a master of many genres, as we would need a diverse array of styles on Cindy's album. On guitar there was old fuddy-dud Jerry McPherson, who once again rubbed it in my face how good he was. We summoned a young bass player named Brent Milligan, who not only stole my first name, but my birthday as well, ten years after mine. And there was Molly Felder, paying dividends again as a background vocalist. With Tom Howard's fabulous help, we strung the first six songs together to make a suite.

Here is a truism about producing: a producer doesn't want to insert too much of his own personality into an artist's album. Throughout this record Cindy's singular artistry and talent shone through. But on one song, "Jamie," I got to do my thing. The Stevie Wonder portamento synth flutes, the vibraphone, the Buzzy Feiten-like jazz guitar noodling, the seconds and ninths in the harmonies all were staples of mine. That was the exception.

Scan me

We saved the best for last. We were determined to capture Cindy playing piano while she sang her ballads. As we rehearsed the ballads, we found she was considerably more passionate and plugged into her voice when she was accompanying herself. For this, we had to do it live. No punch-ins, no overdubs. We did "The Promise", "To Fly", and "Gravity" all live. She was amazing. Craig Hansen recorded her brilliantly. *Listen* is a powerful record that holds up today.

I had been introduced to Michael W. Smith a few times, first in Sacramento, then in Colorado when we were both almost killed by a falling light fixture. He lived nearby in Franklin, and a couple of his kids were the same ages as ours so we would get them together for playdates. Michael would get on a roll with a writer; for a long time, his primary lyricist was Wayne Kirkpatrick, and it was a very successful collaboration. Michael wrote tracks prolifically, and he had dozens stored in his computer, so many that he would scroll around and discover something he had completely forgotten about. He was a very busy guy, and sometimes I had to appear in his line of sight for him to remember he had something for me to work on. We had entered the era of ubiquitous cell phones. Michael and I passed each other many mornings on a small two-lane road taking our kids to school, which would trigger his memory and five seconds later my phone would ring. "Hey! I have a track for you. I'm gonna put it in your mailbox." This was how we worked, and it was perfect. Like Lyle, the track was already there. Michael would hum a melody with nonsense words over part of it and that helped. In this way, we wrote a dozen songs over the years. One in particular stands out.

Michael had almost finished recording a song for his album *I'll Lead You Home*. It was a big, expensive sounding track, but he didn't like the top line (the melody and lyrics) so he and his producer, Patrick Leonard, were about to trash it. He called me up as a last resort and asked me if I would like to take a quick crack at a new melody and lyric. They were almost out of time. I said sure—I loved that kind of challenge. Michael dropped the cassette off at my house. He had his nonsense lyrics in just the chorus and had ended each phrase with "cry for love." I cleared the rest of the family out of the living room and got down on the floor on my stomach with a notebook and pen, like a kid doing his homework. It was a lively track and it sounded great, as it was a near-finished production. In the past, I did my best work with Lyle when I approached the melody counterintuitively, playing off the track rather than going along with it. I immediately thought of Paul Simon and his wordiness on *Graceland* and *Rhythm of the Saints* albums.

My life is like a racing car
Hurtling towards the wall
At the speed of sound
My time has been so finely tuned
But I've never seen a human being
So tightly wound
At times it seems beyond belief
I just need a bit of relief
Like a war-weary soldier
Marching up and over the edge
Take my hand and pull me up
'Cause I'm falling too fast
Somehow I've lost my way
I'm crying save me

Can You hear me? I'm calling out
I'm crying out, a cry for love
I can feel You, You're touching me
You're healing me, my cry for love

I will be the first to admit
I don't have strength
To handle it alone anymore
I don't have to fret, don't have to explain
All my worrying's in vain
I'm not alone anymore
Why is this so hard to believe?
What is mine is mine to freely receive
Like the changing of seasons
This is the beauty of the word
And for all that I have seen and heard
Oh, I want to come home
Somehow I'll make my way
My way home to You

Can You hear me? I'm calling out
I'm crying out, a cry for love
I can feel You, You're touching me
You're healing me, my cry for love

It took a couple of hours, but when I got rolling, nothing would stop me. Because the cadence was so fast and complicated, I had to record a demo of me singing it so Michael would be able to pick it up quickly. I brought it over to the studio and they loved it! Michael put my demo in his headphones and just copied what I had sung line by line. We have the same vocal range, so in the end, it sounded like me.

Scan me

I had another co-write on that album, "Straight to the Heart." Because of this and several other factors, including being on the same label, Michael asked me to be his Music Director and play keyboards on his tour. He also asked me to sing three of my songs with the band in the middle of the set. I agreed and soon after, I was off on another extensive tour of North America.

Golf was currency in Nashville. Many country and Christian artists, record company executives, musicians, songwriters, lawyers, and crew were avid and competent golfers. Golf has its own code inside the Nashville music business. You are taking a "meeting outside the office" if you are going golfing with just about anyone during business hours. Before I moved to Nashville, I had hardly ever played golf. It felt a bit like the German at the beer garden saying, "You might not drink in America, but you're drinking here!" Except this time, it went, "You may not have played golf in California, but you're playing golf here!" Call it peer pressure, but it got to me. I bought just about every book on golf ever written. I purchased a nice set of clubs and started practicing in the back yard with a wiffle golf ball. I then moved on to the practice range. You should never just go out and play golf on a real course without a significant amount of practice. The people behind you don't appreciate players in front of them spraying the ball all over the place and searching in the weeds forever for their errant shots. (It happens enough when you are merely competent.) I took to it quickly and soon I was ready to play.

Being on tour offered the perfect opportunity to improve my game. Michael W. Smith was a good athlete and loved to play golf. I played on his softball team, and on tour we played tennis and racquetball (resulting in a shoulder sprain for me) and then there was ping-pong, which I will get to in a minute.

This was a bus tour; we played a gig at an arena and were in the bus and on our way to the next city by the time the encore ovation died down. We slept in three levels of bunks. The middle bunks were the best and went to the star (when he was there), the road manager, and the music director (me). A whole book could be written about bus stories in rock music. We would wake up early in the morning in a hotel parking lot in whatever city we were playing next. Sometimes I'd roll out of the bus and literally not know what state I was in. We would have "day" rooms at the hotel to shower and shave. Sound-check was at 4:30PM, giving us eight glorious hours to fill with golf, a sport that normally extracts a heavy toll on one's time. It was a great way to see the sights, mingle with locals, and spend four hours out in the sunshine. Michael was a good golfer, and due to his position in the entertainment world, had some fancy friends. We played eighteen holes with the 1987 US Open winner, Scott Simpson, and another eighteen with the 1987 Master's winner, Larry Mize.

Michael was a master himself at combining the sport he loved with the faith he followed. Sometimes, on the course, he had to multitask. I was playing with him one day when he had to do an interview with a Christian radio station. He was on his cell phone talking about "the grace of the Lord, and the meaning of redemption," when it was his turn at the tee. Without missing a beat, he said, "Can you hold on just a sec?" stepped up and whacked his tee shot flush down the fairway.

"Anyway," he continued, "God has granted me the grace with which...blah, blah, blah..." I took notes.

Michael had also co-leased a private Lear jet, which sounds extravagant, but after seeing him use it, I admired him for it. He went to this great expense (of his own) so he could do a gig in Pittsburgh, or St. Louis, or Kansas City, then hop in the jet and spend the night with his wife and family in his own bed and take his kids to school in the morning. That was one of the beauties of living in a centrally located place like Nashville. I saw him do it a dozen times on this tour and was the beneficiary of a few rides.

I had to hold down the keyboard seat, which for a pianist like Michael, wasn't an easy commission. Like Todd Rundgren, he knew exactly what he wanted and how he wanted it played and wasn't shy about showing me. We were fitted with in-ear monitors, a great advantage on stage because with the monitor engineer's help I could set the mix exactly like I wanted to hear it. It was amazing what other people in the band wanted to hear. We would play tapes of each other's monitor mixes on the bus, and I frankly was dumbfounded at some of them. Mine was mixed like a record, and it sounded great every night.

We also listened to something darker and funnier on the bus. Making the rounds of A&R people in Nashville were the worst of the worst demo tapes that had been submitted over time, all collected on one master tape. It was mind-boggling what people would submit. This tradition continued for as long as I was in Nashville.

One of the highlights of the tour, and a genius move on Michael's part, was installing two ping-pong tables directly behind the stage. There were many serious ping-pong players among the band and crew, Michael being one of them. Let me take you backstage on a typical afternoon on tour. Soundcheck was usually around 4:30-5:00 PM. The catered dinner in the bowels of the venue followed at around 5:30 or 6:00. After dinner, one's body experiences a lull in energy as the food digests. This usually happened, unfortunately, at the very time that the musicians were supposed to be amping up their energy for the show, which almost always started at 7:30 or 8:00. The brilliance of the ping-pong tables was that just when the energy would begin to lag, the nightly tournament commenced. And it was serious. People brought their own special paddles in cases. Night after night it was extremely competitive, and no one was more competitive than Michael. We would all be dressed for the gig, bathed in sweat, the crowd would be ramping up to the loud pre-recorded music, and Michael, if he lost two out of three games, which wasn't often, would demand that we go three out of five. We started several shows five or ten minutes late to finish that night's tournament. But it was absolutely the best way to bring up the energy of the band and head out on stage on a high.

Remember that accordion my parents bought me in New Jersey when I was twelve? I kept it all those years and the first time I played it other than a joke was in front of ten thousand people every night when Michael and I did a short acoustic set on a circular stage in the middle of the crowd. Those accordion lessons finally paid off! And my proud parents were there to see it.

The tour climaxed with two Billy Graham Crusades in NFL football stadiums in Minneapolis and Charlotte, North Carolina. Seventy-five thousand people attended each event. I had to take stock of where I was. I felt like a fraud, and I'm sure I wasn't alone. Several warm-up preachers preceded an old time Gospel singer or two, then our band played a thirty-minute set. After that came the highlight of the gathering: the altar call. This is a distinctly evangelical Christian activity; I had never seen it until I saw Michael W. Smith's at his show in Sacramento. The preacher, in this case Billy Graham, started "calling" on people in the audience to make a decision for Jesus Christ, a highly charged resolution. One or two brave souls came forward, usually sobbing, and like the leading edge of anything, they would be followed by the early adopters, who gained strength from the first courageous few, and then the floodgates open, releasing a steady stream of crying, but happy souls who dedicated their life to Jesus. Behind Billy Graham's emotional altar call, quiet, heartfelt piano was always required (Jesus's favorite piano sound). You've heard it a thousand times. And guess who was tapped to play that music behind the Reverend Billy Graham? In both stadiums the big screen displayed a split-view of Billy Graham on the left, and yours truly on the right. From Bill Graham to Billy Graham. If he only knew...

After this tour Reunion Records and I decided that there would be no second album for me with the label. I think the president of the company, Terry Hemmings, knew something about me that I didn't yet know about myself. I made good Christian records, but that alone didn't make a good Christian artist, which was fine with me, because I wanted to produce records more than I wanted to make another one for myself.

I had finally gotten a country cut, this one a co-write with Michael W. called "Some Say I'm Running" on Martina McBride's *Evolution* album. I thought it was a bonafide country yarn.

Here I go restless heart
Another lovely misadventure in the dark
All my friends who knew me when
Tell me not to wander down that road again

What they don't know what they can't see
It's being on that road that makes me free
Some say I'm running
I know I'm falling back to you

The water's deep under the bridge
As I pass by our old house upon the ridge
All our sins have washed away
Now all that's left are all the things we didn't say
Oh restless heart you beat so fast
While my mind is telling me that it won't last
Some say I'm running
I know I'm falling back to you

Against the odds I'll roll the dice
I guess my heart has won despite all good advice
So grab your things and come on in
And get to know your children once again
When does a fool stop being a fool?
And since when is love obliged to any rules?
Some say I'm running
I know I'm falling back to you

While I awaited my next production, I got a phone call that would alter the direction of my life for the next five years.

"Hey Brent–this is Loren Balman at Word Records. Are you sitting down?"

"Uhhh, I am now. What's up?"

"Well, I know this is kind of out of the blue, but how would you like to come work for us?"

"Doing what?"

"A&R. As a matter of fact, we would like you to run the A&R department. You would be the vice-president of A&R."

My brain was scrambled. I delighted in my rebel reputation as one of the guys who threw rocks at the windows of outfits like Word. I quickly tried to think of all the artists on Word Records, and the only one I liked was Cindy Morgan. Word was mainly known at the time for the enormously popular four-piece female vocal group Point of Grace.

"But Loren," I said as gently as I could. "I don't even...like what you guys do."

"We don't either. *I* don't either," he quickly and shockingly replied. "That's why I'm calling you."

Then Loren Balman mentioned two major things in Word's favor. "There's a nice salary and health benefits."

He had me at "health benefits." I was the father of three children, one with special needs. I had been making a living at music since I was fourteen, but I had never had a job with a real salary or health insurance. Maybe it was time to become a responsible adult. I was about to turn forty. Plus, it appeared that he was hiring me to come and shake the tree. Basically, what he was saying to me was, "If you don't like it, why don't you try and fix it?"

"Let me talk to Mary Ann," I replied, but I knew what she would say. Security at last.

Ironically, I would be replacing John Mays, a great guy who I'd almost signed with as a solo artist. John was moving across town to Sparrow Records. One Word group dearly wished they could go with him: Point of Grace. John had signed the female vocal quartet out of a Bible college in Arkansas and deftly guided them to great success. He had come to mean more to them than simply their A&R guy. Now he was leaving, and they were bound by contract to Word Records. And then, to add

insult to injury, the guy replacing him was *me*! (It reminded me
of our situation at Island Records after the sudden death of Joel
Webber, our A&R guy right when the Beatle-ish single "I Don't
Mind At All" was coming out. Joel's replacement, Steve Pross, a
southern rock fan from Atlantic Records, had called me up, and
before even saying hello blurted, "I jus' gotta tell you, I *hate* the
Beatles.") Point of Grace, Word Records' number one act, must
have felt betrayed. Oil and water would have made more sense.

I came up to the Word Records office to have a "get to know
you" meeting with label president Roland Lundy. Loren may
have been holding my hand. Roland was loved by all, but he
was a bit gruff at first, and I could tell my hiring was not his
idea, and it made him a bit uncomfortable. He gave me the
half-an-hour "This is how we do it at Word" speech while I
was on my best behavior. "Health benefits" kept repeating on a
loop in my mind. As we were leaving Roland's office, Loren
leaned over and said in a low voice, "Now your job is to disre-
gard 80 percent of what you just heard." More prescient words
had never been spoken.

Job One at Word was to gain a semblance of trust with
Point of Grace. The only way for me to do that was to spend
some time with them out in the wild. Within days, I flew to
Anaheim, following along to a few shows at a couple of
Southern California megachurches. I caught up with them on
their tour bus, decked out like an American Girl birthday party,
all pink ribbons, balloons, flowers, streamers and cuddly
stuffed animals. *Lord, what have I done?* I'm sure when I
stepped on to the bus, the four of them said, "Lord, what have
we done to deserve this?" We made uncomfortable small talk,
all of us professional enough not to give away our feelings in
the first five minutes. I said how I was looking forward to
seeing them perform, and, truthfully, I was as I wanted to learn
their magic formula.

BRENT BOURGEOIS

I took a seat along with the young mothers and their daughters in the large, sold-out modern facility, an example of today's megachurch. CCM acts have about five thousand venues to perform in not available to secular artists. What I saw fairly blew my mind and emotionally moved me beyond anything my formerly cynical self thought possible. All four of them, Terry, Denise, Heather and Shelley, were good singers. Only Heather qualified as a notch above that. But this is where my foreknowledge of the group stopped. I had only heard their radio songs, well-produced Christian clichés, with catch-phrase hooks and what we derisively called "JPMs," or Jesus-per-minute lyrics. Pleasant-sounding poppy fluff. As I watched them on stage, I had the revelation that this music, these songs, were merely the key to the front door of what they were all about and why they were there in the first place. In my music-centric worldview, songs mattered most. Everything flowed through the lens of great songs. For Point of Grace, souls mattered most, and songs were just vehicles to get those souls into the church. That night I saw four evangelists, each as good a preacher as the next, speaking individually for twenty minutes without an "umm" or a "you know" or a "like" and clearly and passionately proclaiming the Gospel of Jesus Christ. Now, you may disagree with some or all of the content. But I defy anyone to doubt the sincerity of their mission. I've been wrong about a lot of things in my professional life, but I doubt that I've ever been so wrong as in my pre-assessment of Point of Grace. They got me that night.

Point of Grace was already about as popular as they could be. What could I do to help? I figured they had maxed out with all the mothers and their daughters and the Southern Baptist crowd. But another group of people disregarded them because of the triteness of their music. Here I felt I could make a differ-ence. But I wasn't sure they cared about that. I came to understand that when the girls listened to a new song, what they were listening for was the lyrical content. Shelley seemed to be the group's lead listener. My goal became to subtly move their music forward in sophistication without losing the evangelical lyric value, and almost without their noticing.

I moved into a nice but plain office at the Word Records building and immediately asked if I could modernize the environment. If they were hiring me for my mainstream music value, it would be nice to have a mainstream-looking music office. The first smart thing I did was hire the immensely overqualified Linda Bourne-Wornell to be my assistant. I had an overload on the right side of my brain, and a serious lack on the left. Linda became my left brain–I couldn't have done that job without her. Linda, who could have been a vice-president at any label in town, not only was my assistant, but even came to be an invaluable helper to Mary Ann and me with the kids at home.

Eager to please and to make my mark, I dove into the overflowing box of demos from points near and far across America. There are a couple of rules that people submitting music to A&R representatives at record companies should follow. I was just beginning my A&R journey but having been a longtime submitter, I knew these rules.

•*Less is more.* This goes for the number of songs, the length of each song, and the length of the intro of each song. If you don't get me in the first two or maybe three songs, nothing will get me on the fifth or eighth song. In fact, I'll never *get* to the fifth song.

•*Get to the point.* This of paramount importance. Nothing you say in the fourth verse will improve your chances. You can only hurt them. Five-minute songs are a luxury that you, the submitter, cannot afford. This goes double for the crafty, slow-building, cool intro. It might be a feature on your album, but it's a fault when submitting a demo. Get to the point as soon as you can.

•*Guitar solos are meaningless* in most demos unless you are qualifying as a guitar hero. If an instrumental part helps move a song along with its own hook, then that is okay, but guitar solos for their own sake are a waste of time. This goes for

•*Long outros* as well. Again, it might be a good idea on the album, but is all but pointless on your demo. We all wish we wrote "Hey Jude." I don't want to hear seven-minute song demos.

Back in the mid-to-late 1990s, you would want to present a nice package with your demo submission. A representative picture and a CD or good-quality cassette would show that there might be something worthwhile to listen to. Artwork was a plus–it gave a first impression of something creative under the hood.

This explanation leads up to the first demo that caught my attention. On my third day, I received a cassette in a regular letter envelope, bulging and wrinkled. The tape was the worst-quality Radio Shack orange cassette. Strike two...The envelope also contained a long letter on notebook paper scrawled in hand-written cursive. The cassette, instead of containing a couple of songs, was covered on both sides with fifteen tracks. These, too, were hand-scrawled in almost unreadable script. Strikes three and four. The letter was from a youth pastor at Auburn University in Alabama who extolled the virtues of the sister act on this tape. If this had been any time other than my first week, I'm fairly sure this cassette would have headed to the circular file before listening. There was just too much working against it. Everything that could be wrong about this submission was wrong.

I was new, and didn't want to leave any stone unturned, so I put the cassette in. What I heard were some decent songs by female voices who sounded like the Indigo Girls. I liked the Indigo Girls okay, but I couldn't get the picture of them (and there weren't any pictures in this "package," another strike) out of my head as I listened. The first thing I *wasn't* going to sign as the new vice president of A&R at Word was a slightly butch lesbian duo, no matter how much Loren Balman wanted me to shake the tree. That wasn't going to fly.

This episode would have ended right there, except that the guy writing this letter said that these two young women were appearing about a three-hour drive south, in Birmingham, Alabama, on Friday night. It was Thursday afternoon. I thought, *what are you being paid for, if not to take a road trip to look under every rock for possible talent?* So, I decided to go.

As I drove down to Birmingham late Friday afternoon, listening to this cassette in my car, I had another thought, one that I am a little embarrassed to reveal: *What if the music is good, but the two girls are unattractive, or overweight? I know what the mainstream answer would be, but how much does this matter in Christian music?* That was a real, existential issue requiring more study. The longer I drove, the more this question bothered me, because for all the weirdness of the presentation, I was starting to like what I heard. What was I going to see?

I drove up to a banquet hall in Birmingham and walked through the front door. Five seconds later the two singers walked towards me. I could not believe what I was seeing. They were stunningly beautiful. *This couldn't be happening.* One brunette, one blonde. Alison and Catherine Pierce. Both in their late teens.

They greeted me warmly, and immediately introduced me

to their parents, who were around my age. They had been waiting for me to arrive, so without much small talk, they performed. Suddenly the opposite problem presented itself. What if they were *too good-looking* for Christian music? The blonde Catherine, in particular, just oozed supermodel looks. It was hard to take my eyes off of them. I listened to the set, and they were good, especially Alison, who played acoustic guitar and sang most of the leads.

I invited the girls to visit the Word office in Nashville the following week, wanting to see what kind of impression they'd make on the staff. Predictably, when they arrived, all the young men in the office were smitten. Thus began a curious song-and-dance that went on for the better part of a year. I waffled between wanting to show off these two beautiful artists, and trying to hide just how good-looking they were. Alison was a talented singer-songwriter, who had to be the focus. I would have signed her on her own. Over the next month or so, I produced a set of demos for the duo that exceeded my expectations. The Pierce Sisters had a very distinctive style.

Their big test was the CBA, or Christian Booksellers Association annual convention, a gathering of the conservative, southern, old-school Christian side of the business. There on a large convention center floor were the worst examples of capitalistic cornball Christianity. Jesus, Mary and Joseph action figures, Testa-mints, Holy Bears, Christian self-help books (oxymoron?), holy diet books, and Thomas Kinkade jigsaw puzzles, along with the requisite Christian music presence. It was an orgy of evangelical insanity. The Pierce Sisters would have to run this gauntlet of staid evangelical commercialism fronted by church lady Southern Baptists to have any chance at CCM success. Dressed in demure turtleneck sweaters, and chastely greeting everyone they met, they passed with flying colors. Two weeks later, Greg Nelson, Word's Art Director, did a flashy, *slightly* racy photo shoot with them that started up a fresh bout of controversy. They weren't *trying* to be over-the-top–they just were.

We did another round of strong, dynamic demo/masters with Wayne Kirkpatrick co-producing. In the end, though, they were too much for Word Records to handle. Their lyrics didn't contain enough "Jesus-per-minutes" or evangelical buzzwords to overcome their gorgeous looks. Alison on her own would have probably been okay, because she was serious and folksy. But they were a sister act, and Catherine, without trying to be, was simply too luxuriously beautiful for Southern Baptists to accept.

Michael Blanton was by now running Word Entertainment and he made the decision to get Epic Records, our mainstream partners in New York, involved. Each Christian record company had a Big Brother mainstream partner. Epic was ours and had always treated Word like their poor cornpone cousins. I felt sick about losing such talented artists, but it was probably the right decision. Here's how Epic's A&R guy, who came down from New York to meet Alison and Catherine in Michael's office, handled it. As we sat chatting, the third and youngest Pierce sister, Louisa, walked into the room. Louisa was a perfect physical combination of Alison and Catherine.

The A&R guy says, "Who is she?!?"

"That's Louisa, our younger sister," said Alison.

"Does she play anything?"

"No, not really–she can play the tambourine," said Catherine sarcastically, a little put off.

"Can she sing?"

"A little bit, but not really."

"Well," said the A&R guy, "doesn't matter. She's in the group! It's now a trio!"

The Pierce Sisters, renamed The Pierces, went on to record

some mildly successful music at Epic. They are best known as the authors and performers of the theme song for the hit TV show *Pretty Little Liars*.

Back on Planet Earth, it was time to look for songs for the next Point of Grace album. The Pierce Sisters were a luxury item but Point of Grace paid the bills. This was my first test to see whether I could provide a positive influence on their song choices. The announcement of a new Point of Grace album cycle was the Great Song Hunt in Christian music, and I knew the best CCM songwriters would bring their "A" list songs. The POGs didn't write, so they needed at least twelve to fifteen new songs from outside writers. As their A&R representative, I was their first and main line of defense.

I made my way through well over a thousand submissions. Out of every hundred or so, I whittled them down to eight or ten and sent them along; the group would sometimes pick one. While I curated, POG had their own backdoor open to their favorite songwriters and friends. It felt a little unfair, but that was their right. After much wrangling, I managed to get two songs on the album they most likely wouldn't have done otherwise, "Amazing" by David Zaffiro, and "Rain Down On Me" by Michelle Tumes and Tony Miracle. This doesn't count my co-write with Michael W. Smith, a ballad called "The Wonder of it All," which was closer to the type of tune I would have vetoed, but they liked it, so it went on. Excellently produced by Brown Bannister, with vocal arrangements by Chris Eaton and me, *Steady On* continued their streak of top sellers, and represented a significant victory for me.

. . .

Six years after the birth of our third child, we found out that Mary Ann was pregnant again. Adrian, Delaney and Corey were all attending a progressive Montessori school, as close to a California-style education as we could give them. Delaney was getting speech therapy and Corey was the peer model for Delaney's group. (Speech therapy in Tennessee: "Alraht Delaney! Say f-l-wah. Flah!") Delaney was also having seizures–so many every day that she had to wear a helmet around the house. I accidentally took over the coaching of Corey and Delaney's soccer team, when the coach suddenly moved. Considering Delaney's special needs, I felt like I could manage her playing time without hurting anyone's feelings. Little did I know how much I would love coaching soccer! Adrian continued his music progression, becoming a good drummer and pounding out songs on the piano and guitar as well.

It was time for another Cindy Morgan album. This time I directed it from within the company. My deal with Word specified that I would still be able to produce records, and Cindy was at the top of that list. She had an idea to expand upon the suite-like nature of her first record. Her husband, author Sigmund Brouwer, was working on a book about the last twelve days of Christ and Cindy wanted to write a companion record for it. The entire album would be one story. It was an ambitious undertaking, but I was all for it. We assembled the previous crew plus about twenty new musicians and vocalists and Cindy made a masterpiece called *The Loving Kind*. She was a woman in full command of her craft and talent.

Two people in the Christian music scene could have been voted "most likely to make a record but haven't done so yet," and I was determined to snag both. The first was

singer/songwriter Nicole C. Mullen, who sang with us on the
Michael W. Smith tour and was bursting with creative energy
and charisma. She spent most of her time on the bus with an
electric guitar strapped around her shoulder, and by the time
the tour was over, she had learned how to play. Nicole wrote
"On My Knees," a mega-hit for Jaci Velasquez and a song that
transcended the word "hit" and had become a church standard. A proud woman, she still had a bad taste in her mouth
from a previous record deal when she was younger, and thus
far had resisted the overtures of Christian record companies to
try again. I was determined to let her tell her own story. With
her husband David Mullen co-producing, we finally signed her.
This was the first album I was involved with in Nashville that
my kids loved and danced around the house to.

It was also past time for singer and guitarist Chris
Rodriguez to make a record. Chris had played and sung on just
about everyone else's records, including mine, but now it was
time for him to show the world what a great songwriter he
was. Chris was so in demand as both a studio and touring
guitarist and singer that he never found the time to make a
record of his own. I put a stop to all that. We signed him and he
asked me to produce. Chris had appeared on so many records,
he knew what he wanted. My job was to facilitate his vision
and expand upon his good ideas.

Chris and I were proud to create the first album recorded at
The Lodge at Dark Horse Recording Studios, Robin Crow's
magical Colorado-style chalet deep in the horse country of
Williamson County, Tennessee. In fact, the studio was so new,
we recorded in the only room that had a door to close. This
would be the first of many recordings I made in The Lodge as a
producer, and it became my favorite place to make music.
Chris made a great record, *Beggar's Paradise*. The one song that
stood out for me above the others was "Mercy Day." It never

stops building until finally Chris McHugh's powerful drums and Chris Rodriguez's wailing vocal and guitar playing take it to a thrilling end.

I was beginning to feel like that plate-spinner guy on *The Ed Sullivan Show*. Right on the heels of the *Steady On* album, Word Records put Point of Grace back in the studio to record their requisite Christmas album. Every CCM artist eventually makes a Christmas album. They are known as "evergreens," meaning that they pay for themselves over and over again every holiday season.

Most Christmas records were made in the thick of July. Some of them were even good. When it was ninety degrees outside with ninety percent humidity, we dressed the studio up with Christmas lights and a half-wilted tree. The artists got in their overcoats, mittens and scarves and sweated through a pretend Christmas photo shoot.

Amy Grant's *Home For Christmas* was considered the industry standard. If anybody had the voices, the tools, and the spirit to top Amy, it was Point of Grace. Because it was a specialty album, they weren't particularly hung up on the lyrics, and were considerably more open-minded about show-casing a wide variety of styles, all good news to me and their ubiquitous producer, Brown Bannister. We got to play in a snow-filled sandbox. Every kind of Christmas song was fair game, from "Carol of the Bells" to "Jingle Bell Rock" and all points in between.

I even persuaded them to agree to a male lead vocal on a song, something they would never have considered on one of their regular albums. The song was one I wrote, called "Light of the World." I suggested featuring Michael Tait from DC Talk, doing his best impression of Nat King Cole. How I managed this was one of my all-time "don't ask for permission, ask for forgiveness" stories. Loren Balman taught me well. First, convincing POG to do this was a big deal, and they graciously said yes. Now I had to win over Mike Tait. It would be out of their "cool" zone for any of the DC Talk guys to appear on a Point of Grace record. But, again, this was Christmas, so all bets were off.

I caught up with DC Talk at a CBA convention, everyone thought it would be great fun for Tait and he said yes! I mentioned I would have to get clearance from Forefront, their record company, and Tait replied, "Oh, don't you worry about that! I'll talk to them!" *Big* mistake. Never trust a musician, no matter what they tell you, to handle a task like that. It really wasn't his call anyway. But Tait had only a brief window when he could record this song. DC Talk was going out on tour in a couple of days, and he would be unavailable until it was too late. So, I did the right *musical* thing instead of doing the proper *legal* thing. Two days later it was a *fait accompli*, boots on the ground, so to speak, and we had our unique duet.

Now, for the pesky "getting permission" part. If I had initiated the process of getting permission *first*, especially as the lawyers got involved, we still would be waiting today. I knew I was possibly in trouble, but I also knew that Loren had my back. This would be a great accomplishment, a bringing together of titans of the Christian music world from opposite poles– all in the spirit of Christmas! What could possibly be wrong about that? Apparently, plenty, starting with the very un-Christian-like rivalry between these allegedly Godly record companies.

Forefront and Word (and Sparrow) were, at best, frenemies. They all knew each other well, half of them at one time had worked for the other half, and they all played golf together. But, at the end of the year they each desperately wanted to beat the crap out of the other guy's numbers. And it was practically all guys. My immediate boss, Elisa Elder, was a woman, but she was as committed to the rivalry as anyone else. I entered the competition as an outsider, having no skin in the game. I thought of all the artists and musicians as one big happy family. That wasn't the way the companies saw it. It was Us vs. Them. And Them. And Them.

In an ironic twist, the lawyer for Michael Tait's company Forefront Records was Richard Greene, who happened to be the attorney *I* had hired to negotiate my artist deal with Reunion Records. *'O, what a tangled web we weave.'* Now, it was me vs. him. I had to go to all sorts of meetings and apologize, agree to things on Point of Grace's behalf that I was in no position to agree to, say ten Hail Marys and ten Our Fathers, and promise to never, ever, ever do it again, but the fact was, it was already done, and it remains a centerpiece of one of the best Christmas albums ever made.

Because it was Point of Grace, and the budget was proportionately larger, we were able to go to London and record strings for the Christmas album at Abbey Road Studios. It was a wonderful experience, watching the London Session Orchestra record in Studio One. We were in the Mecca of recording studios, the home of all those iconic Beatles albums. I had to lead Point of Grace into Ground Zero, Studio Two, where most of the Fab Four magic had occurred. Gamely, if unenthusiastically, they followed me onto the floor of the hallowed shrine and stood a bit uneasily in the middle of the room while I took the opportunity to pound out "Martha My Dear" and "Lady Madonna" on the legendary upright piano nestled against one of the walls. I turned to the girls and said, "You're in the most famous studio in the world. You have to sing a Beatles song in here–at least so you can someday tell your children that you did." They looked at one another uncomfortably, shifting from one foot to another, until Heather finally broke the silence and asked timidly, "I think 'Yesterday' was a Beatle song?" {Sigh} They had been brought up in the airtight Christian bubble. Adding insult to injury, I took them outside and, conveniently because there were four of them, persuaded them to do the famous walk across the crosswalk that was the cover image of *Abbey Road*. I asked Terry to take her shoes off. They were dumbfounded and had no idea why they were doing this. But they were kind enough to let crazy Brent do his thing and take a picture, now unfortunately lost to history.

*Side note: Michael Tait, as I finish writing this book, has finally admitted what has been rumored for years. He is gay and has been accused of sexually assaulting numerous young men, acts of 'grooming', while plying them full of drugs and alcohol. A whole book could be written on this and probably will be.

On December 14, 1998, we welcomed Natalie, our fourth child. Natalie was a welcome and lovely surprise. She and my sister Coral, have the distinction of being born, unlike any of their siblings, in Nashville Tennessee. Our family was now complete.

A highlight of every year was the Dove Awards, the Christian music world's version of the Grammy's. In 1998, my co-write with Michael, "Cry For Love," was nominated for Song of the Year. The night before the show, each company had a gala concert followed by a party. At the Word party, it was time to let the holy hair down and perform secular songs. I performed the Prince's "1999" with Chris Rodriguez. I snared Point of Grace singer Heather Floyd to sing the female part and she nailed it. Another highlight was Tom Howard, our erstwhile string arranger, taking the mic and slaying the song "I Love You More Today Than Yesterday."

***

Tom Howard

Cindy Morgan "Listen"

With Cindy Morgan

With Michael W. Smith

Michael W. Smith Touring Band

Accordion Lessons Paid Off

Billy Graham Crusade Chrlotte

Billy Graham Crusade Charlotte

Beginning Golf

"I'll Lead You Home" Gold

Me

Nashville Music II 1996-1998

The Pierce Sisters

Loren Balman

Point of Grace "Steady On"

Chris Rodriguez "Beggar's Paradise"

Dark Horse Studio

Point of Grace "A Christmas Story"

Cindy Morgan "The Loving Kind"

The House on Winter Hill Road

Nicole C. Mullen

VP of A&R at Word Records 1998-2000

12

THE END IS NIGH

999. Laptops and cellphones. The Internet. Napster. I remember being in New York with Mike Blanton and each of us buying Apple Newtons, a completely useless device that I couldn't afford. The end was nigh, but no one knew it. There were discussions about the free downloading of music, but like a lot of things that became commonplace in the near future, at that moment downloading seemed complicated and cumbersome. Considering the speed of dial-up internet, and the speed and memory of current computers, it wasn't yet considered a threat. Most people didn't understand how fast technology was moving. Speed was just a speed bump. Memory was getting cheaper by the day.

One anecdote is worth a billion dollars. A vocal group of pre-teens and teens called Jump5 was signed to Sparrow Records. The marketing team brought them into the office to get to know them better and prepare for the PR Sparrow would be doing soon. When the group was asked, "What was the last music you bought?" the kids all looked at each other quizzically, and laughingly replied, "We don't buy music." They downloaded it from Napster. That was the beginning of the end of the music industry as we knew it.

Music in the Rockies, held in Estes Park, Colorado in August, was summer's annual rite and a great opportunity to get out of Nashville when the weather was the stickiest. Estes Park was high up in the mountains and a gorgeous escape for a week. There were seminars during the day and concerts every night. The concerts featured CCM artists, usually with new albums coming out, or passing through on tour. A smaller coffeehouse show for either emerging artists or seminar participants followed the main nightly concert. The A&R reps, including me, stood in the back of the coffeehouse, hands in our pockets, bouncing on our heels, making snarky comments and generally acting like the smartest kids in the room.

One day, I had been tipped off by Cam Florio, who ran the seminar, that there was a local teenage girl singing that night who I wouldn't want to miss. The way he leaned into it made me believe him. That night, I positioned myself casually against the back wall of the café and suffered through a few acts–and then *she* came out.

Under five feet tall and looking all of fourteen, as soon as she started singing it was obvious she was on another level, a rough cross between Mariah Carey and Christina Aguilera. She didn't sound thin when she went up for the high notes as expected of someone her age. Her tone was rich, and she also possessed a wonderfully airy, breathy soft voice. When I heard a talent of her caliber, I knew it right away. I was sold by the second verse of the first song, already calculating what I would do with her. Generally, I wasn't into *just* singers because I had to find all the material for them, and thus it isn't as authentic a process as with a singer-songwriter. But this young singer

transcended all such fine points. She had a once-in-a-genera-
tion voice.

I knew she would be singing only two songs. When the
second one began, I quietly picked my jaw up off the floor and
back-pedaled behind the rest of the A&R line. I slid through a
heavy curtain on the left side of the room, guessing that wherever that led was where I would find her when she was done. I
found myself in a small, dark space with a grandstand, resem-
bling a high school gym and foolishly stood there–what if she
didn't come out this way but came out through the stage, then I
would be the only one *not* meeting her. But to my great relief,
she and her mother appeared around the corner of the grandstand and I all but pounced on them (metaphorically! C'mon).
I asked them to please sit down and introduced myself, leaning
on the *VP* part of A&R for Word Records. I don't remember
exactly what I said, but paraphrasing, "If you turn around and
leave without talking to any of those other losers out there,
several of whom have criminal records, I will not only promise
you an embarrassment of riches courtesy of Word Entertainment, but I will personally introduce you to Jaci Velasquez
tomorrow night."

I had her at Jaci Velasquez. Of all the people in our CCM
world, she already sounded like a more thrilling version of Jaci,
who was the best young singer in the industry. I guessed Jaci
was a role model for her, and I knew Jaci. Jaci Velasquez just
happened to be appearing at our Word-sponsored concert the
next night. I planned to take it one step further. I would have
her sing for Jaci.

Rachael Lampa was still fourteen. She was half Filipino
(her father), and her mother was Irish. Her mom's name was
Marianne, so that didn't hurt. From Aurora, a suburb of
Denver, not far from where we were, she called herself a
Charismatic Catholic–whatever that was, it was good enough

for me. Rachael and her mom took the deal. They left out the back door without talking to anyone else. When I came out from behind the curtain into the café, I saw the other A&R guys turning around in circles, looking for the *wunderkind*. I was David Copperfield. I had made Rachael Lampa disappear.

The first thing next morning, I called Michael Blanton, who was the architect behind the mainstream rise of Amy Grant. He and Dan Harrell had been Amy's managers from the very beginning, but it was Mike who was the dream-caster and visionary. He was the head of Reunion Records when I got there, and now, along with Harrell, was the head of Word Entertainment. One good thing about not being an overly enthusiastic person was that when I did get excited over someone, or something, you could believe me. I told Mike I had found the best singer of the next generation and we needed to sign her no matter what it took. He heard me loud and clear.

That night I met Rachael and her mom in a covert rendezvous because I wanted to keep her away from the other A&R folks as long as I could. I had tipped off Jaci that there was someone special that I wanted her to meet so she was ready. I ushered Rachael and mom backstage before the concert and introduced her to Jaci.

Jaci was only eighteen, but she was already an old pro. She had had a huge hit with Nicole C. Mullen's "On My Knees" which was already becoming a standard. Then and there I had Rachael sing it for Jaci, thrilling both Rachael and her mom. Rachael nailed it, and Jaci said all the right things. Then I escorted mother and daughter to special seating for the concert, keeping them out of the line of sight of the other A&R people. Over the next month, a one-sided contest for Rachael Lampa was fought by Mike Blanton at his finest, resulting in the largest debut contract in CCM history.

As soon as I got home, another artist got my attention for a completely different reason. I received a tape featuring three rough demos from a young singer/songwriter and worship leader from Katy, Texas named Paige Lewis. It was simple and raw. Most people would have concluded that there wasn't enough "there" there, but I heard something. When you know, you know. I decided to fly down to Katy to meet her. She was an all-state catcher on her high school softball team, and barely fifteen. When I asked her to play for me, I could tell she had already gotten better than the tape she'd sent. She had a clear, direct style of singing and her songs were catchy. Although she would get very little of the hype that Rachael Lampa received, Paige ended up making a great debut record on Word, and she remains a friend of our family to this day as well as a longtime music partner of my son Adrian.

Now that I had Rachael Lampa, I had to figure out what to do with Rachael Lampa. The last thing I wanted was a giant publisher's orgy of Point of Grace song rejects, yet that's exactly what came my way. I was deluged with tapes and CDs from well-meaning publishers. I would put it in, press play, and then think, *Haven't I heard this song before?* Indeed, I had—for Point of Grace. You couldn't blame the publishers for trying, but they had no idea who I had on my hands. "B" and "C" songs weren't going to do. The best writers hesitated to give up their "A" songs to an untested new artist for the obvious reason that they would make far better royalties on albums by bigger acts.

I hated the whole publisher song hunt idea, and decided I wasn't going to play that game. First, Rachael didn't just need the best writers; she needed the best singers who were also great writers. Only the best singers knew what it would take in each song to maximize Rachael's performance and provide *that* moment in every song. I would say to these great singers, "If you get to the climax of the song and you can't quite sing it, *then* you might be onto something!" Second, I wanted to provide a place where these singer-writers could come and write with each other, push each other, and outdo each other. And third, I wanted Rachael to test-drive their songs as soon as they were ready to be sampled. We were going to build this album around her voice in real time.

I found a farmhouse in rural Franklin with an owner willing to donate the large, beautiful home to a unique and worthy cause. I installed five workstations in the house so that each writer could have the space to work either alone or teamed with another writer. I carefully chose my team. In the end, more writers worked at the house than ended up on the album, but they still contributed to the overall vibe and cama-raderie.

As captain of the ship, I chose English singer-songwriter Chris Eaton, a powerhouse writer who knew how to create melodies, write hooks, craft lyrics, and was a great singer. Chris Rodriguez was another great singer and songwriter, but he came to the project with a guitar player's perspective, whereas Eaton was a keyboardist. My good friend and liber-ated writer Cindy Morgan had a place on the team because she was also such a good singer and could identify the sweet vocal spots in each song. And I had a station there as well, although I was more invested in how everyone else was doing. Other singer/songwriters who came and went were Michelle Tumes, Nicole C. Mullen, and Ginny Owens.

We treated it like a camp, arriving every day mid-morning and writing until we felt like leaving. It was a uniquely creative experience. Because the songs were written exclusively for her, we were able to home in on the top of Rachael's range, discover where her sweet spot was, and then have her sing to make sure we were putting each song in the right key. We would come together at the end of the day and play each other our songs, always looking for "the moment" in each one.

Ginny Owens and Cindy Morgan wrote what has come to be a standard in Christian music, the transcendent ballad "Blessed." We all knew it when we heard it. It became Rachael's signature song. Chris Eaton wrote a beautiful ballad as well, "Always Be My Home," that so intrigued the booker of *The Tonight Show* that she invited Rachael to perform that and her hit single, "Live For You" written by Chris Eaton and Chris Rodriguez. One outside song, "Shaken," was written by Nicole C. Mullen's husband David.

It was one of the most rewarding experiences of my life. I felt if I never did anything else for Word, I might be remembered for this.

Brown Bannister and I co-produced the record. Brown brought his steady hand and experience, while I guided Rachael to the licks that would make her famous. I could think 'em up, even if I couldn't quite sing 'em. I would hint, "Do something like" and then do a run I was hearing in my head. She would say, "Oh you mean this?" and do it ten times better. It was similar to Tommy Sims playing my bass parts. And it worked. She turned fifteen while we were making the record. I knew what it was like to be fifteen and a prodigy. She was a lot more mature than fifteen-year-old me. She took direction incredibly well. We had a large cast, including an amazing choir of Nashville studio all-stars on "Blessed." Plus, we went again to London and recorded strings for the album at Abbey Road with the London Session Orchestra.

Rachael sang "Blessed" that year at the Dove Awards, where she was nominated for Best New Artist and lost to her best friend Stacie Orrico. There was a lot of great new talent to look forward to in Christian music. A cover of the Campus

Christian magazine that year featured Rachael, Stacie, Paige Lewis, Joy Williams (Civil Wars) and a young emo girl named Katie Hudson, who later blew them all out of the water as Katy Perry.

The time I spent in the Christian music world was in inverse proportion to the time I gave to AA. The more of the former, the less of the latter. I had been thinking that because my life was completely different now–I wasn't in bars or clubs, I was a responsible family man in Christian society, and most importantly, I had long since been relieved of my cocaine obsession–that maybe I could try a little wine, like a normal human. I always associated alcohol with drugs; I had never tried drinking on its own. I hadn't even considered that I might be an alcoholic when I came into AA. I quickly learned that it was the "ic" part that was important. The method of delivery was secondary. Once I stopped going to meetings and drifted away from the program, I lost sight of the "ic."

I was also learning a good lesson about anonymity. There is a reason why it's called Alcoholics *Anonymous*. If part of your public story is about sobriety and recovery, then you automatically carry the burden of it on your shoulders. I was known in the Christian world as a "recovery" guy. It was part of my story. It was a way of identifying the "outsiders." It made for a nice, juicy interest piece, whether in print or onscreen. People surreptitiously came to me to talk about their drinking. After all, this was the evangelical Christian world, and drinking was only mildly approved of.

More darkly, there was intractable unhappiness in my home. The problem had no bad guys. My wife was deeply unhappy about the world she was forced to inhabit, away from her support, her family. She was forced to rely on a me, a man who was incredibly busy and succeeding in the world *he* was inhabiting. In what to her was initially billed as a temporary relocation, the better I did, the more success I had, the deeper our roots grew and another tentpole was stuck in the ground. We had made a deal: If she didn't like our life in Nashville after three-to-five years, we would move back to California. My thinking was, either it wouldn't go as well as I expected, and I would accept this and move back, or Mary Ann would slowly become acclimated to Nashville, and feel no need to move back. What happened was, for her, the worst of both. I did *better* than could have possibly been forecast, and she *never* acclimated.

What didn't she like? It was as basic as the air. Mary Ann had a lung condition, at the time diagnosed as asthma, later as bronchiectasis. She had one functioning lung from birth with a total capacity of around 40 percent. The air in Nashville throughout much of the year was humid, stuffy, and sticky. In California, Mary Ann could open the windows in the morning and at night and get cool air circulating. Not so much of the time in Nashville. Then there were the critters and bugs. The cicadas got us off to a bad start. The snakes in the yard didn't help. There were bats in our fireplace–so many that they would come down the flue and bang on the fireplace screen until we had to shoo them back up where they came. I found a *very large* snakeskin that had been shed right behind our dryer. (It was in the summer, and I never told Mary Ann about it until we were safely back in California.) I got stung a couple of times by wasps, as did my daughter. It was all part of the beautiful, semi-tropical humid climate that was completely foreign to a native Californian who had never lived anywhere else. And there were the southern "bless yer heart" conservative, Baptist, submissive women that Mary Ann had to deal with daily who, being in the music business, I saw only glimpses of.

She was very close to her sister Kathi, who had no children of her own, and had adopted ours to care for as a very hands-on Auntie. Now *she* was twenty-five hundred miles away. You could read the last ten pages and see where I was. I loved my kids, and I loved Mary Ann, and I was really busy. All of this was true. Mary Ann's resentment about her suffocating situation led to my resentment that no matter what I accomplished, it would never make the situation better or make her happy. This was one factor in my faulty reasoning about attempting to drink again. My family's summer-long absences from Nashville didn't help. The guardrails came off. It made sense that my decision to drink again would come when the daily rhythm of home life was disrupted. All I needed now was a trigger.

One afternoon I was approached by a person at work whom I respected. We stopped in the stairwell to talk. Eventually, the subject turned to drinking. "Do you think I'm an alcoholic?" they asked. I flashed back to my visit with Robert Palmer. "I can't say," I replied, "I've never really seen you in action." "We're having a party Friday night," they said, "why don't you come by?" What could go wrong?

In a moment of Déja Vu, I recalled an unsettling story from one of my first AA sponsors, a recovering heroin addict with thirteen years of sobriety. Driving down a country road near where he lived, he spotted his old drug dealer sitting underneath a tree, stopped the car and got out to ostensibly twelve-step his former friend. The next thing he knew, he was at the drug dealer's house shooting up. He was on methadone for the rest of his life.

On Friday, I showed up at my friend's party, and saw a bottle of Jack Daniels keeping a bottle of Diet Coke company in the kitchen. This was one of my go-to drinks when I drank. Before I knew it, I had made myself a stiff Jack and Coke and just like that, was off and running. Twelve years of sobriety down the drain.

I didn't immediately drown myself in an ocean of booze. I hardly drank at all. I kept it to myself. There was never any alcohol in our house. I was usually careful when I did drink, which was rarely. Too many factors worked against it. Too many people knew that I didn't drink, as it was part of my story in Nashville. But once in a while when I chose to drink, it was like a pressure cooker exploding. I wouldn't drink at all for a long stretch of time, then indulge in a night of heavy imbibing. The pattern repeated itself for the next decade and followed me back to Sacramento.

Loren Balman was a man of big ideas. He had conceived of the hit CCM album *My Utmost For His Highest*, a musical tribute to Oswald Chambers' classic daily devotional using Christian artists from different labels. Next, he wanted to tackle a recording loosely based on L.B. Cowman's popular book *Streams In the Desert*. The idea was to pair mainstream and Christian artists in duets around the subject of healing. He generously asked me to produce. I left the "getting permission from the other labels" part to Loren while I began to develop the outlines of the album.

Healing was a subject everyone could relate to. I foresaw a strong orchestral element to the music. We had signed the Irish singer Máire Brennan (pronounced Moya), her sister being the wildly successful Enya, and as part of the Irish family group Clannad I thought right away she would be an element of the project. From our family of labels, we drew on Máire, Cindy Morgan, Chris Rodriguez, Jaci Velasquez, Point of Grace, Amy Grant and Sixpence None the Richer. Loren secured the participation of 4Him, the top male vocal group in CCM, and I brought along Michelle Tumes from Sparrow to write and sing, although she wouldn't write what she sang, and wouldn't sing what she wrote.

While I was in Colorado for the 1999 Music in the Rockies, I rented a keyboard and wrote for the album. The song I ended up with came together in a single sitting and was one of the better I had written in years:

Eyes closed in a veil of tears
When I hear the sound
Once more You've come to me
You've calmed me down
You still the raging sea inside of me
My Lord has come for me, so why
Why is it so hard for me to see?
Why is it so hard to just believe?
Show me what it means to be free
The only thing I need I already have
The fullness of Your mercy in my hand
The only one who loves me as I am
The only thing I need I already have

To perform "The Only Thing I Need," I immediatcly thought of 4Him. The verse was in a moderate key, which would suit Mark Harris, as his voice was similar to mine. The "B" section was made for a tenor, as was the soaring chorus, which was perfect for Andy Chrisman, who had the purest high male voice I knew. I played it for them, and they loved it. Eventually it became a standard in their set.

The Australian singer/songwriter Michelle Tumes shined on this record. Her presence is felt all over *Streams*. She brought in a song that she started, and I wrote these lyrics for it:

Tell me I'm a fool
Tell me that You love me for the fool I am
comfort me like only You can
And tell me there's a place
Where I can feel Your breath
Like sweet caresses on my face again.
Take me back to You.
The place that I once knew as a little child
Constantly the eyes of God watched over me
Oh, I want to be
In the place that I once knew as a little child
Fall into the bed of faith prepared for me.
I will rest in You

"I Will Rest In You" was a perfect song for Michelle Tumes to sing, but we needed a song for Jaci Velasquez, and because it also fit her perfectly, we gave it to Jaci. Michelle sang all the background vocals. She wrote the better part of "Breathe," another one she was born to sing, but we needed a song for Leigh Nash and Sixpence None the Richer, so we gave them "Breathe" and Michelle was all over it with her signature background sound.

Finally, Cindy Morgan and I wrote a nice song for Michelle to sing. I'm sure she would have preferred to sing one she wrote herself, but this wasn't a bad consolation prize. "Hold On" had a soaring, Fleetwood Mac-like chorus with counterpoint melodies featuring Michelle, Shelley Breen from Point of

Grace and me. The bridge, though, was all Michelle and the Irish Film Orchestra.

From Point of Grace, we got "Forever On and On," which I had pitched to them but was a little too sultry for *Steady On*. It was my favorite track they cut. If it is possible to be sensual and spiritual at the same time, this song is. (My interest in Heather Floyd as a possible solo artist can be heard in the outro of this song. It is intense.)

On *Streams*, Cindy Morgan gave a goosebump performance of the type we had perfected on her own albums. We set up her vocal and piano to record the whole song in one take. Very few artists can do this. Most don't even try because you can't fix anything. If you get the vocal completely nailed, but one finger slips a half-note for a quarter-second on the piano, you're done. The brilliant "Job" is a masterpiece, made all the better by the Irish Film Orchestra and Tom Howard's arrangement.

We plucked one song from the secular world that fit the theme of healing perfectly–Peter Gabriel's classic "Don't Give Up," originally sung by Gabriel as the protagonist and Kate Bush as his encouraging wife. I flipped the genders and had Máire Brennan sing Gabriel's part. Her partner would be the voice of God, and I knew exactly who to call–Michael McDonald. There was no one better to sing "Don't Give Up" than the voice of "What A Fool Believes" and a dozen other classic rock hits.

This set up one of many dramatic moments during the recording. Máire Brennan bore all the suffering from her deep Irish roots while Michael brought the song home in his way of singing that many have tried to copy but only he can deliver. They were accompanied by a full roster of musicians, including Robin Crow (the owner of Dark Horse Studios), Chris Rodriguez and Phil Keaggy on guitars, my old band mate Larry Tagg on bass, Chris McHugh on drums, Eric Darken on percussion, Davy Spillane on Uilleann pipes and low whistle, and me on the piano and keyboards. It remains a memorable track.

One light moment I'll never forget is Michael McDonald coming back to the studio to improvise on the outro, a long, cool instrumental section on top of which I wanted Michael to do his thing. He put his headphones on and said, "Go ahead and feed me what you want me to sing." *Wha?* I was one of many singers who had been "doing" Michael McDonald licks and impressions for years. He is perhaps the most imitated singer in the world. And now I was going to feed Michael McDonald licks and phrases to sing?? You would have had to be there to fully appreciate what happened. At one point I asked him if he thought it would be okay for him to sing "'cause you belong to me," one of his signature lines, at the fade. He felt there would be no problem and I fed it to him like I heard it.

One more huge surprise awaited me on this record. Earlier I wrote that there were two times in my life I composed a song with a particular singer in mind without any chance that they would actually sing it. The first was "Can't Feel the Pain" and Christine McVie. The second was "The Only Thing I Need" and Jon Anderson, the lead singer from the legendary progressive rock group Yes. I wrote "The Only Thing I Need" in Colorado looking out at a beautiful snow-capped mountain. When I sang this chorus, I heard Jon's voice:

The only thing I need I already have
The fullness of Your mercy in my hand
The only one who loves me as I am
The only thing I need I already have

Andy Chrisman was as good a substitute as anyone was going to get–he was the Jon Anderson of Christian music. So, when I gave the song to 4Him, it was in good hands. While we recorded the track at Dark Horse, owner Robin Crow was doing double duty in another studio on the property, working on music with an old friend–Jon Anderson. This coincidence made it my sacred cosmic duty to get Jon to sing on the song. I asked Robin if there was any possibility. He replied, "Why don't you ask him? He's sitting in the kitchen right now." Beside myself, I nervously walked across the yard. This was a delicate ask, because Jon was well-known for his New Age philosophy, and his embrace of Mother Earth, and I was about to ask him to sing a Christian lyric on a Christian album on a Christian label. I wasn't sure who was going to have more of an issue with it, him or the Christian music world, but that wasn't my problem. If I got Jon Anderson to sing on this song, I would definitely ask for forgiveness.

Introducing myself, I sat down at the table with him. He is a small man, and his speaking voice is as high as he sings with a strong Northern English tinge. I began to explain that we were doing a healing album, that it was indeed on a Christian label, but we were involving artists from the mainstream as well. Before I could continue my spiel, he laughed and said in a jolly voice, "I'm a Christian! You're a Christian! We're ALL Christians! Hahaha!" Whatever that meant to him was good enough for me. "Sure! I'll sing on it!" he cried. I had to pinch myself. This was too easy. "Let's do it now!" For every parking space I've ever missed out on, every DMV line I had to stand in, every plane that was delayed, this was payback for them all.

We walked right over to the studio and took engineer David Schober by surprise. David wasn't planning on doing any vocals that day. He thought I was just *asking* Jon Anderson. But now meant *now*. I didn't want to give him the opportunity to change his mind. We quickly converted into a vocal setup. Now came the magic. There is an opening section to "The Only

Thing I Need" that I had honestly thought I could make into a Jon Anderson-like collage of vocal harmonies before there was any thought of the Yes singer. Now I had Jon standing in front of me, ready to sing. It was tailor-made for him. When I explained what I wanted, he knew exactly what to do. We recorded about sixteen tracks of pure blissful harmony that transcended words, doing it again in the bridge, and then added his voice as the lead in the chorus. Add in another cup of beautiful Michelle Tumes vocal pads, and when we were done, we had a masterpiece.

After the album was finished, I paid a visit to Jon Rivers, the most popular DJ in Christian radio, and brought a copy of "The Only Thing I Need." He played it on the air, got to the uber-climax of the bridge, and stopped the song live on the radio. "*What was* that*? I have to hear that again!*" he exclaimed before rewinding twenty seconds and playing it over. It was a singular moment in radio.

Scan me

This monumental coming together as one for the sake of healing had its sour side. A "Church Lady" element still existed in the Christian radio and bookseller world whose worldview was stuck somewhere in the 1950s. They couldn't accept the idea that *those* words were coming out of a "heathen's" mouth. The whole point was exactly *that* we got Jon Anderson to sing those words. Wasn't that the evangelical thing to do? But it was a bridge too far for a slew of radio stations in the Bible Belt. After the song was already released to Christian radio, there was enough flak that Andy Chrisman had to come back into the studio and sing a version with his voice on the chorus. He was embarrassed and dumbfounded, as we all were. It delayed the song's progress at radio just enough to deny it its proper place at #1.

Another highlight was in store for us, however. Máire Brennan had extolled the virtues and talents of her native Irish Film Orchestra to discourage us from making the usual trip to record strings in rival London. It was cheaper to pay the airfares and hotel costs to record strings overseas than to do them in the US, and the result was often better. In this instance, the idea of Irish string players performing on an album about healing made a lot of sense. Máire hosted several of us for a week in Dublin, and we took turns recording at famous Windmill Lane Studios and touring the countryside. There is no place where the grass is greener than Ireland (though Tennessee comes close). Part of this recording included four instrumental orchestral pieces culled from already-recorded songs. I wrote one for my daughter called "Delaney McDowell" that still chokes me up when I hear it.

Scan me

I was nominated for a Dove Award as Producer of the Year for *Streams*. The nomination meant more to me than any award–it felt like the culmination of my time in Nashville, and, as it turned out, it was. "The Only Thing I Need" was also nominated for Song of the Year, and *Streams* won Special Album of the Year. My father attended the show, and as he drove me to the theater, it was pouring buckets of rain, like only Nashville can, and we got stuck in traffic. We were so late he had to drop me off outside of the auditorium while he parked. Soaking wet, I ran into the theater only to hear my name announced as the winner. I kept going straight up the aisle to the stage, dripping all the way. My poor dad missed it!

I still had a few exciting things to do before we moved back West. I was asked to produce an OC Supertones album, which was fun. The OC Supertones were a venerable California surf'n ska horn band with a frenetic lead singer named Mojo. The challenge with them was to capture that live energy in the studio. The solution? Give Mojo a hand-held microphone and turn him loose in a large, soundproof room. It worked out great.

After that, it was time for a second Rachael Lampa album. *Kaleidoscope* featured a more youthful sound in both the songwriting and arrangements. Writers included Philip and Natalie LaRue, as well as Paige Lewis. Rachael's vocals on this record are stunning. Listening back to it I hear the connection we made when I led her with ideas and she turned it all into magic. Her range was amazing both in pitch and in texture–she could belt *and* she had a beautiful whispery breathy tone.

One aside to this recording: Rachael and Stacie Orrico, two incredible artists performing and recording in the spotlight in their mid-teens, became close friends because they shared so much in common. However, they were on *rival* labels, so they were supposed to be *rivals*. In Christian music! On *Kaleidoscope*, Rachael wanted Stacie to sing a "call and response"-type song with her. Stacie, of course, readily agreed, as did Brown and me. What could be cuter? But Stacie's management team nixed the idea, saying it wouldn't be good for her career. Good for a fifteen-year-old's career? Honestly, we all take ourselves way too seriously...

Cindy Morgan recorded her third album with me, "Elementary," which I loved producing but felt the label didn't put its full heart into. We signed singer-songwriter Sarah Masen, a personal favorite, to make a record that the label promptly forgot about. In fact, Word Records, like the music business, was changing fast. Profits plummeted alongside sales of music. Why buy when you could download for free?

I was asked to contribute a composition on Steve Taylor and Squint Records' *Roaring Lambs* compilation album, recording a sweet duet with Ginny Owens called "One Thing." I co-wrote three well-received songs with Mark Harris for 4Him, "Mystery of Grace," and "Who's At the Wheel" on their *Obvious* album, and Lay It All On the Line," on their *Greatest Hits* album, and subsequently was asked to produce six tracks on their next album *Walk On.*

Oh—and one I will never live down with my kids. I had to decide whether to sign a Broadway actress who wanted to make a Christian album. At that time, I knew nothing about Broadway, musicals, or anything associated with them. While this would drastically change in the years to come, at that moment, I had no interest. I thought about the reasons I was hired to begin with—to help change the impression of Word Records as a stodgy Christian label. I admit contempt prior to investigation. I was too cool for school. In another Paul Harvey moment, that Broadway actress was named Kristen Chenoweth, and for her next project, she would be originating the role of Glinda in *Wicked*. My Broadway actress daughter Natalie and her sisters have never quite forgiven me for that one.

. . .

Gaylord Entertainment, the owner of Word, smelling disaster, put the label up for sale, hiring a music attorney, Malcolm Mims, to serve as President of the Titanic. In doing so, they fired everyone's favorite father figure, Roland Lundy. Roland had literally come up through the mailroom and had been with Word for twenty-eight years. Now this "Christian" Record company was being run by an atheist lawyer whose job was to cut, cancel, suspend payment on, do without, or outright fire anything or anyone to get the capital costs down for the sale of the company, which eventually went to a Curb/Warner consortium. We had to account for every paper clip, every eraser. I wasn't built for moments like these, a pattern that would repeat itself a quarter century later.

I admit to a bit of a Don Quixote complex. I'm generally about as successful as the errant Spanish knight. I saw the carnage happening at Word and took it upon myself to create the opposition. Friends, both staff members and artists, were being dismissed left and right. I held covert meetings in my office with disgruntled employees (Why is no one ever "gruntled"?). There were many self-righteous complaints, many expressions of disbelief and anxiety over the firing of Roland and what would happen when they sold the company.

Soon I organized a more comprehensive meeting with as many of the whole team as could fit in my office and proposed that we all go out on strike next Thursday (I'm making that up, because I don't remember what day it was). Thursday morning came, and I gathered my things, along with the hammer-and-sickle flag and a kerchief around my head and marched out to my car. I looked behind me and... nothing. Nobody. The employees one hundred percent chickened out.

I proceeded to go on a one-man strike. I stayed at home.

Loren, who had as much patience as Mandela, called me. "Hey, you really think this is a good idea? I mean, I'm not entirely sure what you think you're going to accomplish." Neither was I. The fact was, I was done. In the end, they paid me well to go away. I knew too much and there were no NDAs (non-disclosure agreements).

Soon after I left, they sold the company and fired almost everyone, including my replacement, Chris Rodriguez. They eliminated the level of VP of A&R. Word Records, like many record companies moving forward, became the landing spot for accountants and lawyers, outsourcing the creative positions like A&R, promotions, and graphic design. I didn't see any of it coming, but it didn't surprise me, either. The music business had entered a period of steep and rapid decline. 9/11 only exacerbated the fall. While I sat at the Sound Kitchen Recording Studios with my friends and owners Dino and John Elefante, talking about the future of the business, we saw the second plane crash into the World Trade Center towers. Nothing would be the same again.

———

Rachael Lampa "Live For You"

Rachael Lampa "Kaleidoscope"

Paige Lewis

Nicole C. Mullen "Talk AboutIt"

Chris Eaton, me, Brown Bannister Michell Tumes, Chris Rodriguez, & Cindy Morgan

Campus Life 2000

Maire Brennan in Ireland

"Streams" Album

4Him "Walk On"

OC Supertones "HiFi Revival"

Nashville Music 2000-2002

13
CALIFORNIA HERE
WE COME (BACK)

The music industry slide began before anybody noticed. Signs that look so easy to see in retrospect were not apparent in real time. The crash of the music business had as many things and people to blame as one might care to list. Greed, complacency, arrogance, a failure to see the signs, then a failure to brace for the future–are just a few.

In my lifetime, the biggest change has been due to technology. I've heard it posited that the eighty years between the advent of recorded music and the coming of Napster was actually the great outlier for music as a business. For a thousand years before that, you couldn't buy recorded music, and in the last twenty-five years almost no one has wanted to buy recorded music.

When I was a kid, young people spent their allowances, baby-sitting money, lawnmowing dollars, and money from small jobs buying singles and albums. If you loved a song you heard on the radio, you had two choices. You could wait to hear it on the radio again, or you could go down to your local record store and buy it. You might be able to go over to a friend's house and hear it if they had bought it, but when you purchased it, you could play it over and over and over again, as many times as you liked.

The first chink in the armor of recorded music might have been the recordable cassette. Suddenly, you could tape a copy of that song you loved, either from the radio or your friend's album. FM DJs would announce the airing of the new ___ album at 9:00 tonight, and you could set up your cassette deck to record the whole thing. If you had a decent cassette player and a high-quality cassette, the recording sounded fine. You could even make a copy for your buddy and not lose too much fidelity. A World Music program aired on the local public radio station on weekend nights, and I would set my cassette recorder up and tape four hours of World Music. Four hours of recorded music I now didn't have to buy.

The CD arrived in the early-to-mid-1980s, and immediately gave a huge boost to the music industry, as boomers rushed to replace their skipping and scratched Beatles and Rolling Stones, etc., album collections with pristine digital copies. From that point until the late 1990s, the business was at its zenith. Albums cost $18 a copy. Money was flowing like champagne and cocaine. Recordable CDs may have been a nagging worry, but Moore's Law, the doubling of chip speed every two years–meant that slow desktop computers would soon be replaced by faster laptops, which would be superseded by even faster devices that fit in your pocket.

Even the advent of the Internet was not an immediate problem. Download speeds were maddeningly slow, and storage was minimal and expensive. But technology was improving at lightning speed. The knife in the gut of the industry was the coming of broadband in the early 2000s. Once households began to install broadband, downloading speed accelerated, and at the same time the price of digital storage plummeted. It was a runaway train. Napster was founded in 1999, and the rest is unfortunate history for the music biz.

In the early 1960s Russ Solomon revolutionized the business of selling albums by opening dedicated record stores (Tower Records) and constantly innovating. He showed the old fuddy-duddies in drugstores and TV shops the huge market they were missing. By 2001, Russ Solomon was an old fuddy-duddy himself, famously saying, "Don't tell *me* how to run a record store!" when faced with digital downloading.

By the end of 2001, everybody was cutting back. Artists were let go. Those who remained were given smaller budgets. Record companies trimmed staff, which created a domino effect with producers and engineers. The top producers were forced to take projects below their usual level, which caused the next level of producer to seek the level below *that*, and onward until there were people with great track records making church choir albums. Nobody could get a handle on how to fix the problem. The general public had found a magic fountain where all the world's music flowed for free. The same technology that had been so helpful to the music business now turned on it in a big way, though the advent of computers and digital technology did make albums cheaper to make. They had to be, because the same technology was rapidly eliminating the buyers of those albums.

The payout I received from Word Records to keep my mouth shut allowed me and my family to survive for about a year, because freelance work had dried up. I made a trip to LA to sound out a couple of record company presidents about the prospects for employment, but everyone was in cutback mode.

There was tension in our home. Mary Ann had reached the end of her road in Nashville. I had run out of reasons to stay.

When we sought marital counseling for the first time, our therapist said something that stuck with me. *"Whenever you reach a fork in the road like this one, whichever road you take, if you take it for the right reasons, will turn out okay."*

I didn't want to leave Nashville, where I had made many friends for life and my career had revived in unimaginable ways. But I wasn't alone, and I wasn't living in a vacuum. We were entering the ninth year of a five-year plan. As long as I was constantly working and receiving a steady paycheck, it didn't make a lot of sense for us to leave. But we had reached the point where there was no reasonable, logical reason to stay now that Mary Ann wanted to go home. At the fork, I chose the family road. We were moving back to California.

We let our children finish out their school year before we moved. We weren't exactly sure where we were going. If I planned to eke out a living in the music business, it wouldn't happen in Sacramento. So, our first inclination was to land in Southern California and see what was available. For Mary Ann, that was a fine alternative to Nashville. On May 31, 2002, we drove away from our home on Winter Hill Drive and picked up our kids at Abintra Montessori School at the end of their graduation day. We crossed the Mississippi River Bridge in Memphis and spent the night in Little Rock, on our way to my parent's house on Duchess Trail in Dallas.

Arriving in Dallas the next day, we celebrated Delaney's eleventh birthday with everyone there. It was painfully obvious that my mother's Alzheimer's Disease had progressed. Nonetheless, we spent a few days there before continuing our drive west. A few days later we were in Southern California, settling in around the Thousand Oaks-Westlake Village-Agoura Hills area. We looked at houses and schools for Adrian while I looked for work. It's hard to remember how depressed the music industry was in the middle of 2002. The response was "no" everywhere I went.

We had no choice but to move back to Sacramento, where Mary Ann's family lived, and where the housing prices were cheaper. I didn't know what I was going to do for employment. I assumed at the time I would spend half my time working in Nashville, and this was an acceptable compromise for Mary Ann. Except that's not what happened. I was out of sight, out of mind in Music City. Things were so slow, it didn't make sense to pay extra to bring someone out from California with so many local producers looking for work.

Our family set up camp at Mary Ann's family's house. It was crowded, but no one minded. Her mother was healthy and strong, and her sister Kathi was overjoyed that she had her nephew and nieces back. We settled in there for six months while Mary Ann and I looked for a house.

Just when I faced the most uncertainty about making a living, Warehouse Christian Ministries' Pastor Louis Neely and his wife Mary threw me a lifeline, offering me a full-time position as Music Director and Worship Leader at the Warehouse. That might not sound like much compared to what I was doing, but it was halfway back from nothing. The job marked the beginning of over ten years in the music wilderness. But it also offered me the time and space to be available for my wife and children during an important decade in a way that was never possible in Nashville.

Mary Neely was the founder of Exit Records, which operated out of the Warehouse and had a major label distribution deal with Island Records for artists Charlie Peacock, The 77s, and Vector. That all collapsed when Charlie took his talents to Nashville in 1989, and Mary's dreams of playing in the bigtime had lain dormant since then. When I arrived, her dreams were temporarily revived.

Pastor Neely has the gift of preaching. A Texan power-house, built like the football lineman he once was, he is able to connect to his faithful with a message in plain South Texan language full of humor and anecdotes. Louis is self-depre-cating and at the same time emotional. Prodded by his wife Mary, he was also open-minded about introducing music trends onto the stage of the Warehouse, and not just at weekend concerts. He offered reggae and ska, hip hop, rap, and emo styles for the "special" music during services. He felt that music was a gateway into the faith. Somewhere along the way music for the church became old and stodgy, but that's not how Bach, Handel and Mozart had seen it. Louis and Mary's conception of music made an impression on me, and I was hired to help them get the ball rolling again, like in the glory days of the 1980s, when the Warehouse was a culture-leading church with exciting weekend rock concerts.

Warehouse Christian Ministries was maybe *the* textbook example of a church that was conservative in worldview, but liberal in the music they allowed on their stage. They had a magnificent state-of-the-art concert venue featuring great sound reinforcement, up-to-date equipment, and a large enough stage to accommodate almost anyone. With my Nash-ville connections, I was able to revive the Warehouse concerts. Over the next few years, I brought Michael W. Smith, Point of Grace (on Halloween no less!), Avalon, Cindy Morgan (twice), Joy Williams, Chris Rice, Rebecca St. James, ZOEgirl, Sara Groves, Mark Schultz, Nicole Nordeman, and BarlowGirl to the Warehouse for weekend evening concerts. If I couldn't work in Nashville, I'd bring Nashville to me!

The Warehouse also had a newer version of the recording studio that Charlie Peacock and I used in the mid-80s. It, too, would get a workout during my time there. With my good friend Ralph Stover manning the controls, we made a record for a powerful gospel leader named Louis Smith, who had *the gift* of singing on Sunday mornings in a way that was half-talking, half-singing, coercive, laughing, imploring, encouraging, and altogether engaging. It was hard to contain all of that in a recording, but we set him up in real time like I did Cindy Morgan and let him wail.

With Louis Smith as part of the team, we took our worship circus to London and performed at their Calvary Chapel. While the trip itself was successful, cracks that had been there from the beginning were widening in my relationship with the evangelical Christian worldview. I was known in Nashville for my left-leaning views, never understanding how a follower of Jesus could not border on being a Socialist. Reading the Bible only reinforced these feelings. Capitalism and Jesus seemed anathema to one another, as did Jesus and homophobia or bigotry. The Christian church had come a long way in their race relations, but many church leaders still regarded women as people to be seen and not heard inside a church. They espoused a senseless "love the sinner, hate the sin" attitude towards the LGBTQ+ community, posting hypocritical "All Are Welcome" banners outside many churches, when, in fact, SOME were only welcome if they completely upended who they were. The Bible was conveniently cherry-picked by all sides. One could say, "The Bible says..." about almost anything, and get across any point you are trying to make.

The "my country right or wrong" stance concerning Israel troubled me, as it turned all Arabs and Palestinians into bad guys. This was harmful enough twenty-five years ago, and it's only gotten worse. The steadily increasing participation of evangelical Christians on the Far Right side of the political spectrum was a deal-breaker for me. Christian preachers marched side by side with Martin Luther King Jr. in Selma, Alabama. Christian pastors and Catholic priests burned draft cards to protest the Vietnam War. Christians died for professing their faith in defiance of the Nazis in Germany. Now, through the calculated manipulation of a group of secular right-wing political operatives, Christians were convinced that their guides on the road to Heaven were upstanding folks like Rush Limbaugh and Jerry Falwell. Even some of my friends from the outside, reformed alkys and addicts, had transformed themselves from liberal thinkers into narrow-minded culture warriors, as likely to agree with Pat Robertson as with Martin Luther King.

The great tragedy of 9/11 brought all Americans together in a common sorrow and a momentary burst of patriotism and love of their fellow man that lasted about three days. That was replaced by the muscle-flexing, tough-talking mentality that this nation pivots to so easily. Suddenly, we were in a macho, "you messed with the wrong dudes" contest, led by the faux-cowboy George W. Bush, and somebody was going to pay big time. Much of this was understandable, and somebody should have paid. But many Americans didn't particularly care who that was, as long as they were "somewhere over there." Going after al-Qaeda in Afghanistan was an unfortunate necessity. Starting a war with Iraq was insanity, conjured up by neo-liberal cold warriors still trying to remake areas of the world into our image, this one teeming with oil reserves they wanted to get their paws on. Saddam Hussein was a nasty fellow, but he had nothing to do with 9/11.

I was turning into a political junkie, and there's nothing more virulent and obnoxious than someone who's born-again about anything. Sitting at a table in London with this group of Christian friends and co-workers, I was completely out-numbered by a jingo-esque, pro-American crowd who viewed the current war like a college football game. At the same time, I realized that while I held what I thought were the right ideas, my knowledge of the facts was wide but shallow. I was another person whose opinions were loud but their expertise thin.

Returning from London, I sat at the piano facing Louis Neely as his Sunday morning Worship Leader while he spewed anti-Muslim tropes about terrorists hiding under every rock and gas station. Later that week, at lunch with Neely and fellow Warehouse youth pastors and leaders, I mentioned to someone over sandwiches that there were both good and bad Israelis and Palestinians, and each side had blood on their hands. Sharped-eared Louis slammed his hand down on the table and shouted, "I don't want to hear another bad word about Israel! Is that clear?"

I wrote a few op-ed pieces for the local newspaper explaining my Christian opposition to the Iraq War. I felt it was my duty to correct the misimpression that Christians were pro-war. What a thing to have to correct! This was too much for Pastor Neely. Actually, it was too much for his big-time tithers, the money-people who kept the church afloat. He brought me into his office and said I had to cease writing these types of opinions, or he would be forced to request my resignation. For the first time in my life, I showed a little political backbone and replied that I couldn't as a faithful follower of Jesus stop speaking my conscience and resigned.

Unemployed for the first time since I was fourteen, I had even more time now to commit to domestic life. I drove the kids to school every morning and coached the girls' soccer team. I bought a sitar, started playing music at a Buddhist Meditation Center, and began to study Buddhism. My resignation from the Warehouse opened the door for Mary Ann to finish up her post-master's studies that enabled her to begin her career as a school psychologist. We had money coming in from my royalties, which tided us over. We purchased a home on a beautiful old-school street in suburban Elk Grove that we live in to this day.

Immediately I began research for the book I was going to write, a kind of anti-apologetic: Why, when I became a Christian had I instinctively turned to the Left, when everyone I knew who became a Christian turned to the Right? The question had bothered me for as long as I had been a part of the evangelical world and occupied my energy for the next two years.

Diving headfirst into writing, I spent a great deal of time at the library and bought nearly a hundred books. I was getting the education I missed by not going to college. However, if I had any chance to be taken seriously as a writer, there would have to be at least a college degree in English writing under my belt, if not more. I enrolled as a full-time student at Sacramento City College for the first two years of my degree. I was in my late forties and starting college!

I must say, I enjoyed college (especially a comparative religions course), despite feeling a little uncomfortable as the old guy in most classes, especially when we did group projects. I was at least as old as most of my teachers. Some of them knew who I was, some didn't. I received an 'F' on a political science paper for writing a parody of the assignment. I went in to complain, but the professor had absolutely no sense of humor. I wouldn't have changed a word.

My book, *Left Behind: Jesus In the Age of the American Empire* found a small publishing company, John Mabry's Apocryphile Press, and was released in paperback and on Amazon. The title was a play on the popular "Left Behind" series of apocalyptic Christian fantasy novels. It was my declaration of independence as a left-wing Christian, an oxymoron to many. I finished it just as the first Black president of the United States, Barack Obama was elected. I hadn't felt so optimistic in years.

Scan me

While occasions of my drinking were few and far between, some scary moments drove me back to the AA community. Here in Sacramento again, it was as if I'd never left, and many of my old friends welcomed me back with open arms. In AA, people are never judged if they return. Instead, we become a cautionary tale, a reminder to stay connected to the program at all costs. I was ready to renew my commitment to sobriety and the program.

Less than a year after I left the Warehouse, a similar job opened on the opposite end of the Christian spectrum. I thought I was done with Christians, but the United Methodists *had* marched with Martin Luther King, *had* burned draft cards and *had* marched against the Vietnam War. Pacifists in the United Methodist church went to jail rather than shoot a gun in World War II. St. Mark's United Methodist church in Sacramento has been the leading LGBTQ+ church in Northern California, performing the most gay weddings. It radiated progressive Christianity in a way that truly resonated in me.

However, like many "high" churches, St. Mark's had seen better days. The average age of the congregants was over seventy. The "young" folks were the LGBTQs in their middle ages. They had spent $250,000 on a huge pipe organ at the very time that evangelical churches were putting on rock shows, complete with concert lighting and dry ice, at their services. They had twenty funerals for every wedding. They were, in a word, dying. The pastor, a wonderful woman named Faith Whitmore, recognized this all too well and wanted to do something radical to bring in a younger generation. We found each other at the right time.

St. Mark's shared none of the modern conveniences of the Warehouse. The sanctuary's vaulted ceilings echoed. Their sound equipment was early 1960s-vintage, and not in a good way. They suffered from the exact opposite situation of the evangelicals: their politics were progressive, but their music was stuck in the 1800s. John Wesley, the father of Methodism, was a prolific composer of hymns as well. Wesley's hymns are sung in Methodist churches today, and Methodists are very possessive of them. Getting the progressive geezers at St. Mark's to start singing modern worship music was going to be a tough sell.

In the final analysis, I gave the whole effort a "C." We didn't bring in the younger cohort that Faith was looking for. The old congregation never quite caught on to the music, which was generally too loud. I had mixed success at St. Mark's. I revived the Moon Lectures, a speaker series that featured progressives of all faiths, or of no particular faith. Some of the speakers I booked included Rabbi Dr. Michael Lerner, political activist Daniel Ellsberg, *Democracy Now!*'s Amy Goodman, and Fr. Gregory Boyle, founder of Homeboy Industries, the largest gang intervention program in the world. When Faith left the church to head the local chapter of The United Way, it signaled the end of my time at St. Mark's as well.

My music career seemingly over, I thought I would transition into writing books. I had already written one. Now I wrote a full-length historical novel called "The ~~Long~~ *Wrong* Way Home." I still have great hopes for this one. Inspired by an article by George Orwell in a British newspaper during World War II, it tells the story of two brothers from far western China named Abu and Mahmud. They are Uyghurs, non-Chinese Muslims living in a forgotten corner of the world at the beginning of WWII, which they have heard nothing about. When their father dies, they are sent to the next nearest big town to find work for a season, only to be shanghaied by the Chinese army fighting the Japanese. Training, fighting, and riding trains all the way across China, they are captured in Manchuria by the Japanese, and put to work as prison guards, only to escape north through Mongolia and into the Soviet Union, where they are promptly jailed and sent to the gulag. Stalin releases all gulag prisoners to fight in punishment battalions at the head of the Soviet army, and shortly after, Abu and Mahmud are captured by the Germans. The Germans turn non-Russian fighters into soldiers, and the brothers are sent to defend the Atlantic Wall to prepare for the invasion of Allied forces. There, they are captured on D-Day by American soldiers and sent as POWs to England, where they meet Winston Churchill and become celebrities for their odd appearance. A diplomatic fight ensues, and they are given back to the Americans as POWs and sent to a German POW camp in Mississippi to pick cotton until the end of the war. There they listen to Black blues musicians and are identified finally for who they are—Uyghurs who know nothing about any of this and are simply trying to get home to their mother. The Americans put them in an intelligence unit bringing supplies from Iran into China, and they ultimately arrive near their starting point, only to find out that gangsters have extorted their small town and kidnapped their little sister. After almost six years of war, in five different armies, they have become tougher than they could have imagined and Abu and Mahmud enjoy a happy ending. I am looking for the right connection to a publisher who will read it. It's a great, cinematic story, and it should be a movie.

I wrote because Nashville was *not* calling. By now, I was out of mind. Nothing was happening in California, either. I did get one call out of the blue to produce a Point of Grace song, "This Is Your Land," from their *I Choose You* album. A sign of a new century: I never saw them. I recorded the track in my friend Ralph Stover's house and sent it to them to sing. We mixed it in Ralph's bedroom. Imagine that. We had gone from Abbey Road Studios in London to Ralph Stover's bedroom. Technology.

For over thirty years, I almost never stood still. I was afraid of stopping. I never took vacations. (Snarky people would say my whole life was a vacation.) Now I had to get used to just being comfortable in my own skin. As in, *"Has my value been wrapped up in what I do, in what I achieve?"* You bet it's been. What about my value as a husband and as a father? Can I just be that now? Is driving the kids to school and coaching soccer enough? For someone who was wired to achieve, it didn't feel like enough.

After sacrificing her career for years so that one of us could be home full-time with the kids, it was finally Mary Ann's turn to be out in the workforce bringing home the tofu-like bacon. Adrian was becoming an excellent singer/songwriter and had started making albums of his own. All three of my daughters became happily established in musical theatre. I have ended up knowing more about musical theatre than I ever thought was possible. And I have to say, I've grown to love it.

In 2008, I got the news that my longtime close friend and former Uncle Rainbow band mate Richard Oates was suffering from hepatitis C and needed a *second* liver transplant. We organized a fundraiser in Sacramento at the Crest Theater, bringing together many friends and musicians important both to Richard and to me.

Sacramento luminary (and former rocker) Kitty O'Neal emceed the night. My son Adrian opened the show, followed by Mike Roe & the 77s. Charlie Peacock came from Nashville to lend a hand. We assembled Uncle Rainbow to do a set, which included George Lawrence and David Perper on drums, Bongo Bob Smith on percussion, Little John Sanders on sax, keys and vocals, and Lance Taber on guitar sitting in for Danny Neal. Larry Tagg and I manned the bass and keys and vocals, and Richard, battling illness, sat in on lead vocals. Roger Smith, the long-time keyboardist from Tower of Power, sat in on Herbie Hancock's "Spank-A-Lee."

Scan me

It was an emotionally fulfilling night. I lent a few solo songs–playing "Can't Feel the Pain" with Lyle Workman on guitar, my kids, Corey and Adrian on harmonies, and Eva Scow on mandolin.

Bourgeois Tagg closed the show like we had never left, performing a tight set that could have been played in 1987. It was amazing. We even had a string quartet accompanying us on "I Don't Mind At All." In a foreshadowing of things to come, the show was professionally recorded by a Bay Area sound design company called Wave Group, headed by Will Littlejohn. Will and his wife Leslie were long time fans of Bourgeois Tagg.

When I was much younger, I remember going to at least one "oldies" show–a novelty event featuring a slew of aging groups from the late '50s and '60s. Each band, which ideally consisted of at least one actual member from the original group, stomachs protruding, guitars pushed further away from their bodies than comfortable and bald heads shining under the lights, played a three-song set that included their hit, and then were on their way to the lounge backstage. Fast forward forty or so years and it was our turn. Bourgeois Tagg was asked to do a couple of "Remember the 80s!"-type shows along with several groups of a similar age. Lyle Workman and Michael Urbano were off doing legitimate things with their talent and weren't available, so Larry and I called on our two old buddies, guitarist Lance Taber and drummer Steve Mitchell, along with Scott Moon. I had reservations from the beginning, and they weren't wrong.

Each band on the bill featured maybe one original member surrounded by either their kids or some twenty-something hired hands. One band, which I will not embarrass by identifying, had a famous MTV video in the 80s. The lead guy was a beanpole with the biggest head of hair ever seen. This same guy was now the shape of a bowling ball with a shiny head to match. After two of these shows, I had had enough. I took home what was left of my pride and vowed "never again."

And then, in late 2011, I ran into Michael Blanton at an event while visiting my dad in Dallas. In the thick of the record company malaise, Mike Blanton had started an entertainment company called BE Entertainment. Working alongside him was my old friend Don Donahue. Mike had been approached by a young woman who marched into his Nashville office and told him he was going to manage her.

She wasn't just any young woman. She was the billionaire heiress of a large corporation who also happened to be a budding singer/songwriter. We will call her KH. She and her family were Christians living in Malibu, California. Mike wondered if I might want to be his West Coast representative with KH, which sounded intriguing.

He flew to Los Angeles, and we met at a hotel in Santa Monica before driving to their stunningly gorgeous Malibu home. Dick Van Dyke, who we saw puttering around in his garage, lived next door. The H's also had a beach house about two miles down the road. We sat with the whole family and discussed K's plans.

She wanted to be a recording artist, but she wasn't entirely sure of her genre. Her ideas as a songwriter were hampered by her lack of guitar skills. She was a decent-enough singer, but she needed help with direction. She needed a Henry Higgins. Mom was a Christian Warrior. Dad, not so much. He gave it lip service and mostly just went along with mom. K was like the vintage SNL teenage Conehead, for the moment trapped with her parents but knowing there was a cooler world out there.

Mike gave them the Blanton Treatment, which no one else was ever as good at. Mike had crossover appeal. He could talk the Christian talk, but he focused on the mainstream as his target, the massive success of Amy Grant backing him up. This pitch appealed to folks like the H's, with money to match their ambition for their daughter. I was the perfect California solution to K's needs, having Christian bonafides, but also mainstream appeal. I was hired and would be spending three days a week in Malibu for the foreseeable future.

I put several plans into motion at once. Money was no object, although the H's weren't crazy. They didn't object to any idea if it made sense. I hired Dan Kalisher, a protégé of Lyle Workman's, to give K emergency guitar lessons. She needed to get up to speed fast. Her mother wanted her to be prepared to perform at a Christian Arts Festival in Paso Robles, California within two months.

I needed to put together a band for K pronto. The first member of that band was at home with me. My son Adrian had developed into a first-class singer/songwriter and multi-instrumentalist. It was hard to tell whether he was better at the drums, keyboards, or guitar, but it was great that he played all three. His music partner was Paige Lewis, my former Word Records signee. Together they became the foundation for our new group, along with K's guitar teacher, Dan Kalisher, who helped us fill out the band on bass and drums with a couple of his friends. At the same time, I spent hours with K developing her nascent ideas into pop songs. She turned out to be a talented songwriter.

It was bizarre to have been toodling along in suburban Sacramento, trying my hand at writing books, coaching soccer, and going nowhere as worship leader at a graying church, to be suddenly spending half of my time at a billionaire's house in Malibu. Mr. Magoo landed on his feet again. Within three months, K successfully performed at the festival. Adrian, Paige and I all co-wrote with K, and I produced three recording sessions–two in LA and one in Nashville at Charlie Peacock's studio. I hadn't planned on making it back to Nashville that way.

In a twist stranger than fiction, we recorded "Christian" K in Tommy Lee's home studio, The Atrium, in Calabasas, California. How did we get into the drummer of Motley Crüe's private studio, especially for something like this? Our engineer was my old buddy Ross Hogarth, who had deep connections in the LA rock world. The Atrium's walls and tables were decorated with many interesting objects, including a giant black-and-white closeup photo of Tommy Lee giving the finger installed right over the toilet in the bathroom. K didn't mind but Mrs. H was another story. We covered up the worst of it before she arrived, though there was no covering up the demonic nine-foot phallic statue in the hall.

Tommy was a gracious host, however. In the Department of You Can't Make This Up, newly sober Tommy Lee was going through a full-on baking phase while we were recording. He came down to the studio one day with apron on delivering a full pan of warm, delicious cinnamon rolls right out of his oven. He was a proud man. This gave me the idea for a YouTube-style show called "Baked with Tommy Lee," where Tommy would invite other rocker friends, like Sammy Hagar, or Vince Neil, into his kitchen and they would trade stories and reminisce about old times while baking croissants, or a cake, or cinnamon rolls. Alas, this idea went where most good ideas go: up in smoke.

K called her music "Calipopacana," a modern version of surf-pop. The problem with billionaires is that they bounce from one idea to another. They "have" to go on that yacht cruise in the Adriatic. They "have" to go skiing in Gstaad. They "have" to fly to that art opening in New York. For someone that privileged, K was a hard worker. She genuinely liked to be down in the trenches, getting her hands dirty in some pretty sleazy rehearsal rooms. But there is a different standard of effort when your whole life depends on your labor rather than doing it because it's something cool to try. K is still out there playing dates occasionally. I was grateful for the opportunity and the work.

The re-connection with Michael Blanton remained the most important part of that endeavor. I started writing music again, using my computer for something more than word processing. During my last years in Nashville and then afterwards, I fell behind in the computer software revolution, as I opted for more organic arrangements. When in need of programming, I called on others rather than doing it myself. I had quite a bit of ground to make up. Mike, offering me another lifeline back into music, gave me a publishing contract to write music for other artists (*uh-oh*.) Instead, I subconsciously started writing songs for a new solo album. This became obvious when the songs I submitted were rejected by Mike's publishing director, Marty Wheeler, as being too idiosyncratic (def.–too *me*). I think his exact words were, "*What am I gonna do with these?*"

Here was another case of my not being able to compose for others from a cold beginning. But this time I had written some good songs, unlike the other times I had tried to write for other artists. I had exercised the muscle with K and got to know my computer software again. So, improbably, twenty years after the last one, I started working on a solo album. Record. Playlist. Download. Stream (we hadn't quite gotten there yet). One thing was clear: I was creating for myself, by myself. No record company was going to help. There were only a few companies left, and they weren't signing fifty-five-year-old white guys who hadn't made a record in twenty years.

I started making an album for the same reason I'm writing this book: on a whim. Maybe I was on the twenty-year cycle like Tennessee cicadas. I sat on the living room floor with my computer and a keyboard on a coffee table and wrote the groove to "Don't Look Back." It's an organ figure. I don't think I ever started writing a song with an organ figure. Go figure. It's funny how I began with the firm idea that I was going to perform and record this album completely on my own, every part and every vocal. Talk about mission creep. By the end of it, almost everyone I had anything to do with in my music life made it onto the album, called *Don't Look Back*.

A list:

"Don't Look Back"–Aaron Smith: drums, John Lee Sanders: saxophone & lead vocals, Rachael Lampa: background vocals, Chris Rodriguez: background vocals, Michelle Tumes: background vocals. Mixed by Ralph Stover.

"Back of My Hand"–Steve Brewster: drums, Chris Rodriguez: guitars, background vocals. Mixed by Ralph Stover.

"Deep Blue Sea"– Chris Rodriguez: guitars, background vocals. Mixed by Ralph Stover.

"The High Road"–Michael Urbano: drums, Larry Tagg: bass, Mike Roe: electric guitar, Tim Pierce: slide guitar, Rich Ayers: acoustic guitar, Adrian Bourgeois: acoustic guitar, Julian Lennon: lead vocal. Co-produced and mixed by Ross Hogarth.

"Poor Me"– Aaron Smith: drums, Kasim Sulton: bass, Jerry McPherson: guitar, Todd Rundgren: vocals, mixed by John Fields.

"Anything is Possible"–Steve Brewster: drums, Jerry McPherson: electric guitar. Mixed by Ralph Stover.

"All She Ever Wanted"–Produced by Charlie Peacock, Charlie Peacock: keyboards, programming, Mark Hill: bass, Jerry McPherson: guitar, Cody Fry: keyboards, Sam Ashworth: background vocals, Mixed by Richie Biggs.

"You & I"– George Lawrence: drums, Chris Rodriguez: guitars, Paige Lewis: vocals, Mixed by Ralph Stover.

"Psycho"–Michael Urbano: drums, percussion, Larry Tagg: bass, Lyle Workman: guitars. Mixed by David J. Holman.

"My Island"–Molly Felder: Background vocals, Vicki Randle: percussion, Mixed by Ralph Stover.

"Without You"–Aaron Smith: drums, Wayne Kirkpatrick: acoustic guitar, vocals, Vicki Randle: percussion, Mixed by Ralph Stover.

Suffice to say, I owe every one of these people. I asked a hundred different favors. It was especially nice to have Larry Tagg, Michael Urbano and Lyle Workman on this record. The song "Psycho," could have been right off a third Bourgeois Tagg album. And it was mixed by David Holman. And what can I say about Todd? He put together a whole package of vocals on "Poor Me" which included parts I didn't ask for. The lyric of "Poor Me" should be sung by a sad clown:

Once again I find myself in a place I don't understand
The Goddess of Fate is showing me the back of her hand
And try as I may I don't understand
Of all the people in the world...O why me?
I grow so weary of the chains I have to bear
And it's killing me

Poor me
Falling again from the same tree
Over my head on the high seas
Drifting from trainwreck to tragedy
Over and over again

So I wound up on the wrong side of the tracks
Walked smack dab into trouble–I've always had the knack
And fool that I am–I've forgotten how to get back
Back to my home-wherever home may be...I don't know
I've traveled halfway 'round the world–I've got another half to go
I'm praying for the winds of change to follow me
O Lord let me be

It was a special honor to have Julian Lennon duet on "The High Road." He was willing from the start and stayed overtime getting his vocal just right. He and I had dinner afterwards, and he mentioned that someone else might be coming along. It turned out to be Whoopi Goldberg, who I hadn't run into in twenty-five years.

I gave Charlie Peacock his choice of songs to produce, and

he chose "All She Ever Wanted," the only song I wrote for the second Reunion album that never came about.

On a Friday night, I went out to Wayne Kirkpatrick's studio in rural Franklin, Tennessee to record the last song on the record, "Without You," which was oddly fitting, because Wayne co-produced the final two songs on my previous solo record. We knocked out the song in an evening, and I followed up with Aaron Smith on drums and Vicki Randle on percussion. That night Wayne told me the story of a musical that he and his brother Karey had been working on for years, a parody about Shakespeare that they had finally found a producer for. The process takes years, and they were moving ahead. The show, *Something Rotten*, became a huge hit on Broadway and is one of my family's favorites.

Writing this book involved finding and re-listening to songs I hadn't heard in decades. While most of the songs on my new album were freshly written in 2014, I also scoured old tapes for any hidden gems or even pieces of songs that may have been lost in the mists of time. "All She Ever Wanted" was one of these. On an old DAT, I found an instrumental track that I loved, and wrote lyrics to what became "Without You," the song Wayne Kirkpatrick and I recorded. Earlier, I mentioned that I wrote three songs for 4 Him. One of these was "Mystery of Grace," a co-write with Mark Harris which I hadn't given a second thought to in over twenty-five years. Listening back to "Mystery of Grace," I realized to my horror that the music was the same instrumental track to which I wrote the song "Without You." I had to ask myself for forgiveness. When I mentioned this to Andy Chrisman in a text, he just laughed it off. What are you gonna do now?

A record release party for *Don't Look Back* was held in Mike Blanton's BE Entertainment office in Nashville. I tried a novel approach to selling the record. More of a GoFundYou, where I paid fans to sell my record. I sold dozens. I wrote a personal note on Facebook to five thousand of my closest friends. I sold dozens more. However, this record was more about finding my creativity again. I had a great time making a joyful noise with so many friends. To top it off, I went to New Orleans with my brother Brian and sister Coral and shot a handheld video during Mardi Gras for the song "Don't Look Back." The fact that it never was released was a minor detail.

After this flurry of activity, I faced another "what's next?" moment. I had forced a little more life out of my dormant music career, but the lemon was just about squeezed dry. In 2015, Keith Hatschek, the Dean of the Music Department at the University of the Pacific, known for being the home of jazz legend Dave Brubeck, threw me another lifeline when he asked if I would like to teach a songwriting class. Me, a professor? I didn't even have a college degree. A rare loophole exists in academia, particularly in the arts, that honors "life experience" over education. Charlie Peacock became the Dean of Music at Lipscomb University in Nashville through the same portal. It makes a lot of sense in music. Nothing replaces doing it. I gratefully accepted, put on my tweed jacket with elbow patches, and thought I would ride off into the sunset as a Professor of Songwriting, not a bad way to cap a long career in music. Boy was I wrong.

But first, one more story that captures my fifty-year journey through the music business. Teaching at UOP was great, but it was only a two-days-a-week job. I had a lot of time to fill between classes. Uber was still a new idea in 2015, and the ability to set your own hours and be your own boss seemed, at the moment, intriguing. I had a nice car, and I thought, *Why not?* It was more about doing *something* productive with my time rather than the money. I should have known better. On my *first* ride, a man climbed into my back seat, and looking at the name of the guy who picked him up, said, "Are you *the* Brent Bourgeois? From Bourgeois Tagg? Wow." He shook his head, embarrassed for me. Sheepishly, I said, "Yeah, it's me." I should have stopped right there, but I decided instead to do my Ubering outside of my local area code and head to San Francisco, which was fun–I got to know the City like never before, and the rides were never-ending.

The biggest humbling was yet to come. *Pollstar*, the live music industry magazine, holds an annual awards show, which was taking place at the venerable Masonic Auditorium in San Francisco. One of their directors, Kelli Richards, invited me to present a couple of awards, an invitation I gratefully accepted. I crammed myself into the only rock outfit that still fit, and drove to the venue, renewing acquaintances with fellow presenters Narada Michael Walden and Night Ranger guitarist Jeff Watson before presenting Roadie of the Year, won by a Rolling Stones roadie, and Tour of the Year, won by U2. Neither were present.

After the show, I returned to my car and decided I might as well do a little Ubering on my way home. As soon as I turned on the app, I got a ride. At the bottom of the steep hill, two men climbed in the back and a woman, who kept staring at me, sat in front. Finally, she asked, "Didn't we just see you giving an award at the *Pollstar* show?" She turned around and the three of them chuckled. I quit Ubering that night.

With Julian Lennon

Todd looking for his name

With Michael Urbano & Larry Tagg

With Jerry McPherson

"Don't Look Back"

With Steve Brewster

Me & Charlie Peacock

Me & Wayne Kirkpatrick

With Aaron Smith

With John Lee Sanders

With George Lawrence

Me & Rachael Lampa

With Chris Rodriguez

"Don't Look Back" 2014

14

AN ACT III TO REMEMBER

The University of the Pacific campus is a beautiful, quiet tree-filled oasis tucked inside valley city of Stockton, California. I started my time as Professor of Songwriting teaching just a couple of classes and lending some help in their studio. I had to make a lesson plan, which felt oxymoronic to the art of songwriting, but not to the craft, I guess. The problem I faced right away was that, despite Dave Brubeck's legacy, UOP was not a music school. I was not teaching at Berklee School of Music. Most of the students were taking my class because, when scanning the available electives, it stood out as being comparatively low stress. How hard could it be? As a new teacher, I wanted to succeed, and I wanted the students to like me.

In family news, Adrian moved to Los Angeles to pursue the difficult profession of singer/songwriter. The life I have described in this book was no longer available to anyone other than a chosen few. Adrian has all the tools and personality traits of an artist who in any other era would have already been on his way to success. But he had of come of age when virtually no one purchases music. Free music has become as expected as tap water.

Corey graduated from Chapman University in Orange, California, down the street from my sister Becky and her husband Ray. Corey took separate courses from Disney University, worked at Disneyland in her spare time, and ended up with a great job at...Walt Disney Headquarters in Burbank.

Natalie had to choose between being a budding soccer star and her love of ballet and musical theatre. She chose the Arts. An indelible image from those years is Natalie, nicknamed "The Wrecking Ball" for her tough, aggressive style, limping to the car after soccer practice, knees grass-stained and bruised, and slipping into ballet gear for an elegant rehearsal at Sacramento City Ballet.

Delaney kept the entire River City Theatre Company running smoothly while simultaneously studying at Sacramento City College. And Mary Ann was well established as a school psychologist in the Sacramento Unified School District, a job not for the faint of heart. I commuted to Stockton a couple of times a week, not a long drive from where we lived, blissfully unaware that my life was about to change again.

A life like mine has a long tail. Newly met people become important in unforeseen ways, and significant older relationships often reignite much later, and to my surprise. It is a lesson to be kind to everyone you meet.

Example number one would be Will Littlejohn and Leslie Barton, formerly of Sacramento and now living in the Bay Area. Will was in the 1980s Sacramento band Leo Swift. His wife Leslie was a manager at Nordstrom. They were big fans of

Bourgeois Tagg and saw us perform as often as possible. Twenty years later Will was the owner of Wave Group, the sound design company that videotaped Bourgeois Tagg and Uncle Rainbow's Sacramento reunion concert in Sacramento in 2008. We had rehearsed for the show in a practice room provided by Will.

Now, almost eight years later, I was attending my friend Bob Cheevers's show in a small club in Sacramento and Will and Leslie were there. When I stopped by their table to say hello, Leslie asked me out of the blue if I would like to write a song for them. At least that is what I thought I heard over the din of the music. One of the silly add-ons I had attached to *Don't Look Back* was a promise to write a song about the subject of your choice in return for twenty-five hundred dollars. I had gotten exactly one taker. Now, I'm thinking, *how cute–she wants me to write a song for their anniversary or his birthday.* We agreed to talk by phone in a couple of days.

Will and Leslie called the following Wednesday evening. Will's company Wave Group was doing a great deal of sound design work for Facebook, including the sound for the "Like" button, one of the most popular sounds in the world. Facebook, not surprisingly, absorbed Will's company and made Will the head of the Sound Design department. Leslie, the manager at Wave Group, followed Will a few months later, as did several Wave Group employees. At that moment, sound design for Facebook involved more sound effects than anything else, with some small musical bits provided for in-house projects.

Will was a visionary thinker. He predicted that as Facebook and Instagram adopted a more visually-oriented platform, original music would be needed to underscore the multiplying videos and pictures. This music process had already begun, but Facebook immediately ran into copyright violations with major labels and publishers, constantly being challenged to remove videos that contained music from mainstream artists. Facebook initiated long and tortuous negotiations with the music industry which ended in a massive general payout for limited copyright protection in non-commercial video usage of mainstream music. In the meantime, Will saw a huge opportunity to fill the hole with copyright-protected music that Facebook would wholly own, and that any user of either Facebook or Instagram could use freely at any time for any reason. And this was what they were calling me about—*not* writing a song for them but writing music for Facebook!

"What kind of music?" I asked.

"All kinds!" Will replied.

"What do you mean *all* kinds?"

"We need everything!"

"*Everything*?"

"We are in almost every country in the world except China, so we need music for everyone."

"So... I can write whatever comes to mind?"

"Yep!"

"And I get paid to do this?"

"Yep!"

"I would seriously need to upgrade my studio to even start."

"No problem!"

"No *problem*?"

"How about if we start with some cool Genelec speakers?"

I looked around and blinked a couple of times to try and tell if I was dreaming.

"Uhhh, yeah, that'll do. I'm also gonna need some new software. My stuff is pretty outdated."

"No problem! We'll get you whatever you need!"

Will Littlejohn was given a substantial budget with the

understanding that he could do with it what he thought was needed. He spent nine months experimenting with the idea of a new kind of music library, one that could compete with the mainstream music that was being pulled down daily from Facebook and Instagram posts, and I was his guinea pig.

I didn't realize it until later, but I had entered Facebook/Meta at the beginning of the end of the freewheelin' "fail forward" days. "Moving fast and breaking things" was more of a working philosophy than a slogan. There was little adult supervision in the Executive Suite, and Mark Zuckerberg was a man/child in one of the most far-reaching, financially successful sandboxes in the world. He held an employee Q&A every Thursday afternoon in the lunchroom near our desks, and he honestly was like a kid holding a new Transformer. (The time coincided with Happy Hour, featuring free wine and beer.) He spoke enthusiastically about the good in the world that Facebook new emphasis on Virtual Reality would do, especially in medicine, and not about money, or stock price, or profits. If he was guilty of anything at that time, it was being naive, not realizing that bad people would find ways to use Facebook he'd never imagined.

I was fifty-seven years old. Facebook was a company made up almost entirely of twenty-somethings. How was this going to work? Zuckerberg was only thirty-one. I would have to trade my tweed jacket for a hoodie. Their campus was in Menlo Park, almost two hours away by car, but I was allowed to work mainly from home, in my studio. I was remote before remote was cool. Still, I couldn't wait to travel down to Facebook headquarters, and when I did, what I saw was beyond what I had pictured.

The two campuses were directly across a highway from each other and connected by a pedestrian and bike tunnel. The first, called Classic Campus (like Classic Coke™), was the former campus of Sun Microsystems, re-imagined by Disney Imagineers. It featured a dozen restaurants (all free) including a noodle shop, a stand-alone barbeque, a pizza window, a hamburger shop, an Indian restaurant, two healthy salad bar-type restaurants, and one Mexican restaurant (Palo Alto Sol, Zuckerberg's favorite), at which you had to pay, but where you could get margaritas, an ice cream shop (everything free), several coffee shops, a Japanese arcade, a hair salon, a bank, and an area called Hacker Square for large outdoor assemblies. The buildings were brightly accented like a Mondrian painting. The Facebook sign with the famous "thumbs-up" that faced the outside world was the back of the Sun Microsystems sign, reminding all who worked there that if they got lax or cocky, they, too, would end up like the back of the sign.

There was free coffee, including espresso machines, everywhere you looked inside the micro kitchens in these buildings, which also featured snacks, sodas, and fruit. But many Millennial workers could not kick the habit of paying for their coffee drinks; coffee shops that charged for their drinks were popular with the rank-and-file twenty-somethings.

Our Sound Design team was located across the roadway, in a newer building, the largest open-office building in the world at over five hundred thousand square feet. Zuckerberg's office was a glassed-in "aquarium" where everyone could catch a glimpse of him in action. Eleven free restaurants. Dry cleaning. Bicycle repair service. Car detailing. Micro kitchens. Free sweet shop. Happy hour. A beautiful park stocked with real foxes and a ginger shot bar on the roof. Every excess you heard about and thought, "that's gotta be an exaggeration" was true. Over the next few years, there would be two even larger buildings next to this one.

The first day I came to work at MPK 20, the US Women's Olympic Table Tennis team was visiting, taking on all comers on the patio *right outside my window*. Facebook was staffed with people from all over the world, especially from East Asia, so many employees lined up to test their skills (and get their asses handed to them).

Like almost all Facebook employees, initially I was hired as a contingent worker, a trial run. If they like you and you do a good job, you are converted to a full-time employee with benefits and stock. Writing "world" music was perfect for me. I loved all kinds of music and had ingested enough styles over the years to be able to approximate a wide variety of genres from all over the planet. The most liberating aspect was that most of it would be instrumental, freeing me from the burden of writing lyrics, and having to complete full songs. I liked writing the music first when I wrote songs, so this would be like composing half of a song idea–the part that came easier to me.

My first compositions were a Brazilian samba, an Indian funk hybrid, a 70s funk track, an East Asian fusion track, and a 1980s synth-rock piece. It didn't take me long to seriously scratch the jazz itch. I leaned heavily into African music. I could choose what I pleased; they needed it all. I would literally wake up in the morning and think, *"Where do I want to go today?"* In the first nine months I wrote one hundred tracks.

Although I was hired by Facebook, we worked for all their subsidiaries, including Instagram, WhatsApp, and Oculus. There was a real problem of users pairing mainstream music with their pictures and videos, especially on Instagram, without permission. This was a copyright violation, and Facebook hadn't yet come to any agreement with the major labels and publishers about the use of their copyrights. Even after Facebook finally came to an expensive arrangement with the industry, there were enough caveats and exceptions that it still made sense to have copyright-free music of their own, especially for commercial use.

At the end of 2016, after nine months of contingent work, I became an FTE, or full-time employee. Thus began an incredible seven-and-a-half years. After watching me write so many tracks in such a short time, Will and Leslie tasked me with finding a whole stable of producers, artists, and songwriters to fill out a roster for what would be known as the Sound Collection. I would be joined in this endeavor six months later by Pamela Roberts.

While Leslie brought in my old bandmates Lyle Workman and Lance Taber, I began reaching out to friends like Charlie Peacock and producer John Fields. Ken Lewis and Scott Dente, musician friends from Nashville, already had a company called Global Genius that engaged in making music like this and I signed them up. Global Genius would reign for many years as our number one producer. Well-known Nashville pop producer and writer Keith Thomas signed on.

My brother-in-law Ray turned me on to a fantastic guitar player from the Baha'i community named JB Eckl, and he, in turn, introduced me to his partner, KC Porter, a Latin producer extraordinaire, and I signed them both up as the entity Kolektivo, and we had our Latin music experts. This would become a vital connection because, as with other parts of the world, it was impossible without "boots on the ground" to develop relationships with authentic indigenous artists. KC already had all those relationships. He, in turn, signed up two artists who would eventually become their own suppliers: Jon Rezin's Afro Sound Machine, which had similar connections to indigenous African artists, and LA pop producer Gia Sky, who concentrated more on North African music.

My son, Adrian, made me aware of a singer/songwriter in

LA named Alex G, who'd been a popular YouTube star mainly doing Disney covers with other YouTube stars and I was immediately intrigued. Like Cindy Morgan, there was a powerful singer/songwriter locked inside just waiting for the opportunity to come out. She would eventually marry and rename herself Alex Blue.

The deal with Facebook was tricky, because it involved the surrender of one's intellectual property, a cardinal sin in many circles until very recently. This was nowhere clearer than at Berklee College of Music in Boston. From the beginning, professors there preached ownership of copyrights. But the ability to earn a living in music had taken such a beating with the advent of free downloading and then streaming that basic principles had to be reassessed.

Coincidentally, in the Fall of 2017, my daughter Natalie was starting college at Boston Conservatory, Berklee's sister school. Our family trip east to drop her off was the perfect opportunity to talk to the powers that be at Berklee, starting with Bonnie Hayes, the Dean of the Songwriting department. I had known Bonnie in the 1980s Bay Area music scene, so I pitched the program to her. The next day she had me pitch it again in front of the entire music hierarchy and administration. While I was initially surprised at the turnout, it just showed how tough things had gotten for Berklee graduates. I proffered the heresy of selling songs outright. They gulped hard and had only one request: that I focus my attention on alumni and not current students; if I pitched it to undergraduates, they wouldn't stay students for long. So, I got complete buy-in from the best resource of young music talent in the world. And the faculty helped me curate lists of the finest of the finest. It was an amazing step forward.

From the list of Berklee alumni came Kiri T from Hong Kong, Ella Joy Meir from Israel, Dhruv Goel from India, and

Giulio Cercato from Italy, all fabulous producer-programmer-songwriters who remain the bedrock of the program today. In future years we signed up Canadian songstress Julia Gartha, Oakland singer/songwriter Jennah Bell, and from Turkey, electronic pop songwriter Sirma Munyar. Ela Minus, a talented electronic music performer from Colombia, headlined the EDM stage at Coachella a year later. Through Berklee alumni contacts came more talented artists: Mexico City's Chela Rivas and her brother Tony Dark Eyes, who quickly became top performers. All the former Berklee students had to be "reprogrammed" to accept the purchase of their copyrights, and in the end did so gladly because, in Will's words, "we are going to pay musicians what they deserve." It was a radical concept, that one.

Country artist Dawn Beyer brought the idea of an electronic tip jar on Facebook Live into our program. We even attracted a small record label, Hitmakers, owned by Australian producer Mark Feist, bringing us seventeen-year-old Australian singer/songwriter Tash, who performed our first rooftop concert at Facebook. Even my good friend and mentor Loren Balman got involved, teaming up with producer Keith Thomas to bring original music from India and the Far East.

We kept the program a secret for the first year, even from people who worked at Facebook. Different departments were so siloed at Facebook you could work virtually next to someone, neither of you knowing what the other was up to. We accumulated a vault of around a thousand songs before we let people inside the company know what we were doing so when requests started coming in for a certain type or genre of music, we could accommodate them. We knew the likely landing spot for our music was, at least at first, the more visually oriented Instagram. The Sound Collection eventually grew to over sixteen thousand songs.

Instagram had camera effects, Boomerang and Superzoom among others. Superzoom became a popular add-on to pictures and videos, especially the "Hearts" effect. This was a soft lens look, with little red and white hearts framing adorable pictures of puppies and loved ones. Superzoom "Hearts" became the number one Instagram camera effect. And the song they used behind the effect was mine.

I had written an R&B track called "Felicia Please," a pun on Alicia Keys, that was the epitome of a "Quiet Storm" late night cuddle-up soul number. I didn't write it for the Superzoom camera effect; it was just one of the songs I turned in that first year. At Facebook HQ one day, a fellow member of our team came up to me and said,

"Congratulations!"

"What for?"

"They (whoever *they* were) picked your song to be the 'Hearts' song on IG Superzoom."

I had no idea what he was talking about or what that even was.

"Uhhh, thanks?" I whimpered.

The "Hearts" effect was used tens of billions of times, was heard as part of a bit on *The Tonight Show*, among others, and was the most played song in the world for a couple of months.

Scan me

Nobody knew it was mine, and I didn't receive a penny for

it after my salary, which shows the dichotomy of writing music for the Sound Collection at Facebook. Billions of people heard and used the tracks, but almost nobody knew the artists who made them. Fans or other people who knew me thought I had retired from writing music.

That was about to change with the advent of Instagram Reels. Facebook played copycat with new social media technologies that they didn't themselves invent. They would either buy the company (Instagram) or create their own version (Snapchat). Reels was Instagram's shot at TikTok. The platform was all video, and videos needed music. The rules for using major label music were still complex. It was allowed, but for only so many seconds, and not in all territories, and not this and not that. The restrictions were most onerous for businesses. If you were a business, and that includes restaurants, Mom & Pop stores, t-shirt sellers, and any other entity advertising anything for a price, you couldn't use licensed music without paying for a license. This meant that our Sound Collection music was the only free choice for over eighty million businesses, large and small, and Reels was set up so that the songwriter's name was at the bottom of the Reel along with the title of the song and a link to their Instagram page. This was a game-changer for our artists.

It was a great feeling to spread work around to musicians, producers and songwriters who were having an increasingly difficult time making money in music. I felt like the Candyman. That the public continues to think of music as a free commodity, like tap water, is a shame. People just expect music to be instantly available at all times, either entirely free or for a small subscription fee. What we were saying was, "Go ahead and take it! We've already paid well for it!" And many surprised, happy musicians and songwriters agreed with us.

The first four years at what is now called Meta were some

of the most fulfilling of my career. I wrote over fifty tracks per year, and the artists I brought into the program were consistently the highest achievers. I provided well for my family while mainly staying at home. I spent a few days a couple of times a month at the Facebook Mothership. Will Littlejohn's lasting legacy would be the twenty-thousand square foot state-of-the-art recording studio he master-minded. Its opening in 2019, just across the Dumbarton Bridge in Fremont, was the crowning achievement of the program.

However, Facebook/Meta, hitherto the darling of the tech industry, experienced severe backlash for its role, intentional or not, in the 2016 US presidential election. The executives were slow to respond to the Cambridge Analytica crisis, a problem that would repeat itself over and over again. The reach of the social media giant had gotten so out of hand that it was virtually beyond the scope of its executives to reign it in. It was like a Super-Kid with no idea of its own strength.

Facebook had been a positive force in the Arab Spring of 2011 but was now perceived to have gone out of control. Internally, there were leaks every time Mark Zuckerberg held a company Q&A. Shareholders demanded more accountability. Mark was going to have to leave the nursery and grow up. Fun times were coming to an end.

In early March 2020, I attended a Herbie Hancock concert at the Walt Disney Concert Hall in downtown Los Angeles, a Christmas present from my son Adrian. This would be the last public event either of us would enjoy before Covid shut the country down. Facebook closed their offices, and everyone went remote. This was less of a burden on me than anyone else, as I was already largely remote. We struggled along for a few more months until Facebook shut the whole program down. We were all still employed, but we wouldn't be doing any new business until the pandemic was under some kind of control. The shutdown lasted six months.

At the same time, I received disturbing health news. In a routine visit to my primary doctor some eighteen months before, he had asked, "How long have you had that heart murmur?" (*You're asking me? You've been my doctor for twenty years–how long* have *I had that heart murmur?*) I was observed and tested many times over the next year-and-a-half until my cardiologist informed me I needed to have an aortic valve replacement, and it would be best at my age to perform it through open-heart surgery, and "as long as we're in there we might as well" remove an enlarged part of my aorta. I had been fortunate all my life health-wise, despite the damage I did to my body in my late-teens and throughout my twenties. This was a huge wake-up call, especially during the pandemic.

The problems started even before the surgery, luckily transpiring when I was unconscious. I was allergic to one of the anesthesias, ironically called rocuronium, and went into anaphylactic shock. I was unaware of my close call until after the surgery. The surgery itself was successful, but immediately following, I went into uncontrollable atrial fibrillation. My heartbeat was continuously over 210 bpms. After several unsuccessful attempts to bring my heartbeat down through medicine and cardioversion, the surgeon decided I needed a second surgery to install a pacemaker. I was in the hospital with no visitors for twelve days. Recovery slow and painful.

After the first follow-up with my cardiologist, his assistant informed me that my MRI showed a "shadow" on one of my ribs, and I should get it looked at. *Oh geez, what's a "shadow?"* It turns out I had cancer on the bone of one of my ribs and it was malignant. Six weeks later, I was back in surgery for the removal of a rib. The surgery was successful, but it led to a more painful recovery than the open-heart surgery. However, that it had been discovered before it had a chance to spread was a major blessing.

While recovering, I started having severe pain in my left shoulder which turned out to be pericarditis, or inflammation of the lining of the heart. It is rare but does happen after aortic valve replacements. After several attempts to bring the inflammation down through medicine, I had to have a fourth surgery to install a drain below my heart. This proved to be only a temporary fix and I underwent fifth surgery to install a second drain.

2020 was a tough year. In April, right before Easter, we suddenly lost Mary Ann's sister Kathi, a traumatic event for our whole family. Kathi was closer than anyone to our children. My daughter Natalie was with Kathi at the time of her death and had tried to revive her.

Then my surgeries started in October. They would continue into 2021. The day after Thanksgiving, my brother Brian, the healthiest of all my siblings, died suddenly in Houston of an apparent lung infection. It was a complete shock. Brian, lean and fit and a great tennis player, was the kind of guy who would run to and from the gym. He didn't die of Covid, but he died because of Covid after sitting for four hours in the ER waiting room because of the overload of Covid patients. By the time they admitted him, he was nearly dead.

In an inspired moment triggered by all the traumatic events, Mary Ann found a wonderful house for rent in Santa Cruz, just a hundred yards from the beach. We decided to take it for a whole year, not knowing about all the surgeries ahead of me. It was an amazing place to recover and rehabilitate, sitting on the front porch, looking at the ocean, taking long walks, and slowly building back my strength. Santa Cruz will always remain a special place for our whole family, especially for the memories of Mary Ann's mother, sister Kathi, and Kathi's husband Joe.

In 2021, Facebook, Instagram, WhatsApp, and Oculus were subsumed into a larger corporate entity, Meta. When we returned as a team from our Covid layoff, we found our budget cut in half. Meta never meant to be a music company, and never understood the power of the music we created. I'm not even sure when it was that Mark Zuckerberg became aware that his company was creating its own music. But to the coders and software engineers, music was a back-burner item, something that would soon be replicated by artificial intelligence.

From this moment forward everything was cut back. Rules were tightened. Layoffs followed. It became more about getting a good performance review than actually doing a good job. I worked almost exclusively with outside music partners, but Meta management became obsessed with cross-functional partnerships, which emphasized how well you worked people in other divisions. This meant if your job enabled you to work with several different internal departments, you were good to go on your performance review, but if your main focus was working with outsiders like I did, then you had to make up fictional relationships and pad small interactions into bigger ones. It was reminiscent of making up fibs before Confession. Because of Peer Reviews, it was also necessary to make unspoken deals with your peers. "I'll scratch your back if you'll scratch mine" was a twice-yearly arrangement around Performance Review time.

The whole folly was capped off by bringing all managers together in a cage-match setting, where they fought for the exalted Exceeds Expectations mark for certain of their favored employees. If they were really aggressive, they occasionally garnered a Really Exceeds Expectations for a lucky coder or two. Otherwise, workers were labeled with a Meets Expectations or worse no matter how well they performed. My manager's strategy revolved around keeping their head down and not calling any attention to either themselves or their reports. For seven straight years I did two jobs while being paid for one. I composed over fifty songs per year and was constantly in the Top Five or Top Ten in number of eyeballs watching the videos my music played behind. My job title was Composer, so fair enough. However, I also was the number one developer of artists every year and it wasn't close. The year I wrote "Felicia Please," which may have been the most viewed song in the world, I got a Meets Expectations twice. Here is the logic behind this rating: "You wrote the song in the first half of the year, but there weren't any views yet, so we couldn't give you a higher rating in the first half; the song got all those views in the second half of the year, but we can't award you in the second half for something you created in the first half." *Huh?* If you are detecting a note of bitterness, it is because I had a manager who took this absurd logic at face value; who never went to bat for me, and who thought it was their job to put me in my place. It soured me on the whole corporate experience.

The real demise of the program came when Will Littlejohn left over the same creative differences that unsettled me. After that, Facebook/Meta became a haven for operations and systems management, efficiency *über alles*, and songs became nothing more than widgets to be ingested by the Great Machine. The epitome of this was CORTEX, the giant data storage *thing* that consumed everyone's time and energy. We spent more time trying to manage CORTEX than thinking about music or the artists who created it.

The structure had devolved into something I would never have signed up for to begin with. Most of my peers couldn't believe I'd hung in there as long as I did. Everyone had to vote on everything. The last few years were about all the various ways to say, "No." Couple that with an over-the-top effort at DEI at all costs, and you have a program designed not to reward the best and the brightest, but one merely to fill slots that say, "Look at how DIVERSE we are!!" As an older white guy, I was strictly bottom of the barrel. As of today, the program is in caretaker mode, just awaiting the day when Meta's enormous AI efforts will swallow it completely. There are no music people in the Meta AI Music department to offer even a small measure of quality control. And they are training their AI model on *our* songs, because they own the copyrights!

The final straw arrived over a nice thing that our program did for our artists. In an effort to reward them for a song that might become a viral hit, we gave the artists a streaming license, allowing them to post the music to their streaming services and keep one hundred percent of any streaming royalties. While this might have the ring of a kind gesture, it was not as altruistic as it sounds. Meta thought so little of streaming royalties that it wasn't even worth it to hire an accountant, much less a lawyer to keep track of such a petty amount of money, even for *all the artists combined.* So, they just decided to give away the paltry droppings, still a positive for the artists because after hearing a song on a video listeners could now trace it back to the artists' Spotify or Apple Music sites. Nobody except the Taylor Swifts of the world releases music on Spotify to make money. It's about the ears. Billions of people heard our music secondarily, and we offered the chance for everyone to find the sources if they so chose.

As an employee, I wasn't allowed a streaming license. I had been writing songs for Facebook/Instagram for over seven years and had generated over three hundred and fifty tracks. The company deemed it "double-dipping." Since I was being paid a salary to write this music, I couldn't be allowed to reap the bountiful financial rewards awaiting me through streaming. Over the course of several years, this might have amounted to dozens of dollars. The company also claimed I would have been releasing proprietary sensitive inside information. And we all know that instrumental music can contain layers of national security-level data that, in the wrong hands, could mount a serious challenge to the corporate bottom line. In either case I was denied.

However, when I finally decided to retire, I was promised at last I could have my streaming license, but just prior to my last day, my manager, as a parting shot, said, "Oh by the way, I checked with HR and Legal, and you're not getting your streaming license." I was floored. This was my legacy–the answer to where I had been (musically) for the past eight years. HR and Legal didn't even know what a streaming license was–they were just *de facto* denying it. It had been up to my manager to fight through this, to advocate for me, but once again, they did their best Pontius Pilate impression.

I was directed to the Conflicts Department. If it sounds like something out of Monty Python, it was. They knew nothing about the Sound Collection, had never heard of us. They didn't even know Meta made music outside of the fits and starts of AI–and they didn't know anything about streaming licenses* or why I would want one ("I'm sorry–you're with?") I was just denied... *because they said so.*

Before retiring, I went to my manager with a proposal to become an outside composer and supplier of music, like the artists I was managing. It made a lot of sense, as I could concentrate on the things I did best for the company without wallowing in the corporate sludge. After all, I was one of

Meta's top composers, and I was *the* top artist developer. It was a no-brainer, right? My boss seemed to agree–in June. It is corporate policy for a full-time employee to sit out six months before converting to a supplier role. I used that time to compose tracks for when I would become a supplier in the beginning of 2025. As summer turned to fall, I began to reach out to new artists and had an exciting mix ready for the new year. Except that in November, I was coldly informed by my courageous former manager that my services would not be needed after all. In classic corporate-speak, they were "moving in a new direction," and they would have to "consult with the team." With AI hot on the trail, and using our music to train the machines, the Creative Audio division put the fate of the entire music program in the hands of a couple of contingent workers and a former sales manager at Nordstrom to guide them musically through the final days of the program. I sincerely wish them all the best.

*In late news, the streaming program has been cancelled.

**In even later news, the whole program has been cancelled.

So here I sit, semi-involuntarily retired, writing down my thoughts.

The good news? I am in fine health. I recently had a successful operation for a medium-sized brain aneurysm. Other than that, I feel better than I have in years. I am actively in the process of releasing music I have recorded for Meta over the past eight years to all the various streaming services. I asked for permission, and now I'm not even asking for forgiveness. I have earned my seat and am a member in good standing in my local 12-step program. Mary Ann has a private therapy practice, which she loves. She runs almost every day. Adrian is committed to his singer/songwriter career in LA and is writing great songs while managing an apartment complex in the middle of Hollywood. Delaney keeps us laughing at home and is the family Jeopardy champion. Corey got married in October 2023, and is climbing the corporate ladder at Disney, and it is simply a matter of time before she takes the reins from Bob Iger. And Natalie is living the dream as an aspiring Broadway actress in maybe the toughest environment of all. We are a family with no rogue elements, no embarrassing problems hidden in our closets. The absence of conflict or a black sheep isn't noticed until hearing the stories of most other families. For all of this, I am truly grateful. It has been a great, wild ride.

———

The Berklee Connection L-to R: Dhruv Goel, Giulio Cercato, Kiri T, Julia Gartha, Ella Joy Meir, Sirma

Ruby Amanfu · Scott Dente & Ken Lewis · Chela Rivas & Tony Dark Eyes

Alex Blue · John Fields

Dig Infinity · KC Porter · Dawn Beyer

Tash

Meta Artists 2017-2024

OUTRO

I wrote this book to get down all the memories I could while I still remember them. Until about thirty years or so ago, people left a paper trail of their lives through letters, diaries, and journals. Now everything is in The Cloud. Clouds can go *poof!* Who knows what will be left of it fifty years from now? The dates were the hardest; I did not keep a journal or even a calendar and some of the dates are just guesses or approximations. I did better overall than I thought I would at first, and most of my contemporaries are similarly challenged. But it's amazing what happened when I got those neurons firing.

I was fortunate to be raised in an era when people still paid for music. I made a living in working bands for over fifteen years until I started earning my daily bread through publishing deals. At the age of thirty-nine, I finally got a job at a record label with health benefits for my family. At fifty-seven, I got the most unexpected job of all, and it still involved writing music and finding and managing others to do the same.

We used to sadly condescend to our cultural cousins in the visual arts. Very few contemporary painters made a living selling paintings. Now we're all in the same boat. I was present at the turning of the music business on its ear by the same technology that had allowed it to thrive. The artists and musicians never recovered. The three remaining record companies figured out how to turn a profit in the streaming game. It's a pyramid scheme: they co-own the means of delivery.

I've talked about identifying with Mr. Magoo, and I realize there is something good about the ability to reinvent yourself. I credit the adaptability I developed to moving around a lot as a kid. I started over as a young teen in Dallas and again as an older teen in California. I was able to start over when I got clean and sober. I was able to start over as a left-leaning Christian in Nashville and then again in California as a middle-aged man working at one of the largest tech companies in the world. There is a Magoo-like quality to it all, but I learned how to carry the best bits with me from the last place and leave the rest behind. I was always the youngest person around doing what I was doing, until one day I found myself saying, "Oh yeah, I made that mistake. That happened to me. Here's what you want to do to avoid that."

I've tried to present an honest picture of life as a popular local musician struggling with an addictive personality. There is nothing more appealing and less healthy than that combination. My upbringing, the era I came of age in, and my singular talent marked me from the beginning as someone headed for danger. It took many years for my head to catch up with my talent. The mistakes I made, especially after my first long stretch of sobriety, were sudden, unpredictable, almost out-of-body experiences. The phrase "cunning, baffling and powerful" is 100 percent true. It remains a daily struggle.

My 2020-2021 health scares convinced me to make some long-needed changes in my diet. Inspired by the works of Drs. David Sinclair, Peter Attila, and Michael Greger, I became a vegetarian bordering on vegan. I say bordering because it's progress, not perfection. I have become a guinea pig for Healthspan supplements and off-market drugs designed to not just increase lifespan, but more importantly, make the last ten or so years of my life worth living. I walk briskly three-and-a-half miles every day. I've become friends with the folks at the Sacramento Natural Foods Co-op. There are many things I cannot undo, but I'm still working on the things I can.

Reducing stress was the number one reason I left Meta. Reducing stress is also why I no longer engage in fruitless political debates on social media. *"I read what you wrote on Facebook, and it changed my whole political outlook. Thank you!"*— said no one ever. I've taken it a step further and do my best to avoid reading political opinion pieces, even those that I agree with; it just raises my blood pressure. I have taken the posture of an ostrich. I am not unaware of the current political climate. I have simply chosen, for my own health, not to engage. Instead, I read books voraciously. And I've written this book. There is so much to catch up on.

Another theme that emerged as I wrote: the long search for spirituality in my life. Raised a practicing Catholic, abandoning that when old enough to think on my own, spending over ten years not thinking much about anything religious or spiritual except for a "foxhole" God with whom I would sadly make deals, getting sober and learning of a Higher Power (which for me was not hard given my upbringing), becoming involved in an evangelical church which led to ten years in the Christian music world while the Higher Power stuff lay dormant, finding the hypocrisy of the evangelicals too much to bear, especially the Nationalist, war-hungry sector, coming back to AA and the Higher Power, moving to an LGBTQ+-friendly version of Christianity, researching world religions and dabbling in Buddhism while writing a book on left-wing Christianity, and then abandoning all pretense of organized religion–it's been a long, frustrating life of false starts and dimmed hopes.

My search has led me to the following still evolving interpretation, opinion, diagnosis, conjecture–

Most religions and sects have similar ideas–many are universal precepts that follow a related code of morals and ethics. Many of these same religions and sects impose a "my way or the highway" set of rules that force one's believers to accept their official version of the truth or The Truth. In Christianity, this dogmatic approach leads to an attitude of, "God said it, I believe it, that settles it!" But it settles nothing. It only settles what you were taught in your Southwest Texas Bible College. I believe that one can learn transformational things from a study of religion. Jesus's Sermon On the Mount, followed closely, is all you really need. But it's like Gandhi said, and I repeat, "I like your Christ. I do not like your Christians. Your Christians are not anything like your Christ." In 2025, that couldn't be any truer.

I spend a fair amount of time on Facebook. Over the years I've accepted thousands of "friend" requests. Other than guitar players and drummers, the most requests over the years have come from Christians who heard and liked my music in the half-decade of the mid-1990s. Many of these folks assume that I think as conservatively as they do, especially politically, and when I don't it's instant betrayal. Heresy! They believe there is only one way to think. And they've twisted the Bible like Silly Putty to back up their beliefs.

After all my searching, the answer I have embraced is Wisdom.

First, there is knowledge. Knowledge is the sum of everything we have ever learned, good and bad, from every input and source. This includes everything we've read, everything we've been told, everything we've watched, all art we've seen, all nature we've experienced, and every bit of music we've ingested. We obviously don't need it all. Discernment is the great sifter of knowledge, which then ideally turns it into Wisdom.

To prepare to receive Wisdom, we need to clear the tremendous clutter from our brains. We have never been force-fed as much mindless claptrap as we are today. This brain-clearing could be called Meditation.

Accessing Wisdom is petitioning the mind to make the right choice; we face a thousand choices a day, most of them binary, from the mundane to the crucial. This might sound awfully secular, but it's not all that different from WWJD–What would Jesus do? Jesus is part of that Wisdom–as large a part of it as you wish to make Him. But so is Mandela, and Gandhi, and that teacher in high school who made a huge impression on you, and your grandmother. Humbly seeking the right answer, to me, is Prayer.

The problem I have with the God of religion is that it has been anthropomorphized to conform to a personality far too small for the Creator of the Universe. We make Him a cranky old man, a gambler with Satan, the Father of all Good Things, and then the Holocaust happens. Or, closer to home, my nephew Sean, the only son of my older brother Bruce and his wife Patricia, both devout Catholics and stellar parents, dies in a one-person car accident. I wrote in the song "God Is Not Dead":

> *God answers prayer sometimes unfortunately*
> *The answer may not be exactly what you planned*

That's because the universe is chaos. Blind praying is wishing, hoping. There may be power in the energy that flows from one organism to another that we have yet to discover. What we can do is make the right decisions based on the skilled discernment of the Wisdom we've accrued. But praying for your son not to get killed in a war? How many mothers prayed for that?

Am I an atheist? No. An atheist can't prove God doesn't exist any more than a Christian can prove that he does. I believe the concept of God is born within us and is accessed through Wisdom. Buddhist monks are probably the closest example of this ideal. The older I get, the less I know, but the thirstier I am for knowledge. I feel like I am in a race with time. I am not advocating or pushing my view on anyone. This is just where I've landed. Honestly, anything that makes you a nicer and more patient husband, wife, mother or father, son or daughter, sister or brother, friend, co-worker or driver is a good thing.

Am I retired? I would say not. Just waiting on the next right thing to happen. At this point I have the luxury of not forcing anything to happen. I still have a lot of music left in me. More than that, I have gained wisdom from success, and more importantly, from failure. With it I can help guide others to avoid some of the traps I stepped in. This book may yet have another chapter to go... *"The rest is still unwritten"*

Jamming with Brian

With Bro-in-law Ray

11 year-old Becky

With Mom & Coral

Brian

Mom & me in Dallas

Mom, Dad & Becky

Coral & Me

With Cousin Petey

The Whole Fam...

Mom, Becky & Coral

At Coral's Wedding

Brian

With Brian and Bro-in-law Scott

Becky

Dancing in the living room with PaPa

With Bruce & Brian

Brother Brother Bruce

Tennis with Scott, Coral and Dad

Dad

Family of Origin

Young Mary Ann

w/Delaney, Adrian & Corey

4 year-old Adrian

1983 Wedding

With Dad & Mom

In England with Adrian

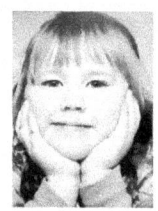
Adrian & Corey

Cut the Cake

Corey

Natalie & Corey

Delaney

Honeymoon Mary Ann

Natalie

Delaney

With toddler Adrian

With Mary Ann & baby Adrian

Mary Ann

The Fam at a gig

Early Family

Adrian

Mary Ann

Natalie in 'Pretty
Woman"

Corey

Corey & Natalie

Corey

Delaney's birthday

Adrian

Natalie at the ballet

Delaney

The Fam

WHERE ARE THEY NOW:

Bruce Bourgeois, my oldest brother, lives in Austin, Texas with his wife Patricia and they are lovingly looked after by their daughter (my niece) Larisa, her husband Jason and their daughter Elodie. Daughter Nicole lives in Houston, Texas with her husband Andrew Chau. Their son, Sean, is deceased.

Coral Bourgeois, my older sister, lives in Providence, Rhode Island with her husband Scott Stenhouse. She is a successful visual artist and an excellent tennis player. Their two children, Miles and Ruby, live in Brooklyn and Queens, New York, respectively.

Becky Bourgeois, my younger sister, lives in Orange, California with her husband Ray Zimmerman. They are both involved in many charitable works through their Baha'i faith. Ray is also a professor of English at Saddleback College. Their son, Daniel lives nearby.

Brian Bourgeois, my older brother, died in November 2020, not from Covid, but from the effects of Covid. He had a lung infection and sat in a waiting room in the ER for four hours before he was seen because there were so many Covid patients. He died shortly thereafter.

Mary Ann Barber Bourgeois, my wife, retired as a school psychologist from the Sacramento Unified School District to open her own thriving private therapy practice. She still runs almost every day. We have been married for forty-two years and counting.

Adrian Bourgeois, my son, lives in Los Angeles, California and is still pursuing his career as a singer/songwriter/producer in a much-changed environment. He keeps an amazingly optimistic attitude about it.

Scan me

Delaney Bourgeois, my oldest daughter, lives at home with us, keeping us on our toes, winning Jeopardy nightly and staying on top of the musical theatre happenings.

Corey Bourgeois Fox, my middle daughter, is newly

married to Kris Fox and works for the Walt Disney organization, which she will one day run.

Natalie Bourgeois, my youngest daughter, lives in Hoboken, New Jersey and is a budding musical theatre actress. Both she and Adrian have chosen careers not for the faint of heart.

Cousin Elizabeth 'Betty' Bourgeois is living in Dallas Texas.

Cousin Henri Wolbrette is living in North Carolina.

Rusty Trevena is Dr. Russ Trevena, retired, a longtime pediatrician living outside Atlanta, Georgia.

Bruce Yamini played bass for years in the Dallas music scene before becoming a Southwest Airlines flight attendant, a job which suited his personality to a 'T'.

Richard Oates passed away in 2010 in Grapevine, Texas. I was with him when he died. His wife, Cindy Ziglar Oates, still lives in the greater Dallas area.

Richard Bannister passed away circa 2016. I had lost touch with him.

Danny Neal still lives in Dallas, Texas and teaches guitar. As The "Answer Dan," he also helped me with some important details in recounting our lives with Uncle Rainbow.

John Lee Sanders lives in Palos de Frontera, Spain with his wife Maria. He has had a long and successful career as a songwriter, performing artist, and a backing musician with several prominent artists. He also helped me with important details for this book.

Steve Mitchell passed away from a brain tumor in 2018. He was living and performing in Sacramento, California at the time.

George Lawrence lives in Memphis, Tennessee and owns his own drum shop, Famous Drum Company, as well as a magazine, Not So Modern Drummer.

David Perper is still a performing drummer in the San Francisco Bay Area.

Jimmy Wallace lives in Dallas, Texas and owns the Dallas Guitar show, as well as his own guitar store. He still performs regularly in the Dallas area, and still owes me a Mexican food meal.

Michael Hossack died of lung cancer in 2012.

Ian Samwell had a heart transplant in the 1990s and died in 2003.

Jerry Sterchi passed away in 2006, followed by his wife, Karen, a few years later.

Narada Michael Walden is still living and producing music in the San Francisco Bay Area.

Larry Tagg still lives and plays music in Sacramento, California and the surrounding areas. He is a retired schoolteacher and Civil War history author and has recorded two solo albums. He is happily married to Lori Jablonski and has two grown children, Erik and Mariel. His memory for dates is even worse than mine.

Lyle Workman lives in Glendale, California with his wife Timi. They have a son, Wyatt. Lyle has toured with many top artists including Sting, Frank Black, and Sarah McLachlan. He has also scored many hit movies, including several for the director Judd Apatow. He probably still owes me $10.

Michael Urbano lives in Berkeley, California and is a popular and successful recording and touring drummer. He still remains, at this time, younger than me.

Scott Moon owns a science fiction fantasy store in Sacramento, California.

Mick Brigden and **Arnie Pustilnik** both died in 2021.

David J. Holman passed away suddenly in April 2025. He mixed a song for me on my *Don't Look Back* album in 2014. He is survived by his wife **Laura**.

Lionel Conway still lives in Los Angeles and is still involved in music publishing and promotion.

Robert Palmer died in 2003.

Anne and Nancy Wilson are still touring with the band Heart.

David Fincher is a major American film director.

Anita Baker has sold tens of millions of albums over the past forty years.

Todd Rundgren lives in Kauai, Hawaii and continues to tour. He appeared on my 2014 album *Don't Look Back*.

Julian Lennon is a world-class photographer as well as recording artist and defines the word "peripatetic." He appeared on my 2014 album *Don't Look Back* and remains a friend.

Ross Hogarth lives in Southern California and continues to be an A list record producer and engineer. He co-produced and engineered a song on my 2014 album *Don't Look Back*.

Danny Kortchmar lives in Los Angeles, California and recently put together an all-star group of legendary musicians called The Immediate Family.

Randy Jackson lives in Los Angeles, California and went on to fame and celebrity as a judge on *American Idol*.

Steve Jordan is currently the drummer in The Rolling Stones.

Christine McVie died in 2022.

Mick Fleetwood is still playing drums in Fleetwood Mac and as of yet has not released his recordings of his poet father.

Phil Quartararo passed away in 2023. **Bob Catania** is still promoting records out of Los Angeles, California.

Glenn Rosenstein continues to produce and engineer records in Nashville, Tennessee while owning Fame Studio in Mussel Shoals, Alabama.

Tommy Sims lives in Nashville, Tennessee and is a prominent singer, songwriter and record producer as well as being one of the finest bass players in the world.

Vicki Randle lives in the Bay Area and had a long stint as the leader of the Tonight Show band. She is still active in the music scene.

Charlie Peacock lives in Nashville, Tennessee with his wife Andi. Their two children, Molly and Sam, live nearby. Charlie is an author, a jazz pianist, a record producer, a songwriter, and one of my closest friends.

Don Donahue lives in Spring Hill, Tennessee with his wife Laura and is the Chief Cook and Bottle Washer of Donahue Creates.

Jerry McPherson lives in Nashville, Tennessee and is looking for work as a guitar tuner or guitar roadie.

Steve Brewster lives in Franklin, Tennessee and continues to be an A List session drummer.

Wayne Kirkpatrick lives with his wife Fran in Brentwood, Tennessee, but has taken his talents to Broadway having co-written the fabulously successful musical *Something Rotten!* as well as the music for *Mrs. Doubtfire*.

Cindy Morgan lives in Nashville, Tennessee with her husband Jonathan and along with her continuing songwriting, is the author of the best-selling book, *The Year of Jubilee*.

Tom Howard died in 2010.

Aaron Smith lives in Nashville, Tennessee and continues playing jazz drums.

Chris Rodriguez lives in Nashville, Tennessee and continues to play guitar and sing in major touring acts and on recording sessions.

Michael W. Smith lives with his wife Debbie in Franklin, Tennessee, and continues to be a leading light in the Christian music scene.

Loren Balman lives with his wife Valerie in Franklin,

Tennessee and continues to have his hand in various aspects of the music industry. He and I resumed working together during my time at Meta.

Point of Grace, which currently consists of original members **Shelley Breen** and **Denise Jones**, along with Leigh Cappillino, are still touring and making records, now leaning more towards country music.

Alison and Catherine Pierce both live in Los Angeles, California, both are married, and both have a small child. Catherine has a line of health and beauty products.

Brown Bannister lives with his wife Debbie in Franklin, Tennessee and after producing a gazillion successful albums, he became the Dean of Music at David Lipscomb University.

Nicole C. Mullen lives in Nashville, Tennessee and is still a popular touring and recording artist in the Christian music world.

Rachael Lampa lives in Nashville Tennessee with her husband Brendan and their two children. Rachael has embarked upon her second act as a Christian music artist after taking almost twenty years off to be a mom.

Paige Lewis lives in Houston, Texas and is a successful Texas country music artist. She spent several years performing and recording with my son, Adrian.

Chris Eaton lives with his wife Abby near London, England and continues to write music.

Michelle Tumes Higgins lives in Southern California with her husband Doug. She appeared on my 2014 album *Don't Look Back*.

Michael McDonald lives in Franklin, Tennessee, and seems to be more popular than ever. He tours with the Doobies, his own band, and in various permutations of Steely Dan.

Andy Chrisman lives in Tulsa, Oklahoma and is the moderator of the podcast *1 Degree of Andy*.

Robin Crow is an author, guitar player and the owner of Dark Horse Recording Studios and Vacation Suites.

Jon Anderson lives with his wife Jane in the Pacific Northwest and continues to tour with his group The Band Geeks.

Louis and Mary Neely live in El Dorado Hills, California and Louis continues to preach at Warehouse Christian Ministries.

Ralph Stover lives in Half Moon Bay, California, and worked alongside me at Meta for many years.

Faith Whitmore lives in Sacramento, California and left the United Methodist ministry to head up the Sacramento United Way and then work for political candidates.

Michael Blanton lives in Nashville, Tennessee and continues to be the definition of a music entrepreneur.

Will Littlejohn left Meta at just the right moment and splits his time between the Bay Area and Kauai, Hawaii.

Thanks

My wife **Mary Ann Bourgeois**, I'm simply not here without you. I love you forever.

Adrian Bourgeois, thanks again for the idea. My muse!

Corey Bourgeois, thanks for the design help.

Natalie, thanks for the cover, and **Delaney**, thanks for the inspiration.

Helen and Harry, thank you for the unconditional support and love.

My sisters **Coral** and **Becky** and my brother **Bruce**, thank you for your unending love and support.

Susan Mathews, thanks for the early help.

Jacob Hoye, thank you for your timely and expert editing advice.

Charlie Peacock, thanks for your wisdom, love, and counsel all through the years.

Lionel Conway, you believed in me far longer than you needed to, and I am forever grateful.

Bruce Yamini, you instilled a love for jazz in me the never left.

Danny Neal, thanks for being the 'Answer Dan' and for being such a creative inspiration in my formative years.

John Lee Sanders, thanks for your memory and for your amazing talent.

Larry Tagg, thanks for being a rock of consistency and immense talent, and my better half.

Lyle Workman, thank you for all the wonderful beginnings—and the laughs

Michael Urbano, you were the rock.

Scott Moon, thanks for having my back.

Todd Rundgren, thanks for insisting on heart over head. And it didn't bother you.

Bob Catania, thanks for your support

Danny Kortchmar, **Randy Jackson**, & **Steve Jordan**, thanks for an amazing record.

Vicki Randle, thanks for your talent and support, over and over again.

Ross Hogarth, thanks for your friendship and your talent throughout my life.

Glenn Rosenstein, thanks for your wisdom and your laughs.

Don Donahue, thanks for constantly reaching out your hand in support.

Michael Blanton, thank you for your vision and your belief in me.

Jerry McPherson & **Steve Brewster**, thanks for thirty years of great music and laughs.

Chris Rodriguez, thanks for your musicianship and your friendship.

Wayne Kirkpatrick, thanks for saying 'yes' when so many say 'no'.

Michael W. Smith, thank you for being such a great songwriting partner and for your belief in me.

Cindy Morgan, thank you for your trust in me. We made beautiful music together.

Loren Balman, thank you for your tremendous belief and support for so many years.

Shelley, **Denise**, **Heather**, and **Terri**, thanks for the inspiration.

Rachael Lampa, you still remain the best singer I have ever heard.

Louis and **Mary Neely**, thanks for providing a lifeline just when I needed it.

Ralph Stover, thanks for your help over the many years, and with the audiobook.

Will Littlejohn and **Leslie Barton**, thanks for surprising me with such a rewarding Act III.

Dr. Russ "Rusty" Trevena, Jimmy Wallace, Bongo Bob Smith, Steve Holzapple, Bob Cheevers, and Daniel Rinne, thanks for your enduring friendships.

To those who are no longer with us, Brian, Richard, Steve, Ian, Jerry, David J., Robert, Christine, Phil Q, Tom, Kathi, and Joe V—your memory lives on inside my heart.

This book is dedicated to my brother, **Brian Bourgeois**, 1951-2020

ABOUT THE AUTHOR

Brent Bourgeois is the co-founder of the 80s pop group Bourgeois Tagg as well as the creator of four solo albums and producer of many more. He was the VP of A&R at Word Records in Nashville, Tennessee for five years in the late 1990s. He is the author of three books, including Left Behind: Jesus in the Age of the American Empire and his new autobiography, The Real Things: The Intimate Journey of a Working Musician from Bill Graham to Billy Graham to Instagram. Brent has been married to Mary Ann Barber Bourgeois for forty-two years and they have four children: Adrian, Delaney, Corey and Natalie. Brent and Mary Ann live in Elk Grove, California.

www.ingramcontent.com/pod-product-compliance
Lightning Source LLC
Chambersburg PA
CBHW071135130626
46553CB00004B/1380

* 9 7 9 8 2 1 8 9 1 0 5 0 1 *